"All the old salty agents in the office couldn't help but ____ Eddie Follis when he arrived. He was like a little windup toy that had been cranked to the max. The kid was going to get the bad guys—whatever it took. He had the grit and resolve of a sheep-dog, wasn't afraid of anything, and we all wondered if that was going to get him killed someday . . . Although we all carry the title, there are only a few who are *truly* 'special agents.' Eddie turned out to be one of those rare special agents who earned his pay and who earned that title. The country owes him a great debt of gratitude. This book is a knockout."   —William Queen,
New York Times bestselling author of *Under and Alone*

"Ed Follis was truly one of the best all-around DEA agents I had the pleasure of working alongside. Calm and cool undercover, Ed was an innovative self-starter, destined to rise to the top. *The Dark Art* is a fascinating read—you won't want to put it down."
—Michael Bansmer, Resident Agent in Charge (Retired),
U.S. Drug Enforcement Administration

"Ed Follis is the epitome of the undercover DEA 'superstar.' Most agents don't volunteer to work in a war zone. Most agents don't work undercover without surveillance in a foreign country. I know. I've been there. Ed's accomplishments, dedication, and sacrifices are universally recognized throughout the DEA and the law enforcement community. This book is a most compelling read."
—Michael Holmes, Assistant Special Agent in Charge (Retired),
Los Angeles Field Division,
U.S. Drug Enforcement Administration

continued . . .

THE DARK ART

UNDERCOVER IN THE GLOBAL WAR AGAINST

NARCO-TERRORISM

EDWARD FOLLIS

AND DOUGLAS CENTURY

BERKLEY BOOKS, NEW YORK

BERKLEY

An imprint of Penguin Random House LLC
375 Hudson Street, New York, New York 10014

Copyright © 2014 by Edward Follis.
Penguin supports copyright. Copyright fuels creativity, encourages diverse voices,
promotes free speech, and creates a vibrant culture. Thank you for buying an authorized
edition of this book and for complying with copyright laws by not reproducing, scanning, or
distributing any part of it in any form without permission. You are supporting writers and
allowing Penguin to continue to publish books for every reader.

BERKLEY® and the "B" design are registered trademarks of Penguin Random House LLC.
For more information, visit penguin.com.

Berkley trade paperback ISBN: 978-1-59240-944-0

The Library of Congress has catalogued the Gotham Books hardcover
edition of this book as follows:

Follis, Edward.
The dark art : my undercover life in global narco-terrorism / Edward Follis
and Douglas Century.
p. cm.
ISBN 978-1-59240-893-1 (hardback)
1. Follis, Edward.   2. Drug enforcement agents—United States—Biography.
3. Drug traffic—Investigation—United States.   4. Drug traffic—
Prevention—United States.   5. United States. Drug Enforcement
Administration—History.   I. Century, Douglas.   II. Title.
HV7911.F64A3 2014
363.45092—dc23
[B]
2014028373

PUBLISHING HISTORY
Gotham Books hardcover edition / October 2014
Berkley trade paperback edition / October 2015

PRINTED IN THE UNITED STATES OF AMERICA

10   9   8   7   6   5   4   3   2   1

Cover photograph © John Moore / Getty Images.

While the author has made every effort to provide accurate telephone numbers, Internet
addresses, and other contact information at the time of publication, neither the publisher
nor the author assumes any responsibility for errors or changes that occur after publication.
Further, the publisher does not have any control over and does not assume any responsibility
for author or third-party websites or their content.

This is a work of nonfiction. All events depicted are true, and the characters are real.
The dialogue has been re-created to the best of my recollection and, wherever possible,
verified against the memories of other participants. In some scenes—due to the sensitive nature
of ongoing investigations and national security—the names of certain federal agents
and confidential informants, as well as some other persons, have been changed.

Penguin
Random
House

CONTENTS

PART THREE

CAST OF CHARACTERS

IN ORDER OF APPEARANCE

THE LAWMEN

Edward Follis: DEA Special Agent; St. Louis–born; former United States Marine Corps military policeman; initially detailed with Group Four of the Los Angeles Division

General Mohammad Daud Daud: a former mujahideen who fought for years against the Soviet invasion; later established and headed Afghanistan's first counter-narcotics police force (CNPA)

Rogelio Guevara: DEA Special Agent; supervisor of Group Four in the Los Angeles Division; gravely wounded while working undercover in Monterrey, Mexico

José Martinez: DEA Special Agent with Group Four of the Los Angeles Division; nearly fatally wounded in a shooting incident with drug traffickers in 1988

Paul Seema: DEA Special Agent; born in Thailand; murdered in a drug deal gone bad in Pasadena, California, in 1988

George Montoya: DEA Special Agent; also murdered in Pasadena, California, in 1988

William "Billy" Queen: Special Agent with the Bureau of Alcohol, Tobacco and Firearms (ATF); detailed the Heroin Enforcement Group in the Los Angeles Division of the DEA

Mike Holm: DEA Special Agent who, after serving many years in Beirut and Cairo, making cases against traffickers in the Middle East, became associate special agent in charge of the Los Angeles Division

John Zienter: assistant special agent in charge of the DEA's Los Angeles Division

Jimmy Soiles: DEA Special Agent; detailed to French country office located in Paris, France; later Deputy Chief of Operations in Office of Global Enforcement for the Drug Enforcement Administration

Rudy Barang: DEA Special Agent; assigned to Bangkok

Mike Bansmer: DEA Special Agent and Resident Agent in Charge, Songkhla, Thailand; spent almost a decade making cases against the Shan United Army

Don Sturn: DEA's assistant attaché in Bangkok

Don Ferrarone: longtime DEA Special Agent in the United States; later DEA's country attaché to Thailand, based in Bangkok

Don Carstensen: head of the Organized Crime Unit in the prosecutor's office in Honolulu, Hawaii

Charles Marsland: prosecutor of Honolulu, Hawaii, whose son Charles "Chuckers" Marsland was killed in a brutal murder in the 1980s

Enrique "Kiki" Camarena: DEA Special Agent who, while in Guadalajara investigating the increasingly powerful cocaine cartels, was brutally tortured and murdered in 1988, spawning a major diplomatic conflict between the governments of Mexico and the United States

Ambassador Ronald Neumann: veteran State Department official; appointed ambassador to Afghanistan, where he served in Kabul from 2005–07

Steve Whipple: DEA Special Agent detailed to Juárez Cartel Task Force in El Paso, Texas, with Special Agent Follis; expert in wiretapping and other legal strategies to combat the Mexican cocaine cartels

THE TRAFFICKERS AND SUSPECTS

Haji Juma Khan: major opium trafficker and Taliban financier; power base was in the Baluchistan region near the Iranian border; estimated to have provided hundreds of millions in funds to Taliban insurgents

Khun Sa: nom de guerre of Chung Chi Fu, leader of the Shan United Army drug-funded insurgency based in Burma and northern Thailand; reputedly responsible for 70 percent of the heroin in the United States during the 1990s

"Dr. Dragan": heroin and arms trafficker; worked in Los Angeles to acquire military weapons for Shan United Army insurgency

Kayed Berro: high-ranking financial officer within the Berro heroin trafficking organization of Lebanon; hiding in Southern California after being sentenced to death in absentia by an Egyptian court for drug trafficking

Mohammad Berro: patriarch of the Lebanon-based Berro heroin trafficking organization; based in Lebanon and the north of Israel

Ling Ching Pan: a major financial officer and lieutenant in the Shan United Army; based in Bangkok, Thailand

Sam Essell: boss of the Essell narcotics and organized crime group; responsible for major importation of narcotics to the United States; based in Lagos, Nigeria

Christian Uzomo: chief lieutenant in the Essell narcotics and organized crime group, based in California

William Brumley and Mike Lancaster: violent associates of the Essell narcotics importation and organized crime group; known for dealing in illegal weapons and producing silencers

Harvey Franklin: associate of the Essell organized crime group; a Crips gang affiliate known for dealing in heroin, stolen bearer bonds, and supernote counterfeit currency

Ronnie Ching: hit man for major Hawaiian drug traffickers and organized crime; ultimately confessed to committing nineteen murders

"Phong": street nickname for a chief lieutenant in the Shan United Army; based in the north of Thailand

Amado Carrillo Fuentes: the so-called Lord of the Skies; boss of Juárez Cartel; the de facto CEO of a sprawling cocaine empire; estimated net worth of $25 billion; ranked by the DEA as the most powerful cocaine trafficker in the world in the mid-1990s

Vicente Carrillo Fuentes: second-in-command in Juárez Cartel; some say the later successor to the position of boss of the cocaine-trafficking organization

Joaquín "El Chapo" Guzmán: originally a lieutenant in the Carrillo-Fuentes cartel; ultimately rose to the position of the most powerful drug lord of all time; ranked by *Forbes* magazine as the eighty-sixth richest man on earth

Mullah Omar: spiritual head of the Taliban; Afghanistan's de facto head of state from 1996 to late 2001; intimately involved in the production, price-fixing, and sale of opium

Haji Bashir Noorzai: Afghan opium warlord and Taliban financier; responsible for much of the opium cultivation and heroin production in the Kandahar region

Haji Bagcho Sherzai: Afghan opium warlord and Taliban financier; a former mujihadeen; responsible for much of the opium cultivation and heroin production in the Kandahar region

Haji Khan Muhammad: major Afghan opium trafficker and Taliban insurgent; based in the Kandahar region

AGENT EDWARD FOLLIS'S GLOBAL INVESTIGATIONS

LOCATIONS: Mexico/Texas border; El Paso, Texas; Ciudad Juárez, Mexico

INVESTIGATING: Cocaine trafficking

CRIMINAL ORGANIZATION: The Juárez Cartel, aka the Amado Carrillo Fuentes organized crime group

LOCATIONS: Los Angeles and Orange County, California; Paris, France; Nicosia, Cyprus; Tyre, Lebanon; Cairo, Egypt; Tel Aviv and Jerusalem, Israel

INVESTIGATING: Heroin trafficking

CRIMINAL ORGANIZATION: The Berro organized crime group of Lebanon and the United States

LOCATION: Honolulu, Hawaii

INVESTIGATING: Methamphetamine and marijuana trafficking

CRIMINAL ORGANIZATION: Various indigenous Hawaiian organized crime groups

LOCATIONS: Riverside, California; Guadalajara, Mexico

INVESTIGATING: Interviewing suspects in the torture and murder of DEA Special Agent Enrique "Kiki" Camarena

CRIMINAL ORGANIZATION: The Guadalajara cartel, aka "The Federation" of Mexican cartels

LOCATION: Riverside, California

INVESTIGATING: Methamphetamine; illegal pharmaceuticals; cocaine, heroin, and marijuana trafficking

CRIMINAL ORGANIZATION: Numerous Asian- and US–based organized crime groups (including Hong Kong; Tinian and Saipan in the Commonwealth of the Northern Mariana Islands)

LOCATIONS: Los Angeles, California; Las Vegas, Nevada; Tel Aviv and Jerusalem, Israel

INVESTIGATING: Ecstasy (MDMA) production and trafficking; homicide

CRIMINAL ORGANIZATION: The Abergil organized crime group of Israel and the United States

LOCATIONS: Los Angeles, California; Las Vegas, Nevada; Lagos, Nigeria; Hong Kong, China

INVESTIGATING: Heroin and marijuana trafficking; illegal firearms; counterfeiting; stolen bearer bonds; illegal steroid distribution

CRIMINAL ORGANIZATION: The Essell organized crime group of Nigeria and the United States

LOCATIONS: Songkhla and Bangkok, Thailand

INVESTIGATING: Opium production and heroin trafficking

CRIMINAL ORGANIZATION: The Shan United Army, aka the Khun Sa Insurgency

GOLDEN CRESCENT

GOLDEN TRIANGLE

LOCATIONS: Kabul and Kandahar, Afghanistan; Balochistan, Pakistan

INVESTIGATING: Opium production and heroin trafficking

CRIMINAL ORGANIZATION: The Taliban and Al Qaeda through the organized crime groups of Haji Juma Khan; Haji Bagcho Sherzai; and Haji Khan Mohammad, aka Haji Baz Mohammad

LOCATIONS: Republic of Korea (South Korea); Democratic People's Republic of Korea (North Korea); as well as the DMZ (Demilitarized Zone)

INVESTIGATING: Illicit, state-sponsored factory production and distribution of methamphetamine by North Korea

CRIMINAL ORGANIZATION: The Democratic People's Republic of Korea (North Korea)

All scenes and conversations have been rendered as faithfully as possible, yet as I have matured over thirty years—some would say I have a few more yet to log—I have realized that events and adventures can sometimes be slightly blurred by a shock-drenched brain, from too much frolicking and from watching other good men pass over to the other side before me. One day I will join them. Until then, I must say: It has been one wild journey, one party celebrating all those who've made everything I've accomplished in my life—and my DEA career—possible.

EDWARD FOLLIS

PART ONE

One must also note the growing convergence of terrorist organizations with criminal cartels like the drug trade to finance their activities. Such cooperative activities will only make terrorism and criminal cartels more dangerous and effective.

US JOINT FORCES COMMAND, "THE JOINT OPERATING ENVIRONMENT," NOVEMBER 2008

No man can serve two masters: for either he will hate the one, and love the other; or else he will hold to the one, and despise the other. Ye cannot serve God and mammon.

MATTHEW 6:24

PRELUDE

Kidnapped in Kabul

ASSIGNMENT: COUNTRY ATTACHÉ: GS-15

POSTING: KABUL, AFGHANISTAN

TARGET: THE HAJI JUMA KHAN NARCO-TERROR ORGANIZATION

DATE: <u>CLASSIFIED</u>

I was responsible for all blood. If anything happened to any of my agents or informants during an operation—even routine travel outside of the secure US Embassy compound—the weight was on me.

By early 2006, I was the country attaché, a senior member of the Drug Enforcement Administration at Level GS-15—in military terms, the pay-grade equivalent of a full-bird colonel. But I kept on doing what I'd always done: working the street. It was unheard of for a GS-15 to be tearing around a war zone in a Land Cruiser, toting an M4 carbine and a Glock 9mm, running undercover ops in the most hostile and lawless regions of Afghanistan. My superiors at DEA headquarters were often none too pleased when they read the stream of cables, emails, and sixes my team were filing from Kabul.*

Honestly, it was the only way I knew how to do my job. I was never a traditional desk boss. Whether in Los Angeles, El Paso, Bangkok, Tel Aviv, Cairo, or Kabul, I was always a street agent.

That's why the DEA boys in the Los Angeles Division started calling me Custer. Fuck the odds: I was always ready to get into the game. They gave me an old framed photograph of General Custer taken a few weeks before Little Bighorn: typical black humor between cops. The portrait was hanging over my desk.

Our embassy in Kabul is a huge complex—the perimeter entrusted to a contingent of Gurkhas from Nepal, experts at security and counterterrorist work. The compound itself, which cost the United States $880 million, is surrounded by thick citadel-like walls. Unlike Baghdad, there's no Green Zone in Kabul. Outside those high concrete walls, things were *never* safe. Every day there were insurgency attacks. I lived in a small apartment directly under the ambassador's residence, and I'd wake up most mornings, ears assaulted by the sound of explosions. When Ramadan began in September 2006, we were hit by bombings for sixty days continuously.

Every time you drove out of the embassy you were a target for a suicide bomber with a VBIED—vehicle-borne improvised explosive device. I had a silver-metallic Land Cruiser with Level 3 body armor, but it could never withstand a direct hit. If you were at an intersection, you had to be ever-vigilant for VBIEDs. Even cruder: In the mob crowding the streets, asking for hand-

---

* The US Drug Enforcement Administration's internal report of an ongoing investigation, known as DEA-6, is commonly referred to by us as a six.

outs, some kid rolls a hand grenade under the chassis and—no last-second prayers—that's the end of it.

* * *

It was a bright June morning, and the mountain bowl of Kabul was already heavy with the promise of a hot, fetid afternoon ahead. I was at my desk, right under the imperious gaze of Custer, when I got a call from Group Supervisor Mike Marsac, who was managing one of our daily undercover operations.

I'd approved an op in which my investigative assistant Tariq, along with an Afghan informant code-named 007, was sent in undercover to purchase three kilograms of heroin for fifteen grand. The dealers we were targeting were a smaller tributary crew, but I had a hunch that infiltrating them could lead us deeper into the orbit of the biggest opium and heroin organization on the planet and the man reputed to be their leader: the mysterious Haji Juma Khan.

It should have been a routine buy: I'd done hundreds of them in my career. But now I heard Marsac out of breath—scared shit-less: "Ed, they're fuckin' gone!"

"Who?"

"Tariq and Double-Oh-Seven. They were just grabbed and bagged."

"What the hell are you talking about?"

"I don't know how—they were snatched off the street."

"Mike, where are our people now?"

"We don't know."

"Shit." The reality stung like some whipped-up mountain sandstorm: There'd been a security breach. We'd had surveillance units, our DEA agents, and a team from the CNPA—the Counter

Narcotics Police of Afghanistan—parked in undercover vehicles at both ends of the street. But somehow during the operation we'd been betrayed.

With geometric precision two compact cars—an older red Toyota Corolla and a gray Honda Civic—came screeching in. The Corolla parked diagonally in front of our undercover vehicle; then the Civic rammed in tight behind. No possible way out. As Mike Marsac described it, four guys—all Afghans—snatched Tariq and 007, pulled them into their vehicle, and made a clean getaway. All in a period of less than ninety seconds. So fast that our surveillance people couldn't race to the scene. Tariq and 007 were gone. The speed of the boxing maneuver told me one thing: Whoever snatched our people were trained intelligence operatives.

"Who're we looking at here?" Marsac asked.

"It's too textbook perfect," I said. "These guys were raised by the fuckin' KGB."

I made a flurry of calls to the Langley boys and to the National Directorate of Security (NDS), the domestic intelligence service of Afghanistan. In effect, I was talking to two heads of the same hydra: Although the NDS was an autonomous branch of the Afghan government, our spooks were the puppet masters of the Afghan intelligence apparatus.

"Listen to me—I just lost *two* people!" I shouted into my Motorola.

Blanket denials. One spook with a midwestern accent kept telling me: "No, we have operations today, but nothing involving counter-narcotics."

I hung up on her midsentence. There was only one *possible* explanation: a rogue group of Afghan intelligence officers. Agents from the NDS who'd been trained by the Soviets at universities in

Moscow and military bases had now gone into side business for themselves. Sure, the *business* of ripping off actual dealers. They must have had me and my people under surveillance and assumed that our guys—Tariq and 007—were real heroin dealers. It was a validation of our undercover disguises and techniques that we were so utterly believable as an authentic Afghan drug-trafficking organization.

The rogue unit had planned an audacious rip: kidnap Tariq and 007, steal the dope, steal the buy money, then sell the three kilograms of heroin at pure profit. A couple of dead heroin dealers in the Afghan desert: Who was going to ask any questions?

No cooperation from the spooks. We'd have to get them ourselves. I grabbed Special Agent Brad Tierney, my right-hand man in Kabul. Brad had been a US marshal in Tulsa before landing at DEA. Fifty-three years old, tall, with thick brown hair, Tierney was a cop's cop. A guy you could trust with your life.

In fact, in the recent past, I'd done just that. Tierney had been stationed in Bangkok with me for my three-and-a-half-year stint, during which I worked to infiltrate the Shan United Army, the world's largest drug insurgency. It was funny that so many agents stationed in Afghanistan had served with me either in Thailand or when I was in El Paso working the Mexican cartels.* As if all the scattered knights and bishops and rooks had been reassembled for one final chess match . . .

From the doorway of my office, I gave Brad a heads-up.

"Grab your shit."

---

* The Drug Enforcement Administration has an elite program of vetted units stationed in hot zones around the globe: Mexico, Colombia, Thailand, Burma, Afghanistan.

Tierney nodded. Each of us had a holstered regulation Glock 17, and we checked the cartridges of our M4 carbines—the reduced version of the standard US military M16 assault rifle, preferable for operating in tight urban spaces. And, of course, I had my Cold Steel bowie knife sheathed on my back. We slung our M4s over our shoulders and raced outside to my Land Cruiser.

Before we hit the street, I'd rung up General Mohammad Daud Daud, the deputy interior minister for counter-narcotics. In the past six months, Mohammad had become my dear friend. We'd gotten down on our knees and prayed together—devout Muslim and Christian—in a Kabul mosque during some of the worst Ramadan terror attacks. Mohammad was Tajik, a venerated mujahideen who'd fought heroically against the Soviet invaders. Indeed, he'd been chief of staff to General Ahmad Shah Massoud, the legendary Lion of Panjshir—the father of Afghan democracy—murdered by Al Qaeda on the eve of September 11, 2001.

Daud was now a three-star general and had a powerful reputation, one of the few high-ranking men in Afghanistan whose integrity was unquestioned.

"General," I said, "two of my guys are gone—kidnapped."

"Who are they, Ed?" he asked.

I told him. "But nobody's talking. NDS all swear it wasn't them."

Working two sets of cell phones, General Daud and I organized a dragnet. If my people had been kidnapped by legit traffickers, they'd be taken out of Kabul, held as hostages, and bartered for ransom. The dragnet consisted of my DEA guys, General Daud's CNPA officers, members of the National Interdiction Unit, and uniformed Afghan police—more than three hundred sets of eyeballs working all investigative leads and exit routes from Kabul.

It's the peril of doing drug enforcement in a war zone: There are *no* blue-on-blue safeguards. Among the DEA, CIA, and various Afghan police and intel agencies, there are no counter-checks to avoid an undercover stepping—unsuspectingly—onto the set of another undercover op and getting popped.

* * *

Mohammad played his trump card: He called the office of the National Directorate of Security and spoke to General Ahmad Nawabi, the second-in-command of the NDS in Kabul. Brad and I raced over to the NDS headquarters. It was a dreamlike vision: We were no longer in Afghanistan. The gates parted to reveal lush foliage, a small garden, a well-groomed soccer field. A verdant oasis amid the outlaw frenzy of downtown Kabul.

The building itself was poured concrete, early-'80s construction; it had been used for interrogations by the KGB. I ran up three flights of stairs and saw grisly reminders of the building's more recent use under the Taliban. On one flight a few of the floor tiles were tinged pink, stained by the blood of "transgressors" who Mullah Omar's henchmen had flogged for blasphemy, adultery, or other violations of Sharia law.

Afghan guards led us at gunpoint straight to General Nawabi. He was waiting for me in his leather desk chair, casually smoking, eyebrows furrowed. He wore a charcoal suit, a striped gray-and-blue tie, his gray beard perfectly trimmed. We wasted no time on handshakes or pleasantries.

"Are you listening to me?" I said. "Don't tell me this was some *random* rip-off. It was done with geometric precision. I *know* these are your people."

Nawabi grimaced and then, without warning, he left us alone

in his office. I couldn't hear what he was saying next door, but he was obviously on his private cell. When he returned, he gave me a straight fucking answer for the first time.

"It seems we have found your people."

"Yeah? Where the hell are they?"

Nawabi cleared the phlegm in his throat. He spat out an address: My guys were being held at a building on the eastern outskirts of Kabul. Brad Tierney and I bolted outside. By now the sun was brutally hot. The streets of Kabul would be surging with mobs of pedestrians, street vendors, Muslims on their way to mosques. I decided we'd have better odds undercover. This wasn't by the book, but then very little in Afghanistan ever was. I grabbed the duffel bag I kept discreetly hidden in the Land Cruiser.

"Haji up," I said. We threw on our UC garb: the white cotton tops of the *shalwar kameez*, black scarves around our faces, and two Massoud caps—tan-colored beret-like hats that were the favored headgear of the Lion of Panjshir himself. I was gunning the gas, on the *edge*, swerving the heavy armored Toyota as if I'd taken a straight shot of adrenaline. The streets of Kabul swarmed around us like a medieval bazaar. I had tunnel vision, oblivious to the thumping as the side mirrors of the Land Cruiser clipped pedestrians, knocking more than a few to the pavement. Tierney had tunnel vision, too. Behind us, we heard angry shouting.

I glanced at Brad. "Look, man," I said. "Whatever we gotta do—I mean *whatever* we've gotta do—we're gonna get them the fuck out today."

"You bet the fuck we are."

As I raced through the Kabul side streets, we made a solemn vow to each other—as *men*, not cops. We weren't anticipating a shoot-out, though anything was possible in Kabul. I drove out on the winding highway that leads to the eastern outskirts. I looked up at those towering humpbacked mountains and saw scores of Afghan women and boys trundling down thousands of feet just to get their daily water.

We pulled up to the curb, double-checking the address. It was an old white-and-gray concrete office building, also from the Soviet era: nondescript and boxlike, pockmarked by decades-old civil war shelling. There wasn't an external threat at the building's entrance or perimeter, so we left our M4s behind. Brad and I stepped outside, drawing the Glocks from our leather holsters.

■ ■ ■

We ran up a rank-smelling stairwell, and by the time we'd reached the fifth floor, I could hear thudding and shouting and moaning and I could feel my heartbeat up into my throat. We burst through an unlocked door and saw that Tariq and 007 had been savagely beaten. They were slumped over on a blood-smeared fabric sofa, drifting between half conscious and half dead.

We immediately faced off with the four kidnappers. They were dressed like Westerners, not Hajis: light-colored polo shirts and khakis and dress shoes.

At first glance, they must have thought we were Taliban, but we ripped off the black-and-tan scarves and identified ourselves as DEA agents.

The commander of the unit, a diminutive Pashtun, spoke an educated—albeit heavily accented—English. His enforcer was wearing a blood-spattered pale linen shirt. He had a damaged eye; a crude gauze patch covered the wound. He also looked Pashtun, about six-two and 230 pounds. Hours later, we learned that he'd been a prizefighter, some Russian-trained heavyweight, and he'd certainly put his boxing skills to creative use. He'd beaten Tariq and 007 professionally, methodically: cracked ribs, smashed eyes, busted noses, knocked-out teeth.

The kidnappers were staring us down. But they weren't showing any weapons, so Brad and I holstered our Glocks. A crazed cacophony of cursing and shouting ensued.

"Who the fuck are you guys?"

"We're conducting a drug investigation," the commander said finally, calmly.

I looked down at the sofa. Tariq had regained consciousness but could scarcely sit upright. It looked like our informant, 007, might already be dead.

"Where's the heroin? Where's the three kilos?" Brad shouted.

"It has been turned in for evidence."

"*Evidence*—what the fuck are you talking about?"

"And where's the money?" I said.

The hulking one-eyed boxer simply shrugged at me.

"There was fifteen Gs for three fuckin' kilograms!"

The room was tight. Things were getting so heated, so explosive—somebody was going to get popped any second. I looked down at Tariq and 007: They were both bleeding heavily, eyes rolling back, drifting away . . .

■ ■ ■

I didn't give a shit about the missing cash or heroin. First and only priority—I needed to get our guys back to our embassy compound, where they could receive medical attention. Brad and I lifted them onto our shoulders, like a couple of firefighters, pushed past the kidnappers, and lugged them down the five flights.

I kicked open the front door, and we burst back into the blinding daylight. A gawking mob had surrounded my Land Cruiser, angry Afghan men, young and middle-aged, pressing in close, undulating like some great human jellyfish. With our black scarves off, they could see our sunburned American faces now; they'd pegged us for imposters—interlopers—infidels.

We pressed forward, through louder shouting, cursing. I felt hot breath on my neck.

The mob parted. We pushed forcibly into the Land Cruiser. Tariq and 007 both slumped over unconscious in the backseat.

"Twenty minutes," Brad said, once I was speeding on the highway into Kabul.

"No doubt," I said, "*if* that . . ."

Tierney was right: If we'd showed up twenty minutes later, our guys would've been *gone*. The boxer would have beaten them to death.

CHAPTER 1

GROUP FOUR

My first day on the job I was terrified.

Wasn't too worried about the work.

I was scared out of my mind that I might be *late*. It seems ludicrous to me now—Los Angeles would soon enough become my adopted hometown—but as a newly minted DEA agent entering strange and frightening territory, I was driving those Los Angeles freeways for the first time. My aunt's place was about thirty miles from the DEA office, and I had no idea how bad the traffic might be.

I hardly slept, got up at four a.m., was showered and dressed in my dark-blue suit, waiting for first light. Drove into downtown LA and was in the office at six a.m. sharp. DEA headquarters was then in the heart of the financial district, right in the Los Angeles World Trade Center, a low-rise office complex on 350 South Figueroa Street, with a staff of about one hundred.

I pulled down South Figueroa, parked, and went upstairs. The only other soul in the place was Lekita Hill, a DEA secretary who was to become one of my closest friends and my emotional rock as

I took on increasingly difficult, logistically complex, and politically sensitive investigations.

In the Los Angeles Division, I was assigned to Enforcement Group Four—the Heroin Task Force, where I was to learn the nitty-gritty of undercover narcotics operations firsthand. The task force was filled with these older, irreplaceable lawmen, veterans who'd been rewriting the playbook on how to be an undercover.

As I arrived on the scene, Group Four had just suffered an intense trauma, one that had played out in the national headlines and was still being written about almost daily when I came on the job. Three sterling men had all been caught in a deadly shoot-out in an undercover operation down in Pasadena. The only one left to talk about it was DEA Special Agent José Martinez; the other two undercover agents, Paul Seema and George Montoya, had been shot to death by a thug wielding a .45 semiautomatic.

José, the driver during the undercover operation, badly wounded in the shoot-out, would receive the Medal of Valor personally from President Reagan.

Shortly before I started in Group Four, the *Los Angeles Times* ran a front-page story that spotlighted the high-risk world I was about to enter. I remember reading the story at my aunt's kitchen table.

A SHADOW WORLD OF LIFE AND DEATH:
WORKING MOSTLY UNDERCOVER, DEA AGENTS LIVE WITH DANGER AND OFTEN DIE UNHERALDED

The article described, in great detail, the brutal killings of agents Seema and Montoya, explaining that no matter the level of street smarts, instinct, and training of the undercover agents, drug dealers almost always have the upper hand, armed with "absolute greed" and a callous willingness to instantly kill both other dealers and "federal officers who play too convincingly their roles" while undercover:

> "Television glorifies us as fun and games and cops and robbers," said Rogelio Guevara, a Los Angeles agent for the Drug Enforcement Administration, a friend of both men. "But [DEA work] is also very real, a very dangerous job, and it is for keeps.
>
> "We have the highest assault rate of any federal law enforcement agency, and if anything, we're seeing an increase. That's nothing to brag about, just a sad truth . . ."

It was daunting to enter into that tight-knit Group Four family. I sensed it immediately: This was a family of trauma, a family of hurt. I didn't know George Montoya or Paul Seema personally—though ironically enough, years later, when I was living in Thailand, I would hear repeatedly from people who'd known Paul as a young man; he'd been with the CIA before he transitioned over to the DEA. People in Thailand regarded the murdered agent with respect bordering on reverence.

When I came on the job, the details of that trauma were still murky to me: I knew that two agents had been murdered in a heroin transaction while working undercover. The one who'd survived, albeit badly wounded, came back to working undercover just a few months after the shooting and was now sitting six feet away from me.

José Martinez was to become my partner, indispensable friend, and invaluable mentor.

José was known as a premier undercover, probably the best UC we had working in Group Four at the time. He stood only about five-five but was strong as a bull, never backed away from anyone. José had been a top collegiate wrestler. He's Mexican-American but has a very pale complexion and jet-black hair— I guess the conquistadors' DNA still runs heavy in his genes, not the more Aztec features so many Mexicans share. José speaks flawless English, but also Castilian Spanish, a variety of Mexican dialects, and Spanglish. His skills on the street were intuitive—stuff you could never learn in a classroom or some practical exercise at the federal academy.

José took me under his wing; I became his junior partner. That first Christmas in LA, I spent with José and his family. We put in a lot of long nights working surveillance, out on undercover jobs, talking about the Pasadena shooting.

The bullet scars on his legs were still pink and cherry red; the trauma was equally fresh in his mind. He needed to talk to somebody about it, needed some clarity, needed to make sense of what had happened to his two dear friends. You never really get *closure* when you've lost two of your partners and nearly died yourself.

José, more than anybody in Group Four, pushed me hard to get into the undercover roles. He read me immediately; he knew that UC work was best suited to my personality. He had an uncanny—almost innate—knack for it, and he immediately recognized the same traits in me.

Rogelio Guevara, the Group Four supervisor, was my immediate boss. He'd been really tight with special agents Seema and Montoya.

Born in Mexico, Rogelio had led a full life before joining the DEA: He'd been a butcher, and then earned his college degree in criminal justice, ultimately becoming a legend among Mexican heroin agents. In another near-fatal undercover operation, while working down in Monterrey, Mexico, Rogelio had very nearly been murdered. He lost the use of one eye for the rest of his life.

Bandits ambushed him, put a bullet in his cranium, but he'd miraculously survived that head shot. He and his partner had come over a ridge and been confronted by a gang of more than thirty banditos, some of whom were riding horses. It was supposed to be a major undercover marijuana buy, but it turned out to be a rip. The traffickers killed Rogelio's partner. A bandit on horseback shot Rogelio in the face. One round went in right over his eye and exited at his temple. Even today, he still has a huge dark scar down the side of his face.

Like José Martinez, Rogelio was fearless. Strongly built, Aztec features, about six-foot-one. The long scar and his damaged eye gave him a particularly intense appearance. When I came to Group Four, he was still hopping back and forth between his supervisory role in LA and undercover work inside Mexico.

Rogelio was a marvelous guy; more than once, he went undercover as a boss with me—which wasn't by the DEA rulebook, especially given that he was virtually blind in one eye. It was something I watched and internalized and would carry over into my own days as a boss, as supervisor, and even higher up the chain of command in the DEA. For Rogelio, rank meant nothing. He knew it was on the street that the real police work gets done.

■ ■ ■

After completing the federal academy in Quantico, Virginia, I had several career options. My application to the US Secret Service was rejected, but I was offered positions with NCIS, the FBI, and the DEA. While still a military policeman in Hawaii, I'd also been recruited by the CIA—even gone through the battery of psychological tests down at Langley. I mulled things over for a day. I didn't ask anyone's opinion. I wanted the decision to be mine. I withdrew from both FBI and NCIS, then called the CIA as well.

"Thanks," I told them, "but my heart is with the DEA."

Honestly, I'd wanted to be a narc—working for the DEA—ever since I was nineteen years old and heard the song "Smuggler's Blues" by Glenn Frey. A few lines in the lyrics, about the '80s cocaine epidemic, just leapt out of the tinny car speakers:

> It's propping up the governments in Colombia and Peru,
> You ask any DEA man,
> He'll say, "There's nothin' we can do . . ."

Driving in my old Chevrolet, something struck a chord—I guess it must have pissed me off—and I couldn't get the song out of my head. Obsessed about it for weeks. Talked about it constantly with my buddies. One of those crystallizing moments: I said to myself, *Fuck it, I'm gonna* become *that DEA man. Let 'em try to tell me there's* nothing *we can do . . .*

Around that same time, I stumbled on the book *Serpico* by Peter Maas, and it blew me away. Today, after years in law enforcement, I realize that I have some of the same personal flaws as Frank

Serpico. But back then, as a very young man, I saw in his crusad-ing, lone-wolf policing style a role model for my life. After reading *Serpico*, I was dead set on becoming an undercover narc. Then the movie, starring Al Pacino, came out: I saw it about six times.

In hindsight, I can see I was an idealist—perhaps naïve—but I really thought I could make a difference. I consolidated my aca-demic goals, focused everything in my life from that day forward toward becoming a narc. Every move and decision I made was with the goal of becoming a DEA special agent working under-cover to take down drug traffickers.

To me there was no better platform for a career in law enforcement than the Drug Enforcement Administration. DEA's roots go back to laws enacted in 1914. Originally under the US Department of the Treasury's Bureau of Prohibition, the agency was created on June 14, 1930. Most people don't realize this, but for years the Federal Bureau of Narcotics (FBN) was the only law enforcement agency tackling the Mafia; J. Edgar Hoover famously denied that there was a national syndicate of organized crime families—until the public embarrassment of the Apalachin conclave in 1957 forced Hoover to admit that there was indeed a nationwide organized-crime conspiracy; Hoover stubbornly refused to use the word "Mafia," preferring to call the gangsters members of La Cosa Nostra (LCN).

Despite the widespread belief that the Mafia bosses wouldn't sanction drug dealing on supposedly moral grounds—a myth per-petuated in films like *The Godfather*—Mob bosses going back to Arnold "The Brain" Rothstein and Charles "Lucky" Luciano traf-ficked in heroin in the 1920s and 1930s. Luciano once famously described heroin as "a million dollars in a suitcase."

It's a long-standing truism: Wherever there are drugs, there's organized crime. The Bureau of Narcotics almost by default was in the vanguard of interdiction, seizures, and arrests. Back in the 1960s and 1970s the big money was in smack. Horse. H. Cases involving the notorious French Connection—the Corsican importers, the Sicilian manufacturers—were all handled by the precursor of the DEA, task forces comprised of the Federal Bureau of Narcotics alongside local cops from the New York State Police and New York Police Department detectives.

The Drug Enforcement Administration, established by President Nixon in 1973, melded the Treasury's Bureau of Narcotics and the Justice Department's Bureau of Narcotics and Dangerous Drugs. Before I came on the job, the DEA headquarters was located at 1405 I Street NW in Washington. With the growth of the agency due to the explosion of illicit narcotics flowing into the country, by 1989 the headquarters had expanded and relocated to Pentagon City in Arlington, Virginia. The DEA was established to spearhead the original "War on Drugs." As I was to see during my years on the street, there could hardly be a greater misnomer than a "War on Drugs." The only "war"—if we insist on that military term—consists of battles targeting individual drug traffickers. For me, the idea of a War on Drugs was irrational; no matter how good a federal agent you are, no matter how big your cases, you could never simply *seize* enough narcotics to make any appreciable difference.

Even early on, fresh out of the academy, I realized that the only difference you could ever make was by pursuing a tactic of *decapitation*: Taking out the actual kingpins. Decimating the organizations themselves not by working your way up the ladder but by going straight at the leadership. If you wanted to win, you had to take out the bosses directly.

It was in those early days in Group Four—barely two weeks on the job—that I learned the nitty-gritty of undercover narcotics operations firsthand. The task force included DEA agents like José and Rogelio, but also a group of special agents from the Bureau of Alcohol, Tobacco and Firearms (ATF).

One was a hard-charging North Carolinian who everyone called Billy-Boy: Special Agent William Queen of the ATF. At the time, Billy was becoming an expert undercover, working one-percenter biker gangs throughout the Southwest; a decade later, he'd chronicle his undercover journey inside the Mongols outlaw motorcycle club in his *New York Times* bestseller, *Under and Alone.**

I was a *baby* the first time I went undercover on a heroin deal. We were going out to buy a pound of smack at this hotel. The traffickers were independent Mexican wholesalers—midlevel distributors connected to one of the cartels south of the border, known as the Riveras organization.

They dealt in a form of black-tar heroin called *chiva*. Supposedly, they had some of the best quality *chiva* in California. I'd learned to talk the talk by now: We had to refer to weights such as "eightballs" and "Mexican ounces." (Mexicans, like much of the rest of the world, use the metric system. A kilogram is 2.2 pounds; there are 35.2 ounces in a kilo. A standard ounce on the decimal scale is 28.35 grams. Rounding down for convenience, a Mexican ounce is actually 25 grams.)

---

* *Under and Alone: The True Story of the Undercover Agent Who Infiltrated America's Most Violent Outlaw Motorcycle Gang* (Random House).

I was going on the set as an undercover alone, but with me that day I had one hell of a backup team: my DEA partner, José, and a few of the ATF boys as well. Billy Queen was there, as was Mike Dawkins—both as seasoned as I was green. Like me, Billy wasn't tall, but he was a fearsome presence, known for his expertise with *any* kind of firearm; Dawkins was more physically imposing, standing six-foot-five—a special agent you would never want to get on the wrong side of.

The operation started off by the playbook; I was being vouched for by our informant, Miguel Green Eyes, who was already inside the Holiday Inn. I was wearing my dark-blue business suit. Before I went in, Billy Queen kept whispering in my ear:

"Be cool, Eddie. Just be cool."

The hotel room was on the ground floor, with open windows facing the street. The curtains were drawn tight. When I knocked, the bad guy wouldn't open the hotel door. And then this nauseating waft hit my nostrils: The room smelled like shit.

Finally, the door swung open very slowly. I squinted and recoiled from the stench. I had our "flash" at the ready—to show the dealers that I'd brought the money in good faith—but it was one of those deals where the crooks immediately got skittish and nervous, their twitchy body language impossible for me to read.

You often get into standoffs, these dangerous games of chicken, where all it takes is for one of the players to have a *yearning* to shoot, be stoned out of his head, psychotic, or paranoid.

"Where's the dope?" I said.

"Don't know, primo. Where's the money?"

"Don't worry about the money, where's the fucking *chiva*?"

"I don't know. Where's the *money*?"

"I don't know. Where's the *chiva*?"

And you go back and forth a dozen times until someone blinks and shows theirs first, and the deal can continue.

No cop wants to be the one to show his cash first, because if you're dealing with some bad players, as soon as you flash the money, they may get the drop on you: Pull out a piece, grab the money, and flee.

What had happened with Paul Seema, George Montoya, and José down in Pasadena was not the typical dope deal gone wrong. Criminals don't kill as often as they steal. They'd rather hold you at gunpoint, take the money, and split.

There I stood, in my crisp business suit, trying not to breathe deeply in that shit-reeking hotel room—back and forth we went. Finally, I reached into my suit jacket pocket and flashed the cash, but the criminals still wouldn't show their dope.

Then, in the time it took me to draw a breath, the whole world went to hell.

My backup team—Mike Dawkins, Billy Queen, Doug "Running Rabbit" DaCosta, and José Martinez—ran up to the window. Dawkins took his shotgun butt and smashed through the glass.

We all reeled back from the sound of the smash.

I was half frozen, in a daze; looked over and saw Billy Queen, calm as can be, using his own shotgun to clear out the jagged shards of glass and then, parting the tan curtains, stepping right through the open window into the room. Next through the bashed-in window: Dawkins, DaCosta, Martinez—all of the backup guys were shouting and charging into the hotel room, taking charge of the set. I'd never seen anything like it.

Sure enough, something had been off, and my guys figured it out instantly after I flashed the cash. The kilogram of black-tar heroin was somewhere else; the traffickers had balked, didn't want to bring out the smack.

Through all the shouting and the swirl of DEA and ATF windbreakers, we did a pat-down of the criminals. After a few minutes, we found an address in Bakersfield. I jumped in my red 1989 Corvette—we'd acquired the car in a seizure and forfeiture from drug traffickers—and hauled ass out to Bakersfield. Went straight before a California State magistrate and obtained a search warrant.

When we entered the address in Bakersfield—*bingo*. We found more than forty guns. In addition to being dopers, these guys were illegal gun merchants. Eventually, José and the rest of the Group Four team, through dogged interrogation, got yet another address and found the black-tar heroin.

Turned out to be a big arrest and seizure. Made the LA papers. My first major undercover operation—didn't go off without a hitch, but in the end we made the bust, and none of our guys got hurt. Given the fresh memories of the Pasadena tragedy, the case was a complete success.

The rush of that first undercover job was crazy. Nothing I'd experienced during my time in the Marine Corps could have prepared me for the surge of adrenaline, the smashing of glass, the newly intensified sounds and colors—almost a heightened sense of reality.

I couldn't get enough. From that first moment, I was hopelessly addicted to undercover.

Undercover work is largely intuitive, as José Martinez always told me. The skills are innate; either you're born to it or you're not.

Undercover is a grand seduction. You build that trust—but

it's never reciprocal. You *never* reciprocate. It's all a facade. You're like a hologram.

Over time, I'd find the drug dealer's appetites, fill or partially fill them, and in short order I'd *own* him. It's human frailty—universal and absolute.

Absent discipline over our vices, *everyone* is always vulnerable. I'm not even sure how—maybe there was some Providence involved—but I always managed to find some trait, flaw, or weakness in the bad guy that I could tap into. Call it his "vulnerability vein." When the time was right, I'd turn the tables. I became the pusher. I made *him* my junkie.

■ ■ ■

What exactly *is* undercover? From a law enforcement perspective, undercover is the dark art of skillfully eliciting incriminating statements. From a personal and psychological standpoint, it's the art of gaining trust—then manipulating that trust. In the simplest terms, it's playing a chess game with the bad guy, getting him to make the moves you want him to make—but without him knowing you're doing so.

As I moved from case to case, I never *touched* an illegal drug other than during a business transaction. I've never been high in my life. After my first UC operation with Group Four— Mike Dawkins and Billy Queen bashing through the motel window—*undercover* became my drug.

I understand this may sound rather twisted, but nothing— nothing—is more satisfying than when you can manipulate and manage someone's actions, his very *thoughts*, so that you get him to behave in a way that works to your strategic advantage. There is no rush more powerful, no high more intoxicating . . .

As an undercover agent, my mantra became:

Just get me in the room.

Once I was in the room, the onus was on me. That's all I ever asked of my informants, of my managers, of my agents, of the criminals—"Get me in the room."

In the DEA, there are two primary kinds of agents: street agents and intel agents. I could do the intelligence work just fine. One of my closest friends and my partner throughout my years in Thailand, Mike Bansmer, likes to call me "Eddie the Academician." I guess that's because, more than most cops, I liked to read and write and do heavy amounts of research.

But it was clear to me—and to everyone in Group Four—that I wasn't an intel guy: I needed to be on the street.

Special Agent John Whelan, on the other hand, was a stellar intelligence agent. We'd started in the DEA together; he showed up probably two months before I did, right after the Pasadena shooting. Whelan's nickname within Group Four was Higgins, because he looked just like the character Higgins on *Magnum, P.I.* He talked just like him, too. His words flowed out at light speed, clipped and proper—unlike any other cop I'd ever met.

Whelan was a Marine, like me, but he'd been an intelligence officer in the Corps, and tended to throw around nautical terms like "azimuth reading" in everyday speech. The more rough-edged agents in Group Four used to stare at Whelan like he'd gulped down *Roget's Thesaurus.*

I quickly became known within Group Four as a case maker. Johnny's strength was intelligence. But if you ask me, both roles are of equal importance.

One of the strangest undercover stings I ever worked, the case of the "Good Doctor," came to us through one of John Whelan's informants, a Chinese-American character named Peter Chin. Peter Chin had actually been a longtime informant for another agent. The drug world is very incestuous. The players almost always know one another. And informants are almost like concubines. They're often passed on from one agent to the other, from case to case.

It was Peter Chin who assembled the entire deal; ironically, like me, he was born and raised in St. Louis. John Whelan was quarterbacking the operation, but this time Billy Queen was my undercover partner. Our job was to go undercover together, guarding the money and the informant. Billy brought all his ATF undercover savvy to the game; I was just some young undercover mope, trying to keep up, holding on to Billy's belt loop.

We were looking to do a deal with some murky figure named Dragan, this smack wholesaler who'd come out of nowhere, started to develop a heavy reputation in Southern California. He was apparently a Vietnam vet—sort of resembled a young Rutger Hauer, six-one, close-cropped blond hair and cobalt-blue eyes. The intel on Dragan was that he had an obsession—bordering on the pathological—with Southeast Asia. The food, the culture, the language, the women—everything.

"Hell, the guy's married to a Thai princess," Billy explained.

"No shit."

"Yeah, imagine that—a smack dealer marrying into the royal family. This princess he married, that's how he got his connections over there."

Then Billy told me something that left me laughing out loud. Our Thai-loving heroin dealer had earned his doctorate.

"A doctor of what?"

"Shit, I don't know—some kind of degree. All I know is that over there they all call him professor. The Good Doctor Dragan."

Most traffickers want to do deals strictly for cash. Dr. Dragan was unusual: His basic commodity in exchange for heroin was armaments.

"He wants heavy-duty US military weapons to bring to Khun Sa," Billy said.

"*Khun* who? Who's that?"

I was so green—four months on the job—I didn't have the faintest clue who Khun Sa was. Billy Queen, smiling patiently, sat me down and explained the geopolitical scope of this deal.

■ ■ ■

At headquarters on Figueroa Street, long after everyone had left for the day, I did all the reading I could on our Golden Triangle operations. The Shan United Army, the largest drug insurgency in history, was headed by this supposedly untouchable general known as the Opium Warlord.

Born in 1934 to a Chinese father and a Burmese mother, he was given the Mandarin name Chang Chi Fu but went by the nom de guerre of Khun Sa, meaning "Prince of Wealth," though among American authorities the name had by now morphed into "Prince of Death."

Khun Sa, known for chain-smoking American cigarettes and welcoming journalists into his forest-cloaked redoubt, saw himself not so much as a drug baron but as a guerrilla leader in the separatist movement of the Shan, a distinct ethnic group numbering about six million, living primarily in the Shan State within Burma but also in adjacent regions of China, Laos, and Thailand. He gradually built a powerful drug empire trading opium for weapons, which were used to consolidate his control over large swaths of the remote and impoverished Shan region.

Now at the height of his power, Khun Sa controlled an estimated 70 percent of the Golden Triangle heroin trade, which enabled him to finance an army of tens of thousands of well-armed soldiers and large-scale heroin laboratories. Almost entirely due to Khun Sa's smuggling routes, according to our intel, the share of New York street heroin coming from the Golden Triangle had skyrocketed in recent years from 5 percent to 80 percent. His product, an estimated 45 percent of the heroin entering the United States, had been tested at nearly 90 percent purity. The US government posted a $2 million bounty for his capture.

There have been populist uprisings around the world since the dawn of civilization, of course, but Khun Sa holds the dubious distinction of leading a full-scale army of insurgents funded entirely by the production and sale of opium. The Sicilian Mafia, the Corsicans, and other organized crime groups had used drug proceeds to advance various illegal enterprises, but the Shan United Army was the first to organize its entire funding structure—from grassroots logistics to the purchase of military-grade armaments—entirely on drug dealing.

After three hours, I had to stop reading our intel reports. I felt like my irises had been burned by a subtropical glare. We were no longer looking at typical midlevel street dealers, or even high-profile international traffickers.

The Opium Warlord was, at the present time, the most powerful illegal drug merchant on earth. *Welcome to the big time, Eddie.*

What Dr. Dragan was asking us to do was completely unprecedented; it required a special joint operation by DEA and ATF, a string of official authorizations going all the way up the chain of command to the Department of Defense.

I was stunned when Billy Queen explained the logistics.

"What you think, Eddie? It's not like we got all these military weapons sitting around in a warehouse in downtown LA."

Somehow or other, he said, we'd got access to a military base. Whelan also had managed to commandeer our own aircraft to fly the armaments to Los Angeles.

"An airplane?"

"How else we gonna do it? We can't *drive* all that explosives and shit across the country."

Within a few weeks Whelan, through his bureaucratic alchemy, obtained an astonishing cache of weapons. No federal law enforcement agency—DEA, ATF, or even FBI—could pull something off like this in today's world. We had a whole warehouse full of C-4 explosives, M60s, general-purpose machine guns, Hawk missiles, LAW rockets, even man-portable air-defense systems (MANPADS). When I entered the warehouse, I stood there in disbelief: wooden cartons stacked upon wooden cartons—LAW rockets? Surface-to-air missiles? How the hell had we got our hands on these things?

We even had the missile guidance systems—in fact, John explained, the Department of Defense was more reticent about us taking those guidance systems than the actual missiles. Guidance systems are compartmentalized independent components, which can lock in precisely on specific targets. All of the missiles and rockets to be used in our sting had been rendered inert as a precaution. Of course, we were never going to let Dragan take possession of the weapons cache.

As the new kid on the team, one of my jobs was to xerox all the serial numbers of the cash we were bringing as part of the flash. Any time you're doing a deal for drugs, weapons, or any kind of contraband, all the money is categorized as OGF—official government funds—and must be accounted for with serial number representation.

Technically, it's against the law to photocopy US currency, but we would xerox all the bills, and then we'd transfer all the data to the 6-A. The official DEA report on an ongoing investigation is known as a six, and the second page (6-A) is known as the Money List. I always called it the Cheese List. "Cheese" was the latest street slang among LA dealers for cash.

Dragan was going to give us seventy units of heroin, but he didn't want a dime in cash; he simply wanted our heavy-duty armaments. So I documented all the serial numbers and specs of the weapons on the Cheese List.

When it came time for the meet, Billy and I were the ones tasked with picking up the "good doctor."

Billy, Mike Dawkins, and I were playing the roles of arms dealers. We didn't have to *sell* ourselves; our flash spoke for itself: How else could we have got our hands on surface-to-air missiles?

Billy Queen always had a heavy undercover presence. Billy had the heavy weapons on him, too. I was just carrying my .38 snub-nose. Something small and concealable. Everybody else on the team carried cannons. I was a good enough shot that as long as I could see you, I could pop you in the head. That was always my philosophy: If you're a good enough shot from a distance, you don't have to carry anything heavy. Billy was a great shot, too, but he was known for his Colt .45 and shotguns. Honestly, Billy carried whatever the *hell* he wanted. By comparison, I was a Boy Scout. I kept quiet, with my little .38 tucked in the front of my pants, right against the hip bone.

I never felt the need to carry anything heavy. When I got to the DEA, I was proficient with both handguns and rifles from my time in the Marines. In the DEA we qualify regularly with a handgun, shotgun, assault rifle, and submachine gun. Since my Marine Corps days I've been known as a good marksman, but only with smaller guns. My friends used to jokingly call me Eddie Pistolero. In my academy class, I finished number one in all the firearms tests, and graduated with an average of 99 percent with all four weapons.

The handgun testing was particularly interesting: There's a rich history and mystique. If you graduate with an aggregate score of 95 percent on the different qualifications in the seventeen-week training, then you are eligible to attempt—three occasions, on the same day—to fire upon a paper silhouette target that is the size of a slender man, at distances of 50 yards, 25 yards, 15 yards, 10 yards, 5 yards, then back to 10 yards.

You fire exactly fifty rounds each time; each of the distance stages is timed—alternating from standing to prone positions, between positions on top of a barricade and on its right and left sides. If all fifty rounds strike within the outline of the silhouette target, then you are inducted into a select fraternity known as the Possible Club.

The Possible Club—essentially a Hall of Fame of federal agent marksmen—dates back to the 1930s, when an FBI firearms instructor named Bill Nitschke devised a target testing system based on the silhouette of an actual special agent.*

When we went to pick up the "good doctor," all of us UCs were professionally dressed—befitting men capable of trafficking in military armaments. We weren't street dealers; we were international arms merchants.

I had on that same dark-blue business suit—my only good suit at the time; Dawkins looked similar, but with a suit in charcoal gray. All of us had on ties, except Billy Queen. Billy wore a sports jacket, but with jeans.

We pulled up in our undercover car: a new blue Firebird. I was the driver, Dawkins next to me. Dragan stepped outside; he was wearing the most gorgeous hand-tailored suit, with Italian loafers, striped silk tie. The doctor got into the backseat next to Billy.

His demeanor remained ice-cold; he didn't say shit. Didn't so much as nod. And he damn sure didn't smile. I don't think he was a white supremacist, but to me, he had an almost neo-Nazi appearance; he held your gaze for too long, and those blue eyes were chilling. I've learned with guys who look like that, guys who think they're badasses, you don't keep your distance from them. You move in *closer.*

When they think they're bad, make sure they *feel* you.

---

* I was only the twenty-fourth man inducted into the Possible Club in DEA's history. These days, they are up to about sixty. The FBI's club goes back to the Depression; the ranks of their Possible Club are much bigger. The DEA's only been in existence since 1973; our membership in the club is small by comparison. Still, I'm honored to have made it into the Possible Club, and still cherish that bullet-riddled silhouette target, which hangs on the wall of my home office.

Dragan had assembled several millions of dollars in cash, as well as some of the purest smack from the Golden Triangle, to trade for those weapons. The Shan United Army, untouchable in their dense forest stronghold in Burma, were waiting for this arms shipment.

Billy walked in first, and I followed. Then Dr. Dragan glanced around inside the warehouse.

Just for a second, I thought I saw Dr. Dragan smiling. He could not believe we had all these crates full of brand-new Hawk missiles, LAW rockets, M60 machine guns. This wasn't some routine cache you could pick up easily on the black market. He was nodding, staring, and spoke for the first time.

"I'm impressed," he said.

I was, too. To my knowledge, no one in the history of US law enforcement had ever put together an armaments flash like we had that day in the warehouse.

With the weapons flash complete, we made plans to consummate the deal. Dr. Dragan, of course, didn't have a million dollars in cash or seventy kilos of heroin on him personally.

But then the transaction went suddenly, inexplicably, off the rails.

The next day—right after we'd done the flash—Dragan showed some surprising savvy. He was sharp enough to drive downtown, and he did exactly what we would have done: He put himself inside *our* minds.

He set up his own surveillance. Posted up in front of the World Trade Center on South Figueroa Street. We'd all been sitting in this local restaurant: Billy Queen, John Whelan, couple of other guys from Group Four. When we finished lunch and were leaving the restaurant, I'll be damned if I didn't see a tall blond guy crossing the footbridge over South Figueroa Street, connecting the Bonaventure Hotel to the World Trade Center. I saw the clean military brush cut and those cobalt-blue eyes.

"Shit."

"What?"

"Guy looks just like Dragan."

And those bright wolflike blue eyes locked, just for a moment, on mine.

"I'll be damned," Billy said. "It *is* fuckin' Dragan."

He'd set up outside by the Bonaventure, scoping out a restaurant where he thought a bunch of agents in the ATF and DEA would go to lunch. No doubt about it: He was looking for me and Billy Queen and Mike Dawkins.

And from that moment when our eyes locked—that mere millisecond—we were burned.

Dr. Dragan disappeared.

The unprecedented arms-for-heroin deal was never consummated.

Within days, Dragan was lost to us—he was no longer in California, had vanished somewhere in the jungles of Burma or northern Thailand. We had all these expensive missiles, MANPADS, explosives, M60s, to give straight back to the military.

Months later, a few of our Southeast Asia–based DEA guys—along with two spooks—made entry into his empty room in Hong Kong. They discovered a letter Dr. Dragan had written to the vice president of the United States, volunteering his services as a "special liaison" to the insurgent forces within Burma. Obviously, the letter was never mailed to the White House.

The fact that we'd come so close to consummating a major arms-for-smack deal was a blow for us. Still, even your mistakes make you smarter.

Dr. Dragan taught me a priceless undercover lesson:

Never underestimate the bad guy's ability to think just like you.

From that point forward, I never ate in any of the restaurants near DEA headquarters. I stayed in the office, brought my lunch in a brown paper bag. I'd take all kinds of different circuitous routes to work, even changed cars from time to time. I operated on the assumption that I might *always* be under surveillance.

And I never got burned again. Not once.

I proceeded with my Group Four duties throughout that summer, going undercover to take down several midlevel distributors.

As an undercover, you're always on the lookout for the big ones, the long-term cases, but every day or two José Martinez and I would put together a smaller deal—a quick rip, we'd call it—buying a couple of ounces of *chiva* from a crew of Mexican retailers. You learn something from all those smaller deals, too. It's like moving from grade school to high school to college to graduate school to getting your PhD.

Billy Queen used to call me the office sheepdog—tenacious, loyal, sometimes overeager. He was sure I was going to get my ass shot. Within a few weeks in Group Four, I'd developed my own style and reputation. I was always the guy who'd schedule a meet for a Friday or Saturday night. I don't care if you're in California, Ohio, Georgia, or New York: No cop wants to work on Friday or Saturday night; they just don't do it. And criminals all know this.

But to my way of thinking, this gave me a psychological edge.

How better to put the criminal at ease? It became one of my undercover rules: Always schedule your meets for times when cops *don't* work. On weekends, cops normally take care of the yard work and home repairs, the kids and long-suffering wife—unhappy because a cop's life is generally so miserable, underpaid, and thankless.

I had no family, just my auntie, and she didn't care whether I came home to sleep in her spare bedroom. I'd schedule all my meets for those Friday and Saturday nights, and right away I'd allay a lot of the traffickers' suspicions.

Didn't make me very popular with the group. Guys had to give up their weekends to work backup and surveillance. It's mandatory: If your case goes to trial, you need them as corroborating witnesses. And if, God forbid, your case goes bad and the guns come out, you need them to step in and have your back.

Group Four had a special chemistry, one I never saw again in nearly thirty years on the job. We were a "multicultural" group before anyone used that term: We had two Japanese agents, a Chinese guy, a Cambodian guy, a Mexican guy, and me—lily-white Irish boy Eddie from St. Louis.

Group Four had been forged in the fire; they'd learned a hard lesson—paid the ultimate price with the lives of two good men. Even today, a lot of the Group Four guys are still suffering with guilt and trauma, feeling that they could have done more to save their brothers.

I believe it's one of the reasons why, more than a decade later, we were so successful when I was sent over as DEA country attaché in Afghanistan. Rather than coming into the country with a hard-charging military mind-set, I wanted my men to meld into the streets of Kabul as I'd done in LA, mimicking our targets, subtly penetrating their mosques and homes and inner sanctums . . .

I took all the undercover tradecraft I'd learned in Group Four and transplanted it to Kabul and then the outlying Afghan provinces. I wasn't looking at that war-torn terrain as foreign soil: To me it was really no different than working the streets of LA with my brothers and sisters in Group Four.

CHAPTER 2

■ ■ ■

MY FAVORITE PHOENICIAN

> How can you say, "I am not unclean, I have not
> gone after the Baals"? Look at your way in the val-
> ley; know what you have done—a restless young
> camel running here and there . . . JEREMIAH 2:23

My time in the Group Four Heroin Task Force was life-
altering in another sense: It turned my outlook *global.* Barely
six months out of the academy, completely green, I got a career-
defining opportunity, working the Kayed Berro case.

The Berro investigation was to become emblematic of the
way the Drug Enforcement Administration was changing its outlook and operational methods. From a local undercover assignment out of the Los Angeles Division office, the case quickly
evolved into a geopolitical investigation taking me over to France
and Cyprus, from Egypt to Israel.

In the early '90s, the Berro family may not have had the name
recognition of Italian-American gangland clans like Gambino or

Genovese, but from a global perspective, they had a more ominous footprint. And as we would see in the years ahead, they were also to emerge as players on the Middle Eastern narco-terrorism scene. From their base in Lebanon's Bekaa Valley, the Berro clan produced some of the purest and most potent heroin on the planet.

The Bekaa is a fertile valley east of Beirut on the northernmost tip of the Jordan rift. Since Roman times, it's been a locus of Middle Eastern agriculture. Even today, it remains Lebanon's most important farming region; hidden among the legal crops, Lebanese traffickers also produce enormous amounts of heroin and hashish.

Three years earlier, in 1988, while I was still a Marine sergeant serving in Hawaii, the Berro family had been embroiled in the infamous *Reef Star* incident. The *Reef Star* was an 878-ton freighter registered in Saint Vincent and the Grenadines.

The mastermind of the deal, the man who put together the consortium of drug traffickers, was a Pakistani heroin kingpin named Muhammad Khan. Khan was widely known and feared, but nobody seemed to have met him—a bit like the Keyser Soze character in *The Usual Suspects*. His name inspired terror in the Northwest Frontier of Pakistan. Our DEA intel people never once got a clear photograph of him.

On July 29, 1988, the *Reef Star* was making passage through the Suez Canal; neither the Berros nor Muhammad Khan realized that the ship's captain was an informant working for ANGA, the Anti-Narcotics General Administration—counterpart of the DEA in Egypt. (ANGA, founded in 1898, is regarded as the oldest drug enforcement agency in the world.) When the *Reef Star* was in the locks of Suez, the Egyptian authorities stopped her, stormed on board, and seized 300 kilograms of heroin, 288 kilo-grams of processed hashish, and three metric tons of opium.

It was the biggest drug bust to date in the Middle East. In June 1989, after a fast-tracked and highly publicized trial, a judge in Egypt convicted nineteen defendants of capital crimes in the *Reef Star* seizure case. Kayed Berro, along with his father and brothers, was sentenced to death in absentia.

When I first got wind that Kayed Berro was living in Southern California, I stood at my desk for minutes in disbelief. The audacity, the sheer balls of it—he wasn't even living under an assumed name. You'd never have guessed he was walking around under a death sentence, that if he set foot anywhere near Egypt, he'd be hanged—but not before undergoing "vigorous interroga-tion" by Egyptian authorities. Around the University of South-ern California campus, Kayed was known as an intense, studious, but enigmatic twenty-eight-year-old finishing up his master's degree in the electrical engineering department.

I went to my boss Rogelio with the news. I heard nothing but laughter around the office.

"The *Reef Star*!"

"Are you fuckin' kidding me, Eddie?"

Everyone in Group Four thought I was a madman to even attempt to get mixed up with the Berros.

The *Reef Star* was far too vast in scope for me to tackle as a lowly GS-9. At that rank, I was essentially a foot soldier work-ing the streets of LA. Nobody wanted to touch the case due to its international complexity. We'd have to attempt to make a historical conspiracy case. That meant we'd have to somehow plug Kayed Berro into the *Reef Star* seizure of July 1988 using electronic records, or possibly flip someone in his inner circle to give testimony.

"Nah, that's not what we're doing," I said. "There's got to be another way."

I took the case file to my desk, stared at it for hours; being a pugnacious twenty-seven-year-old, I just sensed—I knew—I could find some way in . . .

In the middle of a sleepless night down in Garden Grove, I had one of those flashes of insight. I didn't care if everyone in Group Four thought I was crazy.

I set out to develop both a historical conspiracy *and* a contemporaneous case on Kayed Berro—working undercover, trying to get next to Kayed, playing the part of a young, up-and-coming drug wholesaler named Eddie McKenzie.

That's what makes the DEA a unique federal law enforcement agency. In the FBI everything is split up and delegated: One agent goes undercover, another works the conspiracy case; one agent handles the administrative work, another works all the phone taps, and the case agent coordinates with the US Attorney's Office, writing the warrants and conspiracy documents. In the DEA—our manpower resources being a fraction of the FBI's—it's all *you*. You're the one guy—you're the lone wolf—doing it all.

I would devise and execute the historical conspiracy case while planning to meet Kayed undercover personally.

■ ■ ■

The investigation was still mind-boggling in scope. I knew I had to develop a sound case on the one person that I could physically *meet*—before I could move over to the Middle East to advance the case at the levels I wanted.

I figured if anyone could help me out it would be my friend Jimmy Soiles, a veteran DEA agent stationed in the US Embassy in Paris.

"Got something for me, Eddie?" Jimmy said when I reached him.

"Kayed Berro's in Orange County."

"Traveling?"

"Jimmy, he *lives* here with his wife."

"He's *living* there?"

"Yes. Got a house, two kids. Full-time grad student. You believe this shit? He's finishing up a master's degree at USC."

Jimmy went quiet; I know he found it all too hard to believe.

"Shit. We knew he'd left Lebanon, but we had no idea he was in the US."

"He's got a student visa and everything."

I told Jimmy about the gumshoe detective work I'd done so far.

"I pulled the luds and tolls—you can't believe the fucking communications and logistics operations he's running out of his place in Huntington Beach."

At the time it was impossible to make direct calls between Pakistan and Lebanon; by scrutinizing Kayed's phone records, I saw how he had made himself the daily communications hub required to run a massive international drug-trafficking organization. Every night, Kayed would conduct conference calls, using various long-distance lines to patch in the *Reef Star* mastermind Muhammad Khan in Pakistan, Kayed's father in Israel, and his brother Ali Berro, the operational chief of their organization, who was living in hiding somewhere in Egypt.

All the other players were essentially untouchable to me, but not Kayed Berro. Kayed was a thirty-minute drive away from Garden Grove on the 405 freeway.

"Look, Jimmy. I need an introduction."

There was a long pause and a squelch on the line to the Paris office. Jimmy laughed. Then he sighed.

"Yeah, I think I've got the guy for you. He's my best stool. The Armenian."

"The Armenian?"

"Philip the Armenian. I might be able to talk him into making the intro."

■ ■ ■

Now Philip the Armenian, one of Jimmy's most valued informants in Paris, began his star turn. He'd already helped Jimmy make some substantial cases in the Middle East and Europe. A former heroin dealer based in Lebanon, Philip had been jammed up, flipped, and relocated to Paris. He was Armenian by birth, but he was a child of the world—had spent time throughout the Middle East, in Europe and the United States, all over the globe.

Philip was not a garden-variety informant. The Armenian was a player. Nobody I'd then met—and nobody I've met since—had the connections, savvy, and swagger of this guy. The Armenian was highly educated, knew seven languages—all of them like a native-born speaker.

Within a few hours, Jimmy got me on the phone with the Armenian. I didn't beat around the bush.

"Can you get me a face-to-face with Kayed Berro?"

"The Berros," he said. "Sure, I know the family well. I know the father the best. But I've also dealt with all his sons."

Jimmy made it happen; by the end of the week, Philip the Armenian was on a flight over from Paris. I scooped him up at LAX.

He was jowly-cheeked, pale complexion, late thirties, well dressed, thick black hair neatly swept back. My Corvette listed when he got in the passenger seat. He was only average in height, but very heavy in stature.

He had clearly never pushed away a plate of baba ghanoush in his life.

We went to a hotel in Orange County, only a ten-minute drive from Kayed's house, mulling over where we could put together a first meet.

In any undercover operation, the first meet is *crucial*. It lays down the tenor and tone for all future meets. You have to ask yourself: Where would you want to go if you were the crook? Where would you feel most at ease? At all costs, you want to avoid the obvious places.

Where do criminals typically hang out? They like expensive restaurants. They go to fancy bars. Criminals hang out all night with top-shelf escorts and hookers. The guys at this level want to be impressed. They want to see Rolexes and private King Air jets.

The Armenian and I spent hours in conversation in the hotel, trying to figure out the best way to disarm Kayed.

"Edward, I won't lie to you," Philip said—always a questionable conversational gambit from an informant. "This isn't going to be easy. How to make Kayed think that you're really a wholesale heroin dealer and a good friend of mine . . . Yet he's never even *heard* of you . . . Still, you're big enough that you can run kilogram loads by truck and car from Los Angeles to—"

"Las Vegas," I said.

The Armenian smiled wryly.

"Las Vegas?"

"Yes. I'm from Las Vegas."

There's something magical about Las Vegas.

Every time I've used Las Vegas as a hub, as the location for my undercover backstory—my fictitious illegal activities—criminals fall in love. Something hypnotic about those three Spanish syllables meaning "The Meadows"—the way they roll sensuously off your tongue . . .

The mere mental image of that wide-open man-made desert wonderland. *I'm from Las Vegas.* It's like a neon-colored key that opens up all the greed and larceny in criminals' hearts.

The Armenian apparently didn't like the look of cockiness in my eyes.

"Let me assure you, Edward," Philip said, "Kayed is *smarter* than you."

"We'll see."

"Kayed is smarter than anyone around him."

"Is Kayed smarter than *you*, Philip?"

"No." The Armenian smiled again.

"Then we should be fine," I said. "Stay focused. Where would he want to go on a free weekend?"

There was complete silence in the bare hotel room. The ice machine halfway down the hall let out a rumbling clatter.

What the Armenian said next had me hooting with laughter.

"Disneyland!" he blurted out.

For a second, I thought he might be suffering from Tourette's.

"What the fuck did you say? *Disney*land?"

"Disneyland. We meet at the parking lot of Disneyland."

"What are you talking about? I can't set up a surveillance operation at Disneyland on such short notice."

"Listen to me carefully. This is perfect. We take him to Disneyland. He'll feel completely secure. That's where I introduce you. No cops go to Disneyland—at least not to work on a Sunday afternoon."

"Damn straight."

"Name me one. I've been there many times. There's never cops working there. Only those foolish-looking guards."

"Those aren't even cops actually. They're paid security."

"Precisely."

I let the Armenian's idea sink in for a while. He was arrogant as hell, but maybe not completely crazy.

"So then," he said loudly, slapping his hand on the cheap coffee table with finality, "we're agreed. No cops would plan a meeting at Disneyland."

"Yeah. We're agreed."

I brought no backup. Disneyland turned into another favorite stage for one of my increasingly common solo operations. I set the whole thing up on my own. Just me and the Armenian. I had no idea if the scheme had a chance of working, so I didn't even tell my boss, Rogelio. Didn't tell my partner, José. Wouldn't have mattered if I did. No one in Group Four had any interest in giving up Sunday afternoons to do a boring-ass surveillance detail in the Magic Kingdom of Anaheim.

Nobody in Group Four shared my obsession for Kayed

Berro—they all thought it would be too hard a case to make stick. The chances of a payoff were far too remote. They wanted me to focus my obsessiveness on our typical LA cases: Colombians and Mexicans. But to me those were routine singles. They weren't grand slams. Those types of cases— Well, you could hit those all day long.

My undercover identity was well honed now. Despite the Armenian's skepticism, I knew I could match Kayed Berro's smarts and sophistication, with a dose of my own street swagger. I had long hair pulled back in a ponytail, and I drove that beautiful candy-red Corvette. The car had been seized from a major heroin trafficker. Driving it at high speeds on the freeway made me *feel* like a major trafficker.

I looked, felt, and believed myself to be a wholesale heroin dealer and money-launderer. That's one of the unbending rules of undercover: Never try to portray yourself as someone you're not comfortable playing. It never works. You slip up.

I was an LA wholesaler and money-transporter working out of Vegas. The cherry on the cake was that I had a fine Latina-American girlfriend named Tina—she was actually another DEA special agent. Another key to your persona as a drug dealer. You have to have the fast car, flashy jewelry, and the most gorgeous girl on your arm all the time.

■ ■ ■

I drove out to Orange County, right near the Angels' stadium, and parked my Corvette. I sat there for a while and got my mental state ready. Out in front of Disneyland I met the three of them: the Armenian, some friend/bodyguard named Marco, and Kayed Berro.

The first thing I noticed: Every one of these three guys was so fat he could barely get through the turnstiles. Kayed was about my height, maybe an inch shorter, about five-seven, but he weighed a good 250 pounds.

"*Mar' haba, keefak.*"

Those were the first words I heard out of Kayed Berro's mouth. It's the traditional warm Lebanese-Arabic hello.

I saw immediately the sophistication and intellect at work behind his coal-black eyes. The Armenian was right. This was no ordinary drug trafficker.

They paid for everything, of course. All we did was hang out in the park, strolling, chatting, and eating junk food. We walked around, didn't go on any rides—their asses couldn't fit on any rides. We didn't talk much business at all—except when I casually mentioned to Kayed that his brother Ali had got mixed up in something. It was an oblique reference to the *Reef Star* case; Kayed simply shrugged noncommittally.

Everything was in code. I didn't push things. When you're dealing with Arabs or Asians—frankly anyone except impatient Americans—you have to talk to them for thirty minutes or an hour about their families, their personal lives. It's part of the etiquette. It's almost sexual. There has to be that sense of courtship, of wooing, long before you even get to foreplay.

■　■　■

The smarter and cagier the crook, the more intense the courtship. All told, I would end up meeting with Kayed more than fifteen times before we ever moved forward on the money. That's just the way things work. That's especially the way Arabs function. We had to become *friends*.

Kayed was truly a Phoenician—a descendant of the Lebanese sailors who worshipped the god Baal and who developed the first written language. In the months ahead, as I wooed him, as we became closer, as he let down his guard, that was my name for him. I used to call him "my favorite Phoenician."

He was always exquisitely groomed and dressed. I never saw him in anything other than crisply pressed slacks, polished black leather shoes, and a nice, well-tailored collared shirt.

He could sit down with businessmen in Silicon Valley or Beverly Hills; he had a solid middle-class Orange County lifestyle. He was finishing up his master's degree while at the same time masterminding the financing and the telecommunications of major international heroin deals.

I've thought about it a lot in the intervening years. What I admired about him, I suppose, is that I saw a lot of *me* in him.

I could hang out with bottom-feeders, buy dope in grungy motel rooms, and exploit their knowledge while moving up the food chain toward the bosses and kingpins, climbing slowly up the ladder of power. But I also did have a bit of the "academician" in me. Later in my career, I'd find myself doing one-on-one briefings with US congressmen, senators, the attorney general—even once gave a briefing face-to-face with the president of the United States.

Kayed could operate in any environment. He could move anywhere in the drug world, could change gears back to legitimacy, without the high-performance sports car lurching. Kayed had trusted connections everywhere: Pakistan, Lebanon; most of the Mediterranean and the Middle East; California and New York. He was smooth. He didn't have an enterprise that he *celebrated*; he had an enterprise he kept under the cloak.

It amazed me how he was juggling this international drug enterprise while still writing his master's thesis in the engineering department at USC. There were many days when I sat in my car down the block from his house, then carefully tailed him to the USC campus—it astonished me the long hours he spent in the computer sciences and engineering library. He was a Lebanese Renaissance man. He spoke flawless English, and his Arabic was about as beautiful as any Arabic I've ever heard.

Kayed taught me more about Middle Eastern engagement than any expert at the DEA academy. We even chatted once or twice about his challenges in defending a graduate thesis. But he could also get down to the most abject levels—deal with uneducated street criminals—without setting off any alarms. That was a remarkable talent.

None of the other drug dealers I'd met to that point could slide into those diverse settings so smoothly. Some would *attempt* it, but they'd always bring some of their other self with them. That other self would invariably trip them up. Not Kayed. He was more than slick, more than clever; he was truly a chameleon. In another life, he would have made a great undercover.

■ ■ ■

Took a few weeks to get the invite, but I started coming by his house. My "girlfriend" Tina gradually became friendly with his wife. Kayed's wife was a well-spoken, college-educated Lebanese woman. I soon learned that she *loved* opera. She played opera CDs all the time in their house.

I don't know the first thing about opera, but I did some calling around. I managed to purchase excellent seats, had them sent to her—some big new production at the opera house in LA. The funds came out of my pocket—nobody in the office even knew about it. Things were different back in those days; I'd probably be sternly reprimanded as some kind of cowboy undercover if I were still on the job today.

But how else could it be done? You want to get a PhD in global drug trafficking? There is no fucking study guide. There are no shortcuts. It's quite simple: Spend more time with traffickers and informants than you do with your friends.

One warm March evening, we went to an exquisite Lebanese restaurant in Anaheim Hills. That night, I was wearing a Kel transmitter, and I had DEA guys from Group Four outside on surveillance. I spent about $400 that Friday night on the meal while my friends were outside eating greasy In-N-Out hamburgers.

After all that wooing, all that careful prep work, I sensed it was now time. While we were enjoying that expensive Lebanese meal of roasted lamb and couscous, we settled on the terms of the deal. Ten kilograms. Ten "Rolexes," we called them, using Kayed's favored code. That's where we decided on the amount I'd pay for the ten kilograms and the $40,000 I'd have to front for his travel and logistical expenses.

Back then, cops—certainly rank-and-file local guys—didn't front big money. That's what started to differentiate the DEA from local police forces, even from the FBI and ATF—it took some red tape, but I could get authorization to front amounts as high as $50,000 or $100,000 to criminals. With Lebanese and other Arabs—just as I would later learn with Chinese traffickers—you almost always have to lay some serious cheese on the table.

Kayed Berro agreed to sell me the ten kilos of 95-percent-pure heroin at $25,000 per key—great wholesale price at that time.

The economics work like this. One kilogram of 95-percent-pure Lebanese can be cut into sixteen kilos of 6 percent purity and still maintain its efficacy. That means that sixteen times the diacetylmorphine hydrochloride can be cut—adulterated—and still induce the desired narcotic effect on the user.

The street language for the adulteration is "stepping" on it—cutting the heroin with bulking agents like powdered lactose and vitamin B; mannitol, an artificial sweetener used by diabetics; Procaine, a topical dental anesthetic; and especially various baby laxatives. Heroin is a powerful analgesic, and users tend to become constipated. Not only does the baby laxative help with the constipation, it looks like and has the consistency of refined heroin.

One half-gram packet is a typical street-user quantity. By that time, the 95-percent-pure Lebanese heroin from the Bekaa Valley has been adulterated down to 5 to 7 percent street-sale packets.

For those ten kilos of Kayed's heroin, I was going to outlay $250,000. Obviously I wasn't really going to step on it—I was a wholesale dealer—but by the terms of our deal, my $250,000 investment would have a potential street retail value of $2.5 million. More than a couple million in profit on *one* deal—any wonder why guys risk going to prison for the rest of their lives?

But here's the rub: Retail sales are *very* risky. A typical retail heroin boss would have, say, thirty dealers out there selling glassine bags. Thirty guys who are constantly risking arrest for felony-weight sale of H. You lose the product, there's always the chance one or more of those thirty becomes a loose cannon, gets flipped by the feds, turning informant.

That's why all the top-echelon organized crime groups will not mess with retail. They deal in kilograms—sometimes *tons*—and walk away. They could give a shit what happens to the product on the street. That full retail value—even that possible tenfold profit—carries too much risk. The street is not their environment anyway; that's not their jungle.

Make no mistake—there have been some highly successful retail heroin dealers, of course, like Frank Lucas of *American Gangster* fame and his rival Nicky Barnes, the self-styled "Mr. Untouchable" smack king of Harlem. But I always said that the distinction between a retail and wholesale doper is the difference between a guy who sells used Chevrolets and a Bentley dealer.

All Kayed wanted from me was $40,000 cash—covering his travel expenses—and he was to have ten kilograms of pure Lebanese heroin brought into LA. I'd assume the transportation risk overland to my people in Las Vegas.

I felt by now that there'd been sufficient foreplay. I'd put in my time, and I could push the envelope with Kayed. I wanted to have him on tape admitting to being the guy who facilitated the movement of the money and ran the logistics from America in those massive Middle Eastern heroin deals like the *Reef Star.*

"Listen," I said, casually sipping my red wine, "I understand that your dad and brother got jammed up over there in Egypt with a boatload of shit."

I knew that line wasn't going to kill our deal, but I felt confident enough by now to gauge his reaction.

His gaze turned to ice. He stared at me like he was going to jab his fork between my eyes.

"I've never, *ever* had my parents involved with anything I'm doing," he said through clenched teeth. "It's just my brothers and myself. Not my father. Don't ever forget it."

Classic familial loyalty among Arabs. He would never implicate the beloved family patriarch, Mohammad.

I backed off. I hadn't blown my cover, but I couldn't speed up the wooing. I could see right then that Kayed was never going to implicate his father in a criminal conspiracy. That avenue of pursuit was immediately shut down.

I handed him five grand cash that night.

Again, it's almost like when you're dating a woman. If she gets offended—and Kayed was *deeply* offended by my remark—you have to do something sweet right away to make it right. You have to do something to take the sting away.

Not the memory. The memory will stay with her forever. Just the immediate sting. So I reached into my suit pocket and gave Kayed five grand.

He nodded. Nothing was sweeter to Kayed than cash. The five grand took the sting right away.

That was the first down payment on our deal, but I still had to give him the other $35,000 before we could proceed any further.

■ ■ ■

Two weeks later, I arranged to deliver the remaining $35,000. I set the meet for Monterey Park, the exact same location where George Montoya and Paul Seema had first picked up the bad guys who murdered them. We needed this interaction to be done under strict surveillance. It was a major meet, and practically the entire Group Four team was working it: Nadine Takeshta, Ralph Partridge, José Martinez, Brian Lee, John Whelan, and Jeannette Ferro.

My boss Rogelio Guevara was initially disturbed about my choice of the park.

"Ed, why are you bringing us back here? Why bring us *here* of all places?"

"Rogelio, this is serious business. This is a dangerous player. This is *exactly* the place to do it."

"Don't you know how much *hurt* there is here in Monterey Park?"

Rogelio wasn't going to argue with me about it; he trusted my judgment enough at this point. In fact, he was going to be my right-hand man, working as a second undercover, at the handoff.

As we waited for Kayed to show up, I explained to Rogelio that I'd thought long and hard, that I'd purposely chosen Monterey Park, specifically because I wanted the team to be reminded of the hurt; I wanted everyone to feel the presence of George and Paul, wanted everyone to feel the weight of our brothers who'd paid the ultimate price. I specifically wanted that sense of import, for them to take the danger of Kayed seriously.

"I had a long talk with José about it," I said.

"And?"

"José said he's fine with it. José said, 'Come on, let's bag this motherfucker.'"

And if José Martinez, who'd been shot and nearly killed right there, was okay working surveillance in Monterey Park, how could anyone else raise objections?

Kayed arrived, and we met in a quiet section of the park—no passersby or nosy eyes. Just Rogelio standing about five feet away from me. I made no explanation at all for his presence.

"Here you go," I said.

I had the money in a small satchel. The cash was crisp—bank bricks of hundred-dollar bills that still had the US Treasury money bands on them. Criminals always love to see those clean paper bands; it reassures them that the money isn't counterfeit.

Kayed accepted the $35,000, slipped it into his own small bag.

I wanted the deal to go through, but I also had to give him a bit of a scare. He needed to see that I wasn't a pussy.

"Kayed, remember: I've been to your house. So I'll know where to find you if we need to *discuss* matters, right?"

Now Rogelio stepped forward with his utterly menacing appearance. That dark scar down the side of his face. That damaged right eye. With his fierce stare, he looked and sounded the part of a feared Mexican cartel henchman. His appearance was so hard that he could afford to speak very softly:

"You understand what he's saying, amigo?"

Kayed nodded. The logical assumption was that I was contracting out some of my "dirty work" to one of the Mexican cartels. Tina, my "girl," was Hispanic, too, and would occasionally speak in Spanish on the phone in front of Kayed. You have to put all these subtle, unexplained threads in their minds.

When you're undercover, the perception that you're capable of posing a risk is absolutely *essential*. But we parted on great terms; Kayed and I warmly shook hands, and I had total confidence the deal would proceed.

We'd patiently done the wooing phase, and sold the undercover, and now successfully added a layer of menace by putting the thought that I was closely connected to Mexican killers in Kayed's mind.

Then out of the blue I received a call from my friend Artie Scalzo, the DEA group supervisor in San Diego. Turned out that one of Artie's informants was a high-ranking member of the Berro organization named Safur.

Safur had called Artie to check me out. Classic Arab underworld behavior: playing both sides against the middle. "Eddie, my stool says Kayed's putting together a ten-kilogram deal, and he wants to make sure this guy Eddie is who he says he is."

Artie didn't sound overly concerned, but he was cautious.

"How much does he know?" I asked.

"A *lot*. He's dropping all these details, about this wholesaler named Eddie, his girl Tina, and this red Corvette that they drive. He just kept asking me, 'Is he the real deal?'"

"How'd you play it?"

"I told him you're definitely the real deal. 'Eddie McKenzie? Hell, yeah. He's a top wholesale heroin guy and a money-launderer connected to some heavy people out of Vegas.'"

"Did he buy it?"

"I think so. But if Kayed's got this guy calling me, better believe they're doing background checks on you. Be careful, man."

"I will."

I didn't go home anymore. For all I knew, Kayed had hired private eyes to tail me night and day. I started sleeping in the Corvette. I couldn't take the chance that I'd lead them to my aunt's house. But I couldn't keep ducking and dodging for too long. If Kayed's people were watching me closely enough, we had to come up with an alternate plan.

We figured the best thing for me to do was to get out of town, hide out for however many weeks it would take for the ten kilograms to get from Lebanon to Los Angeles.

It was Jimmy Soiles who suggested I come over to Paris.

Still relatively young, Jimmy already had a semilegendary rep in federal law enforcement. That reputation was to grow exponentially in the next few decades. By 2007, Jimmy had gained international fame as the agent who caught and arrested Monzer al-Kassar, the Syrian-born arms dealer and one of the masterminds of the *Achille Lauro* hijacking in 1985, during which Leon Klinghoffer, a retired Jewish-American, had been thrown mercilessly overboard to drown—one of the first acts of radical Islamist terror directed against US citizens.

By going abroad—though I was too stressed-out to ruminate much about it at the time—I was stepping into a history that predated me, that predated the existence of the DEA.

Back in the days of the Federal Bureau of Narcotics, Harry J. Anslinger had been appointed its first commissioner by Secretary of the Treasury Andrew Mellon. Unlike the more domestic-based branches of federal law enforcement, the main focus of the FBN was fighting opium and heroin smuggling. Anslinger realized it wasn't enough to make seizures after the dope got into American ports and on the streets of our cities. So over time the FBN established several offices overseas in France, Italy, Turkey, Lebanon, Thailand, and other hot spots of international narcotics smuggling. These agents cooperated with local drug enforcement agencies in gathering intelligence on smugglers and also made undercover busts locally.

The modern DEA inherited—and then greatly expanded—the original global interdiction strategy of the FBN.

As soon as I landed at de Gaulle, I was surprised by who picked me up at the airport: Philip the Armenian. I didn't see Jimmy or anyone else from the DEA or the US Embassy. Jimmy was prudently waiting outside in the car. This was an important safeguard, because if anyone was watching us and saw a law enforcement agent picking me up, my cover was blown forever.

That's the low-key style that DEA rolled overseas. Not to knock the FBI, but I'll be honest: The FBI would have had a half dozen surveillance agents swarming all over the airport with dark shades, khaki cargo pants, and walkie-talkies.

Not us. The only guy there to meet me at the airport was Philip the Armenian. Outside in the car, I warmly greeted Jimmy. Six-foot-four, heavy Boston brogue—he was about to give me my tutorial on how to be an international undercover player:

"Are you ready to *learn*, son?"

"Yeah, Jimmy, you bet I am. That's why I'm here. I'll go anywhere you want."

"You ain't gonna sleep tonight. I'll see you in a couple of days. Go with him."

We had to keep it low-key, couldn't be open about the fact we were DEA.

"The Frogs"—that was how Jimmy referred to our French police counterparts—"always have an eye on me."

But with Philip the Armenian—a confidential informant rather than a US federal agent—I could ride along under the radar.

For eighteen hours straight, the Armenian took me around Paris.

We must have hit seven or eight different spots that first night.

He took me to see all of Paris's drug underworld heavyweights. The Corsicans, the Sicilians, the Romanians, the Persians, the Germans, the Greeks, the Algerians—all these different hangouts and bars for the elite criminals of Paris. All the nightspots where dope dealers—both wholesalers and retailers—hung out.

"Don't be obvious. Don't make eye contact. I'm not going to be pointing. You're going to have to listen," he said.

From Left Bank to Right Bank. From Montparnasse to Montmartre. We rolled in taxis all over the city. He'd talk in a half-whisper at every bar. And at every bar the Armenian seemed to have a bottle of a top-shelf Scotch or vodka—there were often reserved bottles on the wall, with your name stickered on the label. He told me he had to pay a few thousand francs to have his special private bottle on reserve at all times.

From an agent's point of view—in terms of pure bureaucracy—this was, of course, taboo. Running around a foreign capital with an informant, writing up no reports, no backup, and no surveillance agents. Back then, as a wet-behind-the-ears GS-9—damn, I could have been barbecued. No questions, no rebuttals:

Bye-bye, Eddie! Hope you find another job!

But I wanted to work the case, wanted to work the streets, so bad. I didn't break any laws; this was just the bureaucratic bullshit protocol of the DEA.

Philip, always whispering, super casual, never making eye contact, was giving me a tutorial in the well-heeled underworld of Paris.

This is how you handle Pakistanis. This is how you handle Lebanese. This is how you handle Corsicans.

I was twenty-seven, sure, but I might as well have been a seventeen-year-old in this world of global drug players. I knew my way around Los Angeles and Honolulu, but I didn't know *anything* about Europe. In my dank, poorly heated hotel room, I kept muttering under my breath:

"This is Paris?"

I was in a very expensive hotel on one of the world's great shopping boulevards, but my bed was off-kilter and squeaked, I could barely fit my ass into the bathroom, and when I did, there was barely any water pressure. A trickle of hot water required twenty minutes of prayer. I was in a rush to meet the Armenian and found myself rinsing off in a lukewarm tub. I was paying close to $500 a night and was living in a place that looked as if it had been furnished in the days of Robespierre.

After the sleepless frenzy of my first forays into the Parisian drug underworld, Jimmy told me to take it easy for a day or two. So the Armenian and I became tourists: went to the Louvre and Notre Dame and the Eiffel Tower; took a nighttime boat cruise on the Seine. Everywhere we went, the Armenian knew somebody— he had an old friend, it seemed to me, everywhere in Paris.

Finally, on the fourth day, Jimmy called me in.

The cab rumbled over bumpy side streets until we got to the US Embassy at 2 Avenue Gabriel. The embassy in Paris was the United States' first-ever diplomatic mission, dating back to our earliest envoys like Benjamin Franklin, John Adams, Thomas Jefferson, and James Madison. The current building was constructed relatively recently by French standards, in 1931, with an elaborate facade that blends in with the other, much older buildings on the Place de la Concorde. It's where the DEA kept its French office; Jimmy had a desk and a window with a view of the Fontaine des Fleuves.

Behind the well-secured walls of that facade, I met directly with Jimmy's boss, the country attaché, a crusty old-time New York agent who had worked the Corsican mobsters in the French Connection case.

This guy was a desk boss, but he was also a badass. I walked into his office, saw the view of traffic circling down below in the Place de la Concorde.

He barely looked up at me.

The first words out of his mouth were:

"Are you one of these LA *fags* coming to my city thinking they know shit?"

"I'm LA, sir, but, uh, I'm no fag."

"Yeah, we'll see."

He went back to looking at his papers for an uncomfortably long time.

"I understand you're into Kayed Berro," he said finally.

"Yes, I am, sir."

He looked up, glanced at me, nodded at Jimmy.

"Look, just do everything Soiles tells you, and you'll walk outta this town fine. You'll knock it down, and I won't have to call Mr. Zienter and Mr. Holm and tell 'em you're an asshole."

John Zienter and Michael Holm were my bosses in the LA Division, the special agent in charge (SAC) and assistant special agent in charge (ASAC) respectively.

"Yes, sir."

That was the end of the conversation.

My ears were burning.

"Asshole" was the last word he ever said to me.

I got the hell out of his office to avoid getting another barrage of abuse.

Jimmy laughed the whole way down the hallway.

▪ ▪ ▪

Now we were off on our own. Without the Armenian as my chaperone, Jimmy and I started prowling Paris. Very quickly, though, we hit a hitch.

The Berro organization had tentacles reaching throughout Europe—some expat Lebanese in Paris were apparently now on to my presence in the city. I called Kayed in LA a few times to tell him I was traveling abroad for a few weeks. But Jimmy felt it wasn't prudent for me to stay in Paris any longer.

"Eddie, no choice—you've gotta get outta sight."

"Where would I go, Jimmy?"

"We can get you down to Cairo. Stay out of sight until they've made the ten-kilo delivery to LA."

▪ ▪ ▪

Jimmy arranged for me to get down to Cairo. En route, I stopped off in Cyprus, settled into the capital city of Nicosia.

Our country attaché, Mike Hurley, was a huge guy—six-foot-four, 250 pounds—and had responsibility for that whole region. His assistant, Fred Ganem, was of Lebanese descent. Hurley said to me:

"Look, Ed, while you're here, you might as well help us with an ongoing investigation."

Hurley's guys had an informant who specialized in hash and weed, and there was a freighter due to pass through the Suez Canal. We assembled the intel, launched a crew of Cypriot police, who boarded the freighter and made a hash seizure of 1.5 tons.

As a reward, Hurley took me to a beach in Cyprus, Ayia Napa, where all these Greek men ogle and attempt to seduce gorgeous Scandinavian women. First time I'd ever been to a topless beach. I went snorkeling. While diving, I was surprised to see that there were no fish—the Cypriots had overfished the entire area. They had used dynamite in the waters and harvested all the fish.

I went down deep. As I surfaced, I saw two women completely naked. Crystal clear blue Mediterranean water. Nude diving girls—perfect, lithe bodies: They seemed like mermaids.

I came up, walked up the beach, and saw all the curly-haired Greeks trying to sweet-talk Swedish and Norwegian women. As I came up the hot sand, I also saw Mike Hurley's wife sitting there completely topless. I averted my eyes, blushing with embarrassment.

■ ■ ■

Shortly thereafter we did briefings with the Cypriot cops; the Berros had been using Cyprus as a way station for their heroin transportation. For the next month an intense crash course in Mediterranean politics and the underworld ensued; I met informants, Cypriot cops, and my DEA bosses—constantly absorbing, nodding, making notes.

They briefed me all about the long-standing pipeline of drugs and counterfeit currency between Lebanon and Cyprus. Cyprus doesn't produce the heroin, hashish, or the counterfeit "supernotes"—the island is merely a way station.

Maybe the most important lesson of that stay in Cyprus was learning about the new age of counterfeiting: the supernote, an undetectable counterfeit US hundred-dollar bill produced in Lebanon's Bekaa Valley. Learning about the advent of the supernote was a valuable education for my next big investigation back in Los Angeles.*

Trafficking in that upper echelon of counterfeit currency, deeply intertwined with narco-terrorism, is the financial equivalent of the worst heroin dealers. Big-time counterfeiters hold *real* power: If they so choose, if they're not just out for personal financial gain, they can act as economic terrorists, potentially disrupting and defaulting a small nation's treasury with an influx of supernotes.

I snuck out one night—again, completely solo. I decided I'd go to Lebanon on a ferryboat. For federal agents, Lebanon had been declared an off-limits country due to the raging civil war. But I wanted to see firsthand the Berro clan's homeland.

I went to Tyre, the ancient biblical city; even read the passages about Tyre and the building of the Temple in Jerusalem in my Bible by my night-light.

Now Hiram king of Tyre sent messengers to David, and timber of cedars, with masons and carpenters, to build him an house.

And David perceived that the LORD had confirmed him king over Israel, for his kingdom was lifted up on high, because of his people Israel . . .

---

* The supernotes are made with the highest quality of ink, printed on a cotton-linen blend, and designed to re-create the various security features of US currency, such as the red and blue security fibers, the security thread, and the watermark.

I already had an affinity for the Bekaa Valley; I'd been studying it so hard. I'd been learning the distinctions between the opium grown in the Golden Crescent versus the Golden Triangle. Now I was doing personal intel: mingling, absorbing the milieu; I never actually *entered* the Bekaa Valley, just skirted the border of the Bekaa outside Tyre.

I've always wanted to personally understand any culture I was investigating. I stayed in a cheap hostel, then took the ferry straight back to Cyprus, told Mike Hurley that I had stayed with a girl in Nicosia the night before. I was scheduled to leave for Egypt to meet with our Egyptian country attaché, Danny Habib.

After that thirty-day sojourn in Cyprus, I flew to Cairo, stayed in a spare bedroom at the house of Danny Habib. I ended up living in Cairo for about forty-five days. I was there during Ramadan, and I lived like an Arab, didn't eat a bite during daylight hours. In the 110-degree heat, it was like a waking dream, finding myself—a midwestern former altar boy—working deep cover in Egypt . . . riding on horseback through the desert, seeing the sunrise over the Pyramids of Giza.

I kept calling Kayed in Los Angeles every few days, telling him I was in Cairo. First, if he got wind of my being in the Middle East, I'd already have explained myself; second, I wanted him to know that, just like him, I was a global player.

My first week in Egypt, I also went on board the freighter that had started it all. I got authorization from ANGA to board the *Reef Star.* As you traveled down the Suez Canal, if you looked to one side, you saw bullet holes in the buildings; the other side of the canal, formerly Israeli-controlled, was all new, fresh, painted over. The Egyptians had left their side of the canal bullet-pocked as a reminder of what the Israeli Defense Forces had done back during the Yom Kippur War of 1973.

My boss back in the LA Division—Michael Holm, the ASAC— was a drug enforcement figure of some repute in the Middle East.

In 1975, Holm had been stationed in Beirut—when the civil war was tearing the nation apart—driving an official government vehicle (OGV) in which a previous DEA agent had been kidnapped; the car was later destroyed during a firefight between two rival militias as it was parked in front of the US Embassy. Holm was assigned to the embassy's Internal Defense Force; he helped to evacuate three thousand Americans from Lebanon. During his time in the war zone, he was shot at three times, twice by snipers and once in an attempted kidnapping as he was driving to the airport to pick up an embassy officer. Later that year, two embassy officers were kidnapped and killed in that same car.

While stationed in Beirut, Mike Holm worked undercover in Egypt and made a five-hundred-kilogram hashish case, delivering the consignment from Damascus to Cairo. Working with ANGA officers, Holm also made a twenty-ton hash bust. Twenty *tons*—no small-time seizure. The hash was being traded for 105 howitzers to be used by Christian militia in Lebanon.

At the request of the Egyptian government, Holm opened the DEA office in Cairo; he made another major heroin seizure from a ship making passage through the Suez Canal. On one of my free days, I went to the ANGA museum in Cairo; there's a whole display paying tribute to the work and diligence of DEA Special Agent Michael Holm.

I was now making plans to leave Cairo and travel to Israel; I had a meet set up with members of the Berro organization in the north of Israel, not far from Haifa.

Mohammad Berro, the family patriarch, owned a successful hotel and resort on the Israeli-Lebanese border. He was already being held in lockup by the Israeli authorities.

But while I was in Cairo, the DEA learned that the Israelis were working the Berro clan as major intel assets. Israeli intelligence had intercepted activity on my case. When they found out I was coming to Israel, working undercover, it created some serious static.

Jimmy called me again from Paris:

"We have another problem, Eddie."

"What kind of problem?"

"Kayed just talked to his younger brother."

"Sure, Safur." The same stool of Artie's whose yapping had started me ducking and dodging from surveillance back in LA. "So what?"

"Well, here's the thing. Now the brother talked to his father, Mohammad. I think that spooked him."

There was no love lost between Mohammad Berro and Israeli authorities. But since he got jammed up with the *Reef Star* case, facing the death penalty in Egypt, Mohammad had been buying himself time, working with the Israelis as an informant. He contacted the Israeli authorities, asking a bunch of questions about some guy called "Eddie in LA."

Israeli intelligence operatives made two calls, one to the DEA in Nicosia and one to headquarters in Arlington, Virginia, and someone—to this day, I don't know exactly *who*—blurted out:

"Sure! Eddie's one of our guys. He's over there right now, matter of fact, ready to close the deal."

I flew into Tel Aviv, desperate to make things right with the Israeli intelligence people. The Israeli cops met me at Ben Gurion Airport, drove me straight up to Jerusalem. But in the blink of an eye, the damage was done. Didn't take more than a few minutes for Kayed to learn I was in Israel, trying to set him up in an undercover sting. That one hiccup sent him into a spiral.

But here's how slick the Berros' operation was. Typical criminals would just flee or immediately lawyer up. But to short-circuit our investigation, Kayed's brother Safur went straight to the DEA office in San Diego—alone—and tried to turn *me* in. He pretended not to know that I was a DEA agent.

"Berro was approached by this guy named Eddie who wants to purchase ten kilograms of Lebanese heroin," he said. "He gave Kayed the money, but we don't want anything to do with it."

But Safur ran into a hard-ass DEA agent in our San Diego office named Gordon Taylor.

"Okay, where's the money?" Taylor demanded.

"Already deposited it."

"Where? Which bank?"

"It's since been transferred overseas."

"Oh really?"

The babe-in-the-woods act was instantly exposed.

Within a few hours, Kayed was under arrest. Honestly, we couldn't charge him with much more than "theft of OGF"—official government funds.

But the damage was done. Our big prize, those ten kilograms

of Bekaa Valley horse, never made it to LA. Nearly six months of work blown due to the unwitting incompetence of some DEA functionary who failed to do the easiest thing: feigning total ignorance.

To the brass in Israeli intelligence, a high-placed confidential source running a thriving hotel business right at the border with Lebanon is worth way more than some ten-kilogram wholesale heroin deal in LA. The Israelis saw Mohammad as a national security asset.

I've been to Israel on cases three times since, and every single cop and intel agent—right up to the brigadier general in their recently formed Organized Crime Unit—shakes his head: "I can't believe you got so close to Kayed."

I played them all the conversations I recorded undercover with Kayed in LA. Nobody could believe I'd had some forty face-to-face meets with the elusive Berro.

All told, because of those forty tapes of Kayed talking about a variety of drug deals with me, always in the code of how many "Rolexes" he could front me, he had no chance beating it at trial. He took a plea and got three years in a federal prison. It wasn't hard time—he served it in a minimum-security lockup—and it was a damn sight better than what he was looking at if we'd consummated the ten-kilo heroin deal. If those kilos had actually got to LA, he'd have been facing twenty-five years in a maximum-security federal pen.

Still, we put some hurt on him. He lost all his material possessions: his nice house in Huntington Beach, his cars. He lost his student visa and couldn't finish his graduate degree at USC.

As usual, the DEA was looking big picture. Since we couldn't put him in prison for a long stretch, we did the next best thing: We flipped him.

He helped out with a bunch of domestic drug cases. We worked him as an undercover informant, made a decent-sized case out of North Carolina. Then we sent him back to the Middle East. Officially, he was deported to Lebanon as an "undesirable" convicted felon. Unofficially, he was going back home as a confidential DEA informant.

In our last face-to-face meeting in LA, I dangled a carrot.

"Listen, Kayed. You do a few good deals for us, maybe we'll see if we can get you back to the States."

That's what he really wanted, more than anything else, to resume his cushy Southern Cali lifestyle. Kayed didn't want to live in the chaos of war-torn Lebanon again.

Working undercover, you need to get intimate with your target. You know his favorite food and drink. You recognize the scent of his wife's perfume; you know what Verdi opera she's dying to see. There's no shortcut: You need to rub skin with him. And more importantly: *You* contribute skin. *You* are the collateral. You are the person he is trusting with his life.

That's what DEA does better than anyone else.

Similarly, dealing with informants, you have to remember: You're always dancing cheek-to-cheek. No one manages your cases or your informants like you. You can't just turn that relationship over to your fellow agents. There's an intimate and unique chemistry, developed face-to-face between two men.

I learned that troubling lesson following my arrest of Kayed Berro. It was one I would *never* repeat again.

■ ■ ■

I was no longer Kayed's handler, and as the years passed, we gradually lost our leverage with him.

Eventually, we lost contact with him entirely.

Flash forward two decades.

The most recent intel photos of Kayed Berro, now middle-aged, show a startling transformation from the pudgy-faced USC engineering student I'd known.

He now has a long salt-and-pepper beard, dresses like a religiously observant jihadist; he has replaced his father, Mohammad, as the family patriarch.

Currently he's considered by the DEA to be a "person of interest," as a financier of Hezbollah.

CHAPTER 3

ENTER THE COBRA

Long before the world awoke to headlines about exploding opium production in Afghanistan, the global heroin hot spot was Southeast Asia—the Golden Triangle ruled by that infamous opium warlord Khun Sa, "Prince of Wealth."

The Shan United Army, along with other Chinese and Thai organized crime groups, smuggled their product from Burma into Thailand and Laos and then eventually into Hong Kong, where wholesale dealers sent out big shipments—500, 600, or 700 kilograms—directly into the ports of New York. These large-scale shipments coming out of Hong Kong were received by powerful Chinese organized crime groups in New York City, who then took over the retail end of the operation.

After my long dance with Kayed Berro had ended, I was feeling more heartbroken than angry. Honestly, it was like having a girlfriend for a while; you think you're getting serious, about to take it to the next level—then she abruptly breaks up with you.

Everyone in Group Four—especially my partner, José Martinez—heard me gripe:

"You know how *bad* I wanted Kayed—and the shit didn't go down. I mean, I stayed at the other side of the planet for two and a half months. Jesus! Who knew that our *own* guys would screw up the deal?"

Luckily, I didn't have too long to ruminate.

Three days after the Kayed case started to settle down, my boss Rogelio called me in. Jimmy Soiles was on the phone again from Paris.

"We have an agent in from Bangkok named Rudy Barang. You know him?"

"No, Jimmy. We never met."

"Doesn't matter. We have a money pickup, and we need an undercover to go with Rudy."

"What's the case?"

"It's kind of complicated. Rudy's in deep over there in Thailand. We need somebody to be the money-courier. Can you do it?"

"Who am I carrying for?"

"Ling Ching Pan."

"Sure, Jimmy." I laughed. "When have I ever said no to an undercover case?"

We had our briefing; as an undercover, I'd often seek out subject-matter experts. I'd get on the horn and speak to people at DEA headquarters in Virginia assigned to the heroin desk. Back then there was a heroin desk, a coke desk, a marijuana desk—agents specializing in Southeast and Southwest Asia, Mexico and Colombia. I did all the research I could, in such a limited amount of time, on the Shan United Army and Khun Sa.

"You'll be flying over to Bangkok and meeting with one of the key lieutenants for Ling Ching Pan," Jimmy explained. "We're going to get you the five hundred thousand in cash. You're going to be the courier. You're personally giving it to the lieutenant."

Ling Ching Pan was the chief financial officer for Khun Sa. This was no small-time operator. A top money-launderer and financier for the Shan United Army, the world's largest drug-fueled insurgency.

■ ■ ▌

The very next day I was staring at more money than I could hope to earn on the job in a decade. Half a million in cash in two black duffel bags. It's not like you've seen in the movies: brand-new leather attaché case filled with neatly nestled stacks of bound hundred-dollar bills—crisp notes straight from the US Mint. Hell no. This wasn't like the fresh bricks of money I'd fronted Kayed in Monterey Park.

These were *real* drug proceeds—half a million in smaller bills, well-handled twenties and tens. It's kind of surprising when you first put your hands on it. Sure, money is *paper*—but you think that's *light*? I challenge anybody to pick up—literally *lift*—half a million in small bills and carry it any distance. Money is heavy. I shouldered the two bags, which had to weigh sixty or sixty-five pounds each.

I threw the duffel bags into the trunk of a black Ford sedan. Driving at high speed on the freeway, Rudy Barang and I were shortly at LAX. A team of our DEA guys was there, and we breezed through.

We couldn't fly nonstop to Bangkok, so we had to make a connection in Hong Kong. We had $500,000 in drug proceeds— no way I was checking *those* bags.

Shows you how much the times—and bureaucracy—have changed.

Today, a DEA agent could *never* get the okay to do an op like that. It would practically take an Act of Congress to authorize this kind of transnational operation. Carrying half a mil in cash, we were going to traverse I don't know how many time zones and jurisdictions.

We got the money past all the airline people: Back in those more innocent, pre–9/11 days, you could still do that. We could have brought *anything* on a flight, and nobody would have blinked. Nobody questioned us. In fact, some security from United Airlines walked us down the boarding bridge—nobody touched us. I didn't let the two duffel bags out of my sight for *fifteen* straight hours. I was watching those bags like they were my newborn twin daughters. Rudy, the quintessential narc, tough-as-nails Filipino, fell fast asleep for the entire flight. Not me. I was the young new jack too skittish to blink or let the money out of his sight.

Landed in Hong Kong, and nobody knew we were there. This op was so covert that our own DEA guys in Hong Kong didn't know we'd arrived. After my Kayed experience of being burned by informants and loose-lipped DEA folks, I was incredibly wary. And even if we could trust our own DEA people in-country, what about their associates? What about the various local and federal police, who might easily have been compromised and have revealed the details of our operation, jeopardizing our lives?

When you tap into figures that high—anywhere approaching a million dollars—you cannot trust *anybody*.

We didn't even have a plan in place for when we landed in Hong Kong. That's the way DEA used to roll; we would simply *engage.* We were known as the most improvisational of all the federal law enforcement agencies.

And sure enough, in the course of that fifteen-hour flight, something had gone wrong. No DEA agents were at the airport to meet us, just a secretary from the embassy. She was one of these older, refined, well-spoken women who'd been in government service for some thirty years. She was our only escort, met us at the gate. The United Air crew simply smiled and waved good-bye.

The secretary from the embassy seemed in a great rush; we didn't have to wait at the baggage carousel. My only luggage was the two duffel bags filled with half a million, as I didn't have clothes, a change of underwear, or even a toothbrush. Figured I would have to buy a bunch of clothes when we got to Thailand.

As we hustled out of the gate, the secretary informed us in a whisper of the latest news. The Hong Kong cops had got word of our arrival and issued arrest warrants for both Rudy and myself. They wanted to detain us as wanted "international drug couriers." Again, we couldn't trust those cops with the details of our real mission.

We didn't take any chances of being spotted by Hong Kong police. The secretary took us down a dark stairwell, went through a few doors, and showed us this narrow passageway. It was a half-lit labyrinth, which, luckily, she knew how to navigate.

It took me a few moments to realize that we were walking *under* the Hong Kong airport. We ended up at the other side without passing through any security. When we finally emerged into daylight, opening a set of baggage doors directly onto the hot and bright tarmac, I knew we were in the clear. Still humping those two back-bending bags of cash, Rudy and I boarded our connecting flight to Bangkok.

Three hours later, we landed in Don Mueang, the bustling international airport of Bangkok. We were met at the gate by Don Sturn. Sturn was the assistant country attaché for Thailand, a GS-15, the number two DEA guy in-country. Tough, diminutive guy—stood about five-foot-five but well over two hundred pounds, barrel-chested, was known as a bench-press champion.

We shook hands. Don's grip was crushing.

He was laughing his ass off.

"What's it like to be an international fugitive, Ed?"

I stood there, staring like a baby fawn.

First time I'd ever been in Asia. First time traveling across the international date line. Rudy Barang was laughing at me, too. In more than twenty years on the job with the DEA, Rudy'd seen it all. Nothing fazed him: Wandering around in the dark passages beneath the Hong Kong airport and humping enormous bags of cash, all while being wanted by the Hong Kong police department—I guess those seemed like everyday occurrences.

"You got the money?" Sturn asked, glancing at my two bags.

"Sir, I haven't let go of this money since we left LA."

We jumped into a car filled with cops from the national Narcotics Suppression Bureau (NSB) of Thailand. Unlike the Hong Kong police, these guys were fully in our camp, fully aware of the mission. To me, they all seemed to have the same look: small, sinewy men with cold black eyes.

The top-ranking police brass among them, General Pornpot—as Don Sturn later explained to me—owned half the real estate in Patpong, the "entertainment" center of Bangkok.

These weren't like any cops I'd ever seen; there was no formality or regalia. They surrounded us in a motley convoy, both uniformed and plainclothes, riding on motorcycles, mopeds, and little three-wheel golf carts they called *tuk-tuks*. In Thailand, I noticed, the steering wheels are all on the right; they drive opposite to Americans, just like the Brits.

With my jet lag, fatigue, and disorientation, it was like stepping through the looking glass.

Our escort of Thai police constantly honking and shouting, we mowed our way through the traffic, not stopping for lights, and made it to the US Embassy. Upstairs in Don Sturn's office, we spilled out the contents of the duffel bags and meticulously counted.

Took us hours. I counted it once; Rudy checked my numbers. Turns out we were over by a few thousand. When you're short in a money-transporting deal, you're in major trouble. Nobody gives a rat's ass if you're a few grand over.

I restuffed the duffel bags. We went straight to Rudy's house, circling around in the side streets to lose any tails. We didn't know who the hell might be following us. I slept at Rudy's, sweating through my top sheet, swatting away mosquitoes. The whole night the duffel bags were within arm's reach.

■ ■ ■

The next morning the traffic in Bangkok was so manic that I now saw why the cops don't use conventional police cars. To move through the throngs and the snarled streets, they're better off on motorcycles, mopeds, and *tuk-tuks*.

Rudy and I hopped in a regular taxi. I had the money right in front of me—still hadn't taken my eyes off it since LAX.

The guy in the front seat was an indigenous assistant—a

Thai national working with us in the embassy—who went by the nickname Bank.

Most of the Thai cops weren't uniformed. I didn't have a clue who was who. There was no briefing or operational plan. I just had to improvise, follow Rudy's lead.

The investigative assistant, Bank, handed me a .25-caliber automatic. Tiny, cheap little bullshit piece. You could conceal it in the palm of your hand. I took the .25 and pulled out the magazine. What the fuck? One of the cartridges was loaded in backward. The thing never would have fired. I reversed the cartridge, got the feel of the gun.

We pulled up to meet the primary informant, the guy responsible for making the introduction to Ling Ching Pan's people. My eyes glazed over. Suddenly, I saw Peter Chin, the same Chinese-American heroin dealer who'd made the introduction to Dr. Dragan back in LA—he seemed to have appeared out of nowhere. I hadn't seen Peter Chin since that day in the warehouse for the armaments flash. Now here he was again, had just materialized somehow.

I started to get an eerie feeling. Almost vertigo. I was processing everything very rapidly. I'd been in Cairo just two weeks before, this was my first full day in Thailand, and the whole scene was dark and ominous. Everybody looked exactly the same. I didn't know who was a cop and who was a crook.

One of the cops barked at me in Thai:

"*Tham-khaw, tham-khaw . . .*"

I stared at Rudy, and he translated:

"He says to follow Peter and do exactly as he says."

I moved along in the dream state, grabbing one of the loops

on Peter Chin's jeans so we couldn't be separated by more than an arm's length in the crushing, confusing, crazy mob.

I held on to that Levi's belt loop so hard, I'm surprised I didn't tear it off his pants.

I had the gun tucked into the front of my own pants. I didn't even know how to shoot the damn thing. I never liked carrying a gun I hadn't trained with, cleaned, and fired. If something bad went down, I'd just have to pull the trigger and hope for the best.

With my finger still crooked to his jeans loop, Peter Chin led me into this storefront apothecary—one of those traditional Chinese pharmacies filled with bottles and jars of the most bizarre medicines: elephant tusks, rhinoceros horns, tiger testicles.

I glanced at the vials of holistic herbs and roots like ginger and ginseng. Peter Chin smiled. He was missing one of his lower front teeth. I kept my mouth shut, slinging my two duffel bags, wobbling under their weight like a drunk. They led me downstairs. The room was filthy: smelled like mold and urine and spilled beer. There were inch-long cockroaches scuttling up the walls.

Suddenly a wiry little Thai guy—evidently a foot soldier from the Khun Sa organization—stepped up with a scowl and slammed his hand hard on my chest. My hands were both occupied holding the bags of money, so I instantly stuck my foot up, karate style, and shoved him back with the sole of my shoe. There were glares and shouts in English and Thai.

But it was just a short-lived scuffle, no guns were drawn, and we quickly got down to exchanging the money.

We unzipped the duffel bags, spilled out the half million in US cash. They counted it out to their satisfaction; then they brought out their own huge mounds of local currency, known as Thai baht, various denominations with the bespectacled face of one of their beloved monarchs, either King Rama III or IV—I wasn't sure. My duffel bags were reloaded with Thai baht, packed down, zipped shut.

Years later, after I'd gone through intensive language training and was fluent in Thai, I would have a better understanding of what we'd been going through, but at that time, I was utterly confused.

I trusted they'd done an honest and fair conversion of US dollars into Thai baht, but who the hell could tell? In the back of yet another taxi with Rudy, I stared at the duffel bags. I didn't know if they contained a *billion* dollars or a hundred.

Rudy ordered the taxi to follow a circuitous route, doing all kinds of sudden turns, until we were back at the US Embassy. Back upstairs, in Don Sturn's office, we didn't even count the Thai baht. We drove straight over to Ling Ching Pan's compound.

I followed Peter Chin to the main gate. The place was ominous. It looked like a citadel. Towering poured-concrete walls. There were two grim-faced armed guards at the gate. I was hoping to get inside, but without a direct invitation, there was just no fucking way.

■ ■ ■

In Los Angeles our boys in Group Four and the US Attorney's Office went to work, trying to obtain a provisional arrest warrant (PAW) for Ling Ching Pan.

Now I got a reality check in the complexities of international criminal law. Many countries with which the United States has friendly diplomatic relations—Mexico, Spain, Thailand—will not honor an extradition request on a PAW if they don't have a corresponding set of laws. And forget about trying to extradite a criminal for a capital crime; even with our staunchest allies like Canada or Great Britain, where there is no statutory death penalty, we won't be able to touch the guy.

The laws in Thailand are vastly different from ours—before a US grand jury, we could have indicted Ling Ching Pan on conspiracy, but under Thai law you need an eyewitness to testify. I *would* have been the eyewitness. But even though I'd delivered the Thai baht equivalent of half a million dollars directly to Ling Ching Pan's compound, I didn't gain entrance to personally see him take the money.

That meant we couldn't indict. We had plenty of wiretap tapes of the bad guys in LA saying this half a mil we were laundering belonged to Ling's boss, Khun Sa, but without eyewitness testimony, it was no-go.

Still, with that wiretap evidence, we started pursuing Ling Ching Pan's people hard. Over the wires we determined that Ling Ching Pan had a shipment of heroin coming in from Hong Kong to LA. We allowed the dope ashore and let his people store it in a warehouse in LA. Then we got the warrants, made the seizure, and nabbed a good haul: fourteen kilos of the Shan United Army's finest heroin, all wrapped up neatly and cleverly in bamboo.

■ ▮ ▯

The money-courier job, however brief, would prove important to my future work in Thailand; we'd developed some key relationships, with the Thai police and especially with General Pornpot.

At the time, I little realized the money-courier job would be the beginning of an intense future focus on the Golden Triangle heroin trade. It would take me years to get back there, but when I did—working under the tutelage of DEA Agent Michael Bansmer—I would make the takedown of Khun Sa, the Opium Warlord, a singular obsession.

By far the strangest moment during that brief trip to Bangkok came right after I'd made the delivery to Ling's compound. I'd broken my cherry as an undercover in Thailand. The Thai cops and Rudy Barang wanted to take me out.

We went downtown for a proper celebration. We were sitting at a big table in the bar when somebody started shouting about a cobra. Thailand is crawling with venomous cobras. These cops would routinely and skillfully catch the deadly snakes by the neck and keep them alive.

I now learned why.

We were in some dive outside Patpong. I really had no clue what was happening. In short order, we were hanging out with a whole bunch of pretty Thai girls. There was a lot of laughing. It was shaping up to be a good night.

But then one of the Thai cops disappeared into a little booth and came out with a live cobra. I was not happy. The cobra was not happy.

Hissing, flaring, and wriggling in the cop's grip.

The cop didn't flinch. He whipped out a big sharp knife and scored the snake right down the middle. He pulled out the intestinal tract and the innards, the liver and kidneys, then drained the blood from the cobra directly into a cup and added the liver, heart, and the intestinal tract.

He added a dose of this strong Thai alcohol to the cup. They handed me the putrid-smelling witch's brew.

They were all chanting in Thai. Rudy quickly translated:

"Drink! Drink! Drink!"

What choice did I have? I had to drink the shit. The whole cup, gulping down the snake's innards along with the liquid like some lumpy, unstirred protein shake. It was the most disgusting thing I've ever tasted.

I started gagging, wanted to puke, but I couldn't do it.

I would have lost face with the cops.

I slammed the empty tin cup back on the table. Now they were all screaming like crazy, slapping me on the back when they saw I'd chugged back that entire mess.

I'm still not sure if it was a traditional Thai ceremony or just cops' fraternal hazing. I was not only nauseated, but the whole scene felt *pagan*.

As soon as we left the bar, trying to clear my conscience, I went out with Rudy Barang. We quickly found a jewelry shop where I bought a twenty-two-carat gold crucifix. It was a nice piece. Only cost about $300.

As we walked out of the shop—obvious targets: a white guy and a Filipino shopping for jewelry—we were immediately approached by two stickup men.

They braced us with knives, snarling, yelling in Thai—which thankfully Rudy understood—wanting us to give them all our money.

We were both armed, probably could have pulled out our

pistols and shot them—with few repercussions from the Thai authorities—but why bother? It was easier to let the stickup men jack us. We gave them a hundred bucks and watched them run away in the crowded streets of Patpong.

The next day, when we told the Thai cops about it, they were absolutely infuriated.

They wasted no time. They went down to some criminal hangouts, asked a few questions, and in short order they'd found these two stickup guys.

There was no interview; there was no interrogation. Due process? Hell no. Those Thai cops were no joke. They beat the two guys to a pulp.

They even brought us back our hundred bucks.

PART TWO

Money only appeals to selfishness and always tempts its owners irresistibly to abuse it. Can anyone imagine Moses, Jesus, or Gandhi armed with the money-bags of Carnegie?

ALBERT EINSTEIN

CHAPTER 4

■ ■ ■

THIS SIDE OF PARADISE

My days with Group Four in the Los Angeles Division came to an abrupt end in the spring of 1990 after I'd gone undercover for months inside a violent Nigerian organized crime ring. In the wake of the investigation, after the arrests, our wiretap people learned that I was being targeted for a hit. We weren't certain if I'd been officially green-lit—the contract killing was still in the planning stages—but the DEA never takes any chances with death threats against special agents. Not after the murders of Paul Seema and George Montoya in Pasadena.

The case had begun with a Nigerian drug trafficker named Sam Essell and spiraled into a large, complex investigation with numerous threats of gun violence. An Ibo chief, Essell was a respected businessman in Lagos, owned an array of legitimate companies whose real purpose was to enable him to launder the tens of millions of dollars coming in through his *other* entrepreneurial enterprise: smuggling heroin and marijuana into the United States.

With a long ponytail, riding a Harley-Davidson Panhead, I took on the undercover role of Eddie McKenzie, a twenty-seven-year-old money-transporter and drug wholesaler for the Mafia, moving significant sums of money out of Las Vegas to Los Angeles.

My introduction into the Sam Essell organization came through one of his LA-based lieutenants, a Nigerian immigrant named Christian Uzomo. Christian was a licensed realtor, but also connected to a wide menagerie of LA gangsters. When we met, Christian looked more like a banker than a drug trafficker. You'd never have guessed he'd just finished up a stint in the Federal Correctional Institution in Lompoc. Sanguine face, round chipmunk cheeks, polite, Christian always spoke perfect—heavily accented—English.

After a few weeks of wooing, I told him I was looking to get my hands on some potent heroin. "My people are tired of that black-tar bullshit," I said. "I'm looking for some serious H." Christian implied—never saying directly—that his connections could bring in the purest of heroin: China white.

"I may have the man for you."

"Yeah, who's that?"

"My dear friend Sam back home," Christian said softly.

"You're gonna let me taste it?"

Tasting—conducting an alkaloid spot test—is always necessary before making a major heroin purchase. We met in a simple second-story office in a complex filled with opticians and mortgage companies. I strolled in, casually carrying my Halliburton aluminum case, an hour late. We worked out the terms: one hundred grams of Southeast Asian heroin, for which I'd pay him $15,000—a fair price for a first purchase.

I put my Halliburton case on the desktop, popped the latch,

took out and assembled my triple-beam scale, then began a Marquis reagent test. There are different formulas out there, but the DEA Marquis reagent kit typically uses a mixture of one hundred milliliters of concentrated sulfuric acid to five milliliters of 40 percent formaldehyde. Different drugs—from opiates to methamphetamine—will react with the reagent mixture by turning a wide variety of hues.

Christian watched intently as I scraped off a small amount of his product and used an eyedropper to add the clear, colorless reagent. After a few seconds the mixture turned reddish brown: the telltale reaction for heroin. "This looks like the good shit," I said. "I think my people in Vegas will be happy." Christian smiled broadly as I handed him the $15,000 for that first taste.

■ ■ ■

After four more deals at the same terms—$15,000 a pop—it was time for me to press the issue, move up the ladder. Sitting down to a lunch, I told Christian:

"Look, man, I'm not moving forward until I can meet with your boss."

He was hesitant, cagey, but finally agreed.

"Yes, of course. We can make that happen."

We started working on setting up the ultimate score, bringing a container ship laden with bales of African-grown marijuana and, hidden within one of those bales, our real prize—what Christian and Sam always referred to as "brown shrimp" from China. "Brown shrimp" was code for ten kilos of heroin produced in Burma by the Shan United Army, smuggled out of the Golden Triangle into Hong Kong, then via container ship over to Lagos.

When I finally met Sam Essell in person, I was impressed: He carried himself like a true Ibo prince: dignified, impeccably dressed in a tailored tan suit and gleamingly shined oxblood shoes. In the days before he touched down on American soil, I had received authorization to pick up $1 million in cash from the US Treasury for a "surprise flash." Given my youth, serious cash was the only way to prove to Sam Essell that I was the real deal. Very few federal agents have ever taken a million dollars from the US Treasury; no one *wants* to, actually, because of the liability.

There was no way I was going to do a surprise flash in the backseat or trunk of a car. That's precisely what had gone bad in 1988 with Paul Seema, George Montoya, and José Martinez. The flash-roll was still in the trunk, and the killers knew it. They shot Paul, George, and José and stole the flash.

His broad smile and warm hug notwithstanding, Sam certainly could try to kill me and rip off the million dollars. After the Pasadena murders, the DEA always tries to *instantly* distance the flash-roll from the dealers; the money needs to get off the set immediately. The best technique is to do a "rolling" or "engineered" flash. We let the criminals see the money, touch the money, then get it the hell out of there. Rogelio and José were the best at this—better than me—strolling up, opening a bag full of tens of thousands, saying, "You see that, man? That could be yours."

Then, *boom*, they'd get the flash-roll off the set. The threat of a rip is neutralized.

I suggested to my bosses that we try a "sky flash," and the DEA obtained a Beechcraft King Air private plane wired up for audio and video. Of course, you're not truly *safe* anywhere you're carrying a million bucks cash, but a US airport, with its magnetometers and surveillance cameras, is probably as locked down as it gets.

I had the duffel bags stashed behind the seats on the King Air. Sam and Christian were both dressed in business suits, sitting across from me in plush leather chairs, thinking they were on a routine sightseeing plane ride up the Pacific Coast. Then, nonchalantly, I turned around.

"I wanna show you guys something," I said.

I pulled out the duffel bag, unzipped it, and showed them the $1 million in bundles of US currency that I was moving for my Mob bosses out in Vegas.

Their eyes opened wide. They couldn't stop grinning.

A flash-roll reveal is like a sexual tease. You want to get them overaroused, so excited that they can't think straight.

As soon as we landed at Riverside Airport, Sam and Christian saw the bag with the million bucks leave the King Air and get carried—by other undercover DEA agents—into the trunk of a Ford.

The million dollars—*their* million dollars—was gone.

But Christian and Sam were still grinning as we went out to a nearby restaurant for lunch and a few beers. They soon got tipsy, loose, and jovial on Budweisers.

"They were really still drunk on the *money*," I said later.

■ ■ ■

Christian seemed to know everyone in the Southern California underworld. If he'd applied his networking skills to a legit life, I often thought, he could have been a successful businessman.

He first introduced me to an ex-con named Harvey Franklin.

Even across the parking lot of the McDonald's on Century Boule-vard, where we first met, Harvey was intimidating. He looked about forty years old, had the swagger of a life spent in the South Central streets and a broad back, chest, and fire-hydrant neck reminiscent of Mike Tyson. As we greeted each other, his power-ful right-hand grip felt rough as sandpaper.

"Look, I'm not dealing in horse now," he said. "How about I set you up in stolen bearer bonds? You interested?"

One of Harvey's confederates down in South Central had heisted half a mil in bearer bonds. Not something you come across every day—even in the most sophisticated organized crime circles.

In addition to selling me the bearer bonds, Harvey told me he had access to counterfeit US currency—untraceable, he claimed—supernotes made using a "brand-new system of printing."

Now I had to bring in Paul Lipscomb, a US Secret Service agent. Paul is six-five, 240 pounds, a former college basketball star. Counterfeiting and other Treasury Department violations fall under the jurisdiction of the US Secret Service.

Paul and I pulled Franklin's pedigree: He had a heavy crim-inal record going back more than two decades and deep ties to the Crips gangs in South Central LA. Franklin was known for being constantly armed. His preference was for the .380 ACP Walther PPK.

We began to meet regularly, casually, became quite friendly—he even talked to me about the details of his personal life, includ-ing the fact that he had thirteen kids by a variety of girlfriends. But no matter how cordial, on every meet we had members of the DEA surveillance team, at a range of a couple of hundred yards—their M-14s with Leupold scopes offering me a sense of security.

Given Harvey's penchant for violence, for the final takedown we assembled a multijurisdictional team: DEA, Secret Service, LAPD, and Los Angeles County Sheriff's Department officers all on surveillance. Harvey was bringing me the $500,000 in stolen bearer bonds, boxes of illegal steroids, and, most importantly, three sample supernotes, with more counterfeit currency to follow.

The technology to make the supernotes had originated in Cyprus—but through Sam Essell's transnational connections, one of the counterfeiting presses had made its way to Harvey Franklin in Los Angeles. Right there in the hardscrabble streets of South Central, they had a printing press capable of making some of the most untraceable counterfeit US hundred-dollar bills anywhere in the world.

None of this had cost me a penny yet; Harvey gave it all to me on consignment. Now I had to come up with some cash. All told I agreed to give him $200,000—with a down payment of $70,000 to start.

We met for the last time down in South Central. Paul and the US Secret Service agents put all the operation planning together on the tactical front; I handled the undercover planning.

My car was a gorgeous white BMW 735—and I backed the ride up against a huge cement wall; Paul had insisted we have a solid backdrop to prevent any innocent bystanders getting hurt in the event of a shoot-out.

As I met him in the parking lot, Harvey suddenly hugged me. He was so damn strong he nearly crushed the breath out of me. He pulled me in tight, and the Walther PPK in his shoulder holster pressed hard into my rib cage.

"You *feel* that?" he said, softly.

"You better believe I feel that."

"I like you, Eddie," he said. "But if anything goes bad, you're *done*."

We went to the trunk. I had the $70,000 in an old brown carry-on bag, but the money inside was brand-new—straight from the US Mint.

The moment Harvey picked up the bag, in the corner of my eye I saw the figure of Paul Lipscomb dashing in—a hulking blur toting an automatic.

Before Harvey could even flinch, Paul had the black barrel of his gun against Harvey's temple.

"You move, you die," he said.

At the same moment, the other members of the backup team were scouring the parking lot. They found a car with two Crips inside, each of whom had a loaded handgun underneath the seat. They were Harvey's point men if anything went bad during the deal.

My DEA backup guys were incensed, dragged these Crips out of the car by their collars and threw them roughly down to the pavement.

"You were going to kill *my* friend?" Special Agent Keith Harding shouted. "You motherfucker! Were you going to kill *my* fucking friend?"

■ ■ ■

William Brumley and Mike Lancaster were two other ex-cons who Christian hired to provide security and off-load the freighter of dope. Brumley had just got out of prison and was living in a half-way house. Lancaster had also done hard time but was finished with his parole. Lancaster and Brumley were white-boy muscle-heads—each one was a rock-solid 220 or 230 pounds. They looked a lot alike, but Brumley wore his hair short, and Lancaster sported a braided ponytail even longer than mine.

Of the two, Lancaster was definitely rougher and more menacing. One night in Riverside, in a restaurant parking lot off I-91, Lancaster agreed to sell me silencers that he'd hand-made from baffles, long metal cylinders designed with a variety of internal mechanisms to reduce the sound of firing by slowing the escaping propellant gas.

"Yeah, I can get you thirty silencers," he said.

Making a detachable sound suppressor isn't easy: You need to be skilled with a lathe, a drill press, a welding torch. Lancaster's handmade silencers were high quality and reportedly very popular with Mexican cartel assassins.

Every word of our conversations was being transmitted to my surveillance team via the Kel device I was wearing right up under my testicles. Lancaster would routinely pat me down before every meeting, run his hand along the front of my pants and between my legs, but never right under my crotch.

He said he could get me more high-powered weapons, including an AR-15 semiauto assault rifle. Things were bristlingly tense between us. I stared at the sinews in his massive forearms. We were openly talking about crimes that carried long prison terms. Lancaster knew that and, suddenly reaching behind him, whipped around with an Uzi and put the barrel directly to my forehead.

"If you fuck me, boy, I'll fuckin' *kill* you."

When you think you're about to take a round to the head, you learn that you're not as tough as you think. Doesn't matter how well trained or experienced you are as an undercover, you can't mask the fear.

My voice jumped up about an octave, and though I couldn't see it, I knew that the backup team would be instantaneously rushing in. Everyone in the DEA—especially within Group Four—had learned the lesson from the black day in Pasadena when Montoya and Seema were murdered. Hearing the change in my voice on the Kel, they were poised to pounce.

But no backup team can move as fast as a trigger finger. I was the only one who could save my ass now, and I started firing back with my only weapon: a verbal barrage.

"What are you talkin' about, Mike? Think I'm a fuckin' cop or something? With all the shit I've already done with Sam? Everything I've done with Christian? How could I be a cop? Listen, man, *I'd* be in fuckin' jail for what I've done with you so far."

That made sense to him. He half nodded, and I could almost feel my surveillance team backing away.

"All right . . ."

He slowly lowered the barrel of the Uzi from between my eyes.

■ ■ ■

Having allayed—at least temporarily—Lancaster and Brumley's suspicions of me being an undercover cop, we consummated a few more firearms deals. I met them at Coco's restaurant in Riverside and purchased a Heckler & Koch Model 91 .308 Winchester, two handguns, and the promised AR-15 semiautomatic assault rifle. Lancaster also gave me, on consignment, his Shelby Mustang, a fast muscle car with a big-block engine, but I couldn't figure out how to shift this six-speed standard transmission. I had to drive it to DEA headquarters downtown, couldn't get it out of third gear, comically doing about twenty-five miles an hour the whole way in the far-right lane of the freeway.

By early April the freighter *Ivangrad* had left Lagos, making passage through the Panama Canal, arriving at Long Beach Port just near LA.

Easter Sunday, with the *Ivangrad* docked, we all came down to the Long Beach Container Terminal near Pier F. It was going according to our ops plan—we would bust them only *after* they'd off-loaded the drug bales. We had DEA agents in a small room, hidden behind a pane of one-way glass; although I was alone in the warehouse, we had eyeballs on me the whole time.

But there was a new variable, always an ominous sign during an undercover op: four fresh faces on the set. Lancaster and Brumley had insisted on a total of six off-loaders—it would take a lot of manpower to get those bales of marijuana and heroin off the *Ivangrad* swiftly and into our white van parked outside. They'd brought two other huge bodybuilder types, a middle-aged guy, and some new young kid. As soon as they entered the warehouse, they all spread out, glancing at the entrances and exits.

The least threatening-looking of the off-loaders turned out to be the most dangerous. He was about twenty-one, slightly built, seemed like a typical college kid; I didn't have a clue who he was, how to manipulate him, how to interpret or maneuver his actions. I'd completely lost control of the set—the worst scenario for an undercover—as the six of them dispersed around the warehouse. Brumley and Lancaster were poking around in various corners, and then suddenly the new kid piped up:

"Hey, there's something wrong."

I turned quickly. His hand was cupped over his eyebrows, and he was staring hard at our pane of one-way glass. He was stroking the glass, kept gazing in, squinting hard. Our takedown team of agents was three feet from his face.

"This is one-way glass."

"What?"

"This glass is only for *one-way* viewing."

Like stirred-up hornets, the six off-loaders converged around me. Lancaster pushed a .22 semiautomatic into my rib cage.

The .22 may be a small-caliber pistol, but it's the perfect weapon for discreet murder. If you take a shot from a .22 to the back of the head, the bullet will squirrel around inside your cranium, and you'll never make it to the emergency room alive.

I was certain now that they were going to try to whack me and take the drugs as soon as the *Ivangrad* was off-loaded. Lancaster growled.

"Move and I'll fuckin' kill you!"

Luckily, my boss, Mike Holm, called out, "Compromise!" over the radio, instantly summoning the backup unit led by Group Supervisor Mark Trouville. There was a frenzy of lowered guns and DEA windbreakers. The team burst out from behind the one-way glass. I broke away from Lancaster, and he dropped the .22 with a clatter to the concrete. Our guys all had their guns out, shouting. In seconds they had all six of the off-loaders belly-down on that cement floor.

"Both hands on the ground!"

"Down! Down!"

"Put your head on the ground!"

"What, you deaf? You want to *die* today?"

■ ■ ■

"You want to die today?"

Those five words kept bouncing around like .22 slugs inside my head. I made it through the afternoon, but by the evening, the reality hit me hard. I had no emotional support network, no outlet for my bottled-up stress. Wasn't married, could never have talked to my family there in California—my aunt and my cousins—about the details of my undercover life.

Everything converged on me at once.

Sam and Christian could easily have killed me for the million dollars in cash if it hadn't been executed as a "sky flash." Lancaster putting the Uzi between my eyes: "If you fuck me, boy, I'll fuckin' *kill* you." The takedown of Harvey—him bear-hugging me, his .380 against my ribs—and the two Crips in the car, their own handguns under their seats, ready to blast my ass . . .

Around nine p.m., in my aunt's house in Garden Grove, I got violently ill. My aunt wanted to drive me to the hospital. I kept dousing my face with cold water, gulping Gatorade. It's visceral: the realization that you've barely escaped being murdered. I sweated and shivered like I had the flu, puked my guts up for almost an hour.

■ ■ ■

With our takedown of the Essell organization in 1990—sixteen arrests; a seizure of more than a ton of marijuana, three machine guns, thirty-two silencers, seven hand grenades, and seven vehicles, plus stolen bearer bonds valued at more than half a million dollars and some of the highest-grade counterfeit US dollar bills—the case earned me a bump up in rank, the Medal of Valor from the Federal Bar Association, and a formal commendation from the US Congress.*

But now, I was learning, there was an imminent death threat, and I could no longer work the streets of my own town.

You want to die today?

We weren't sure exactly who was planning on killing me. The case had been so wide-reaching, it could have been any number of players: most likely Nigerian organized crime figures or Harvey Franklin, who had a reputation both on the street and behind bars as a "shot caller."

When I got summoned into the office of John Zienter, the special agent in charge in the LA Division, he was concerned enough about the death threat that he wanted me transferred immediately out of Los Angeles.

Through the office grapevine, Zienter also knew that I'd been maintaining a long-distance relationship with a girl I'd first met in Hawaii when I was a Marine Corps military police officer. Her name was Desiree England. Gorgeous and sweet, Hawaiian born and raised—from a well-to-do family yet still a *tita*, a tough, independent island girl.

"All right, Eddie, don't worry about it, I'll take care of you," Zienter said.

---

* On April 28, 1992, the US Senate rose to offer its highest commendation to "Special Agent Edward Follis for his extraordinary efforts above and beyond the call of duty" in taking down the Nigerian drug-trafficking organization. "Follis, through highly skilled and tireless undercover work, was able to penetrate this organization at the highest level, and completely dismantle this complex international heroin and marijuana smuggling operation. He frequently met suspects while they were heavily armed and the threat of violence was ever-present."

He took care of me, all right. Got me out of LA, where my life would have been at risk, but also rewarded me for my work on the Essell case by reuniting me in Hawaii with my *tita* girlfriend.

◼ ◼ ◼

Being posted in Hawaii was a pleasant sort of homecoming.

It was in Honolulu that I had first learned the tradecraft of detective work while serving as a Marine Corps MP. I had been lucky enough to fall under the tutelage of one of the titans of the Hawaiian law enforcement community, Don Carstensen. Little did I realize that, about five years later, in 1996, Don would save my life while I was diving in Kona . . .

My first stint in Hawaii, I'd completed my master's degree in criminology, then been assigned by the provost marshal to the Hawaiian Armed Services Police (HASP); all US service branches contributed personnel to form a specialized strike force. We had our headquarters in the Old Naval Station on Ala Moana Boulevard at the edge of the Honolulu business district.

I left normal Marine Corps duties and was acting as military liaison between the police department and all the various branches of the armed forces. At any one time, there are approximately sixty thousand members of the US Armed Forces—Army, Navy, Air Force, Marines, Coast Guard—stationed on the islands.

Along with my HASP liaison duties, I was simultaneously assigned to the city and county of Honolulu's prosecutor's office, detailed to the Organized Crime Strike Force, which was headed by Don Carstensen.

Working in the OC Strike Force, I was suddenly out of my Marine Corps spit and polish; it was the first glimmerings of an undercover life to come. I wore regular "soft" clothes to work every day, let my Marine haircut get shaggy and my reddish beard grow in. Every morning, I rolled with Don and his team.

Don was tall, weighed about 260; he was a black belt in karate, so for such a big guy, he could move remarkably quickly. He was in charge of fifteen investigators, most of whom were in prosecutorial support duties—ranging from child abuse to robbery and murder. But he had six guys—including me—who were detailed exclusively to the Organized Crime Strike Force.

■ ■ ■

Mainlanders may visualize the pristine beaches and curling waves of Waikiki, or the mist-cloaked peaks of Mauna Loa and Kilauea, but Hawaii is also a hotbed of organized crime, much of it drug-related. In fact, the organized crime groups based in Hawaii are some of the most ruthless throughout the Pacific region.

When I first arrived at the Strike Force, Don Carstensen was working a murder investigation that had been unsolved for years. In 1975, Charles F. Marsland—later the chief prosecuting attorney in Honolulu—suffered a devastating personal loss. Marsland's nineteen-year-old son, Charles "Chuckers" Marsland III, was brutally killed. Chuckers was working as the assistant manager of the Infinity disco downtown the night he was killed. Investigative theories swirled: The elder Marsland had been fearless about going after major crime figures in Honolulu.

Though it was now essentially a cold case, Don had committed his life to finding the murderer of Marsland's son.

Meanwhile, I was kick-starting a few of my own cases, almost always involving US military personnel—everything from domestic violence to assault to murder. Within a few weeks of my arrival,

I launched the Deserter Retrieval Program. Don and I arrested nine Vietnam-era deserters, guys who'd gone AWOL and found a nice quiet corner of paradise to lay low, let their beards grow gray, and hang out for decades. Most of them weren't bad dudes, but we still brought them in. It was the first time I'd taken the initiative to step up and develop my own investigative program, something I would later become known for in my years with the DEA.

I played a very minor role on the Marsland murder case, only worked the military angles, talking to guys from the various service branches stationed on the island. I didn't think any of them were potential triggermen—I was simply asking if they'd heard word on the street. Eventually, working my military contacts and informants, I was able to gather some useful leads that helped Don in his investigation.

▪ ▪ ▪

The primary investigative theory of the case was that the elder Marsland was getting too close to taking down Larry Mehau, allegedly the godfather of organized crime in Hawaii. Described in the press as the most powerful Mob figure on the islands, Mehau was a state sumo wrestler and a former Honolulu cop turned multimillionaire rancher, a power broker in the political scene of Hawaii. Mehau owned vast cattle ranches on the island, and unlike a legit business mogul, he liked to surround himself with a fierce criminal crew, hulking Samoan and Japanese guys, all expert martial artists.

For years, Marsland was a thorn in the side of the island's organized crime underworld. In 1975, Marsland's son Chuckers was killed by Ronnie Ching, one of the island's most notorious killers.

When I first started on the OC Strike Force, Don was working Ronnie Ching relentlessly—until he established that Ronnie was indeed responsible for the Chuckers Marsland murder.

In the end, Ronnie Ching would go down in the annals of Hawaiian crime as one of the most feared hit men ever to work in the Pacific. Don ultimately got him for fourteen murders; he admitted to killing state senator Larry Kuriyama in his own Aiea carport, burying a DEA informant alive at Maili Beach, riddling another informant named Bobby Fukumoto with bullets from an M16 at the Brass Door Lounge on Kapiolani Boulevard, and murdering Chuckers Marsland on a Waimanalo roadside.

Ching finally admitted to Don where all the bodies were buried. He'd personally dug a graveyard on the North Shore—right in sight of the famous pipeline waves, a beach the world's best surfers hold as one of their meccas. Don's investigators went up there and did a series of exhumations, dug up dozens of skeletons and decomposed corpses.

■ ■ ■

Working the Marsland murder and other organized crime cases, I learned the essentials of police work you can never learn in a federal academy. The academy teaches you a series of "practicals"—potential street scenarios and your best and worst ways to respond. But Don taught me how to *really* work the streets.

Morning, afternoon, and evening, I was the young military police puppy trailing after Don. He was the boss, in charge of the entire office. He ran all the investigators, managed the prosecutorial support. That's a full-time day job, but he was still out in the street working cases at night.

In later years, when I was a GS-15 in the Drug Enforcement Administration, I realized I'd modeled myself entirely on Don. Just like Don, I could never stay stapled to a desk. I always had to work the street, too.

Through Don, I met all these veteran police officers and DEA agents. That's also when I started learning—firsthand, not from books—about the drug trade. There was no shortage of sizable narcotics cases on the islands.

In my stint with the OC Strike Force I first started to go undercover. Hawaii was a fascinating place to be a UC, given the diversity and complexity of its ethnic communities. Don Carstensen would certainly have made one hell of an undercover, but he couldn't go unnoticed or disguised on those islands. He was just too well known. I recall one news story describing Don as being as "big as a house and a black belt in karate." Hard for a guy with that kind of profile to slip onto a drug set without drawing undue attention.

■ ■ ■

What Don truly taught me wasn't just old-school gumshoe detective work or the tricks of the undercover trade. Don taught me the art of the interview.

He always said it was *his* room. I would never take the lead—I'd sit back, watching, making mental notes. As soon as the door shut behind us, the first thing Don would do was get the suspect a cup of coffee or a can of Coke. Immediately he'd try to determine the guy's ethnic and cultural orientation: Was he Filipino? Fijian? Samoan? Japanese? Chinese? A white American with roots in the South or Appalachia? Was he a military guy, an ex-con, or a straight civilian?

Then he'd tap into his cultural knowledge—which was not insubstantial—for each interview. I watched, fascinated, as Don applied this kind of cultural filter to all his interactions.

He *never* went at criminals hard. Despite his powerful presence—or perhaps because of it—Don never used physical intimidation. No matter what the crime—whether he was engaging an eyewitness or a Mob guy suspected of murder—he rarely raised his voice or lost his composure.

He was remarkably skilled at developing a genuine rapport. Habitual criminals are not stupid; their whole lives they've been manipulating people: They've been observing the weaknesses—as well as the strengths—of those around them, looking to use the other person to best advantage.

"Eddie," Don told me, "you need to identify both the weaknesses and the strengths. One or the other is not enough. You need to know both. If you go too directly at their strengths or weaknesses, they'll know exactly what you're up to. They'll know you're trying to manipulate and maneuver them. They've been doing that same thing their whole lives."

Don would allow them to express themselves for a few minutes and not immediately bear down. He'd give them a measure of respect, a measure of standing—standing that they'd probably never had in their lives. But he would never do it in a pandering manner.

He would look for the malleable areas of the individuals, the wet clay within their personalities. Over time—minutes, hours, days—he would work that wet clay.

If a guy was from Samoa, for example, those are some tough island men, and there are specific cultural norms and mores—

rest assured that Don knew all the traditional societal expectations as well as the taboos.

It's not just a matter of being respectful and humane. No, that's too simplistic, and any reasonably trained investigator can do that. What Don did was more subtle: By constantly identifying the strengths and the weaknesses, and then that third, hidden slice of the personality—that which was still malleable— he'd find those areas over which the interviewee did not have total control. These were the soft areas of the personality that were not yet hardened—by poor parenting, society, or prison time.

As he constantly worked those malleable areas, slowly, with a sculptor's skill and patience, the guys he was interviewing would begin to grant him trust. Sounds *easy*, I know, but it is a very difficult concept to master.

Don's first interview was always so smooth you scarcely knew it was an interview. Interviewing is a highly theatrical process, and Don saw it in exactly those terms. Maybe by the second or third act in the play, Don would start to work the wet clay.

I could never have been a carbon copy or clone of Don Carstensen. It wouldn't have worked for me. But much later in my career, I found myself transferring many of those skills he taught me as an interviewer directly into my undercover work.

That was Don's personal gift: teaching me how to interview, and then amalgamating and tailoring those skills to undercover.

Years later, when I was undercover working major Mexican, Thai, and Afghan drug players, I would instinctively fall back on those first principles of engagement and human response, how to elicit from your target what you need, what you want, and do so in a manner that's so smooth and subtle they don't even *realize* that it's happening . . .

And now I was back in those islands, not as a twenty-one-year-old military policeman but as a DEA special agent, GS-11—I had been bumped up in rank due to the success of the Essell investigation. I was answering to a new boss, Assistant Special Agent in Charge Joe Penda down at the federal building in downtown Honolulu.

The good news—from an investigative perspective—was that I was a fresh face. I knew Hawaii well, but the bad guys didn't know me. I could still play the part of Eddie McKenzie, a drug wholesaler and money-transporter working out of Los Angeles and Las Vegas.

In Hawaii I quickly began to make solid cases: never smack or blow, mostly crystal meth and marijuana. All my targets reflected the cosmopolitan nature of Hawaii itself: Filipinos, Samoans, Fijians, Hawaiian islanders, and Jamaicans. For some strange reason—it wasn't premeditated—I worked undercover within every major ethnic community on the islands except white people.

My first undercover case in Honolulu also happened to be my first big meth case. I was assigned to the Ice Task Force—a group of DEA special agents strictly working on the exploding crystal meth crisis.

Working ice for the first time was *disturbing*. I felt—and still feel to this day—that methamphetamine is the dirtiest of all the drug businesses.

Weed is a party drug. Honestly, I could give a damn if the government legalized marijuana in every single state. But meth and heroin—their effects on users are a different order of magnitude.

Those two drugs steal *souls*.

■ ■ ■

Just a few weeks into my Hawaii posting, I was deep into this meth dealer named Nanoy. He was a Filipino kid: bone-skinny, gaunt, about twenty-five years old. He'd agreed to sell me a pound of pure crystal.

Of course, working undercover on a buy-and-bust, I had a standard backup team from the DEA office: most of the Ice Task Force team on surveillance.

We went out to the set—the parking lot of a strip mall—where I was to consummate the deal with Nanoy: $40,000 for a pound of crystal. Nanoy casually came to my Acura. He had the pound of meth in a small bag.

You always establish an arrest signal before you go out on a buy-and-bust case. The arrest signal for the surveillance team was the moment I opened the trunk of my white Acura.

I opened the trunk, but when I closed it, my backup team didn't move.

I closed and opened the trunk again.

Again.

Five times I kept opening and closing the trunk, muttering excuses to Nanoy.

Nothing.

No raid. No windbreakers, no drawn guns: *Freeze, motherfucker.*

Just me opening and closing the trunk, like a jackass.

It's the scariest feeling undercover: the moment when you realize that your backup team has *lost* you. The phrase we use is "eyes on." I realized, with an icy chill, that they no longer had eyes on me.

Once again, I was on my own.

I ran through various scenarios. We'd exchanged the $40,000 for the pound, but what if he resisted? I figured I might need to get rough to make an arrest.

Nanoy was this little Filipino kid, all eaten up by meth, bad teeth, his pupils tiny black pinpoints—could not have weighed more than 130 pounds.

I'd boxed in the Marine Corps, wasn't the most technical pugilist but I do have a strong overhand right. One right-hand punch from me—if he resisted arrest—might have taken his head off. What were my other options?

I thought of my old mentor Don Carstensen. I thought of how Don wouldn't use his size or strength for intimidation, never used excessive force when making a bust. I thought long and hard about the ethical ramifications of how best to make this arrest.

Also, as Don had taught me, I'd established a genuine rapport: I *knew* this guy Nanoy; I'd been undercover working him for almost a month. We weren't friends, but we had a human *relationship*—no way I was going to punch him senseless.

I pulled out my .38, told him he was under arrest, spun him gently around, put him in handcuffs.

I had no choice but to violate one of the cardinal undercover rules: As the UC, you *never* make the arrest.

Why?

Because emotionally and personally you are not prepared to do it. You are too *invested*, too wrapped up on a *human* level with the guy you've been working. The defense attorneys will question your credibility later during the judicial process.

By now I had little Nanoy in cuffs in the Acura. We drove a short distance, to a neighborhood of nondescript single-family houses in a suburb of Honolulu—a small pocket of Filipinos living right near Pearl Harbor—to Nanoy's known stash house.

The Honolulu Ice Task Force was made up of solid agents, but that night—for whatever reason—they were behaving like the Keystone Cops.

They'd lost eyes on me—already a huge screwup. And now, when they stormed onto the scene to get inside the stash house—honest to God, they hit the *wrong* address.

Making a warrantless entry—based on my engagements with Nanoy—they hit the house next door to Nanoy's stash house.

I went crazy.

"What the fuck—*over*! That's *not* the house! It's the house next door! Shit! The dope is in the house next door! That's the house right there, not *that* one!"

But when they stormed into the *wrong* house, they stumbled upon this strange Filipino cockfighting festival. There was cash and blood and feathers all over the floor. They froze the house—technically it was a crime scene as well. They simply called in the Honolulu Police Department, who locked all these guys up for illegal gambling and animal cruelty. All the fighting cocks had these vicious razor-sharp spurs, and possession of spurs is classified as a third-degree misdemeanor.

I was so pissed off, I could hardly speak coherently.

"Are you fucking *shitting* me? You guys hit the *wrong* house?"

I'd just purchased a pound of meth. I had to take Nanoy down myself, and didn't hurt a hair on his head. Luckily, there were felonies occurring in the wrong house, and in the right house, we found even more meth than we'd bargained for. It was a very successful undercover buy-and-bust. Little Nanoy got locked up, copped a plea, and was sentenced to a decade in federal prison.

■ ■ ■

Years later, Americans would see this kind of super-pure meth in the hit show *Breaking Bad*. But the meth Nanoy sold me wasn't made in America. Wasn't made in Hawaii. He was dealing in pure North Korean–manufactured methamphetamine.

At this stage, we were just on the cusp of one of the biggest drug crises in our new age of narco-terrorism. Yes, the nuclear threat of North Korea is, of course, well known; few people understand how this rogue dictatorship became one the largest methamphetamine producers on earth. These aren't the rudimentary Sudafed-cooking operations for which outlaw biker gangs are frequently arrested in the United States, nor the sophisticated test-tube alchemy that Walter White manages to pull off in *Breaking Bad*.

Today, North Korea is unlike anywhere else on earth: full-bore government-controlled industrial production of the highest-quality ice. They've got the perfect cover: normal-looking pharmaceutical plants making supposedly legitimate drugs. But what they're secretly doing is mass-producing highly powerful meth to pump out into Thailand, Cambodia, the Philippines, Laos, Japan, and Australia.

Recently, the Congressional Research Service (CRS), which provides briefing papers for members of the US Congress, published a fourteen-page report titled "North Korean Crime-for-Profit Activities." The report alleges that North Korea is producing and smuggling major amounts of methamphetamine—along with heroin, counterfeit currency, and cigarettes: "North Korea's maximum methamphetamine production capacity is estimated to be 10 to 15 metric tons of the highest quality product for export."

Due to draconian penalties for its own citizens, North Korea's drugs are destined for export. In March 2002, Kim Jong-il announced—with typical over-the-top bravado—that all North Koreans found using illegal drugs would be "executed by firing squad." The most profitable destination for North Korean drugs is Japan, where the abuse of amphetamines and methamphetamines has been widespread since the end of World War II. Though heroin use is comparatively low, Japan has an estimated 600,000 amphetamine and methamphetamine addicts and more than two million casual users. Japanese mafiosi work closely with the North Korean government to smuggle and distribute this top-quality crystal meth in Japan.

Throughout the South Pacific islands, on down into Australia and New Zealand, you can easily see the grim impact on the population.

North Korea's links with Chinese organized crime networks outside Asia were discovered during two federal operations, code-named Smoking Dragon and Royal Charm. Fifty-nine members of a Chinese organized crime gang were arrested in Atlantic City, Los Angeles, Las Vegas, Chicago, and Philadelphia; the DEA and FBI seized half a kilogram of crystal meth, 36,000 Ecstasy pills, and counterfeit cigarettes and pharmaceuticals, as well as $4.5 million in supernotes—all produced in North Korea.

If you want to understand how an isolated rogue state like North Korea actually survives today economically, it's important to recognize that a vast swath of the North Korean economy is financed by illegal drugs—a meth pipeline originating north of the 38th parallel and ending in the hands of addicts in the democracies of the South Pacific and the United States, particularly our little archipelago paradise of Hawaii.

■ ■ ■

At this point in Hawaii I was almost like a predator in the Serengeti: always looking for my next target. The other DEA agents in Honolulu were well known to the criminal underworld: It was next to impossible for any of them to successfully infiltrate a criminal organization. But I was a fresh face in Hawaii. The criminals never saw me coming.

A few short weeks after the Nanoy bust, I was working another deep-cover case with some Jamaican ganja wholesalers.

I was rolling with a Honolulu PD detective named Janice— gorgeous young Hawaiian woman—assigned to our DEA task force. She was in love with one of my old partners back in LA. Janice was an exotic mix, Portuguese and Hawaiian, and like my girl Desiree, she was a *tita*—a tough-as-nails island girl.

We were out one night working undercover; Janice was playing the role of my girlfriend, as usual. We went to this restaurant right outside of the University of Hawaii and hooked up with these Jamaican weed wholesalers.

When I got to Hawaii, the weed scene was changing fast. Back when I was an MP, the best grass used to be called "Maui Wowie." But we started to get aerial images—known as FLIR (forward-looking infrared)—from various aircraft. From high altitude, FLIR could differentiate shades of green, and the DEA could zero in on where fields of marijuana were being cultivated.

The eradication was so successful that the heavy weed growers soon moved into "volcano tubes"—actually lava caves. These were sprawling operations. We couldn't catch them on the electrical grid; all the electricity was being produced by diesel-powered generators. The local island growers were savvy; they knew that inside those volcano tubes our FLIR planes could not grab their aerial signature.

Our DEA guys did one raid in which we found twenty thousand plants—all produced with grow lights. It was brilliant science: These lava caves absorbed all the energy of the grow lights. We'd never have caught them except for an interpersonal spat; we broke the case because one of the growers got mad at his lover, came in and turned informant, and gave up the whole volcano tube weed-growing operation.

■ ■ ■

It was a balmy midsummer island evening, and Janice and I had had a few meetings undercover on these Jamaican weed wholesalers.

"Let's go do it," Janice said, as we pulled up at the set.

Yes, she was fearless: Diminutive, very feminine, but she was a *tita*—a little island-girl badass.

We went inside this nondescript pizza shop; for some reason, a lot of major wholesale deals get consummated inside cheap little pizza shops. We ordered a pie, some sodas and beers, just shooting the shit with the Jamaicans—all tough-looking, dreadlocked guys.

We were sitting there, eating our pizza, when a DEA special

agent I knew very well—Marty Dundas—came barreling in, loud as all hell, shouting and laughing. Dundas was a desk agent and, frankly, not the sharpest blade in the drawer.

"Hey, Ed!" Dundas shouted when he spotted me.

I ignored him entirely.

"Ed, think you're such a big *badass* coming into my office?"

I stared daggers.

"*Eddie!*"

"Who the *fuck* are you?"

Dundas was so dense, so obtuse—he didn't understand that I was working with Janice as a UC.

He pressed into our table.

"Hey, *shove* over, let me sit with you guys."

I had to do something—anything—or the Jamaicans would figure out in an instant that I was a DEA agent.

I didn't want to punch Dundas. Instead, I put both palms on his chest and shoved him so hard that he fell out of the booth. I'd learned that is a very effective fighting and self-defense technique. One of the best points of leverage on the human body is dead center of the chest.

He fell to the linoleum floor. I dragged Dundas a few feet away, got right down in his face, whispering, spittle flying into his face.

"You fucker. You stupid *ass*. Get out of here. Can't you see I'm on the *job*?"

Janice was a badass little girl; she was ready to jump in and kick Marty's ass, too. I was dumbfounded: This *idiot* was going to blow weeks' worth of our undercover operation?

He was so dazed from my blow to his chest that he didn't know what day of the week it was.

Meanwhile, the Jamaicans were staring, concerned but mostly confused. At last they smiled. My actions proved to the wholesalers that I was legit. They assumed that no cop would beat the crap out of another cop like that in public.

Dundas was dazed, but now he finally got the message, and he dragged his ass up and went away.

Later on, he almost got fired for this whole incident: He was such a *pendejo*.

I sat back down calmly with the Jamaicans as if nothing had happened.

We consummated the weed deal in that greasy little pizza shop.

Three days later they delivered ten pounds of weed in a park in Honolulu, for which I paid them $50,000. Not a big case, but it was a good undercover buy-and-bust.

After that, we got search warrants, nailed the Jamaicans with more than forty pounds of high-potency weed.

I never saw the Jamaicans again.

No question of going to trial. We had them dead to rights. All three pleaded out to possession with intent to distribute, violation of US Code 841. All got some heavy prison time.

■ ■ ■

Talk about burning the candle at both ends. In the midst of doing all this undercover work, I had another major commitment: I was about to get married to Desiree England. Desiree was part Portuguese, part Chinese, part Hawaiian, part white. In Hawaii they irreverently call that the "Chinese menu," meaning a person of mixed ethnicity. We'd planned an idyllic ceremony, on an orchid farm that her grandfather owned. The view was surreal—the volcanoes in the backdrop, the intoxicating smell of the orchids: It was like a tropical dream.

But even as we were planning the wedding, the job completely overtook my life. I was about to have two permanent changes of duty station in one year—pretty much unheard of for a young DEA man.

First, I was going to language training school in Arlington, Virginia, for nearly a year; then I'd put in for a posting overseas.

She said, "If this is the life I gotta live, Eddie, I can't do it."

■ ■ ■

I felt—and *still* feel—that I let Desiree down. We were deeply in love, and she expected me to be her husband. Instead, I was flying off to the mainland and then God knows where, and the whole time that I was in Honolulu, living with her, I was barely *home* at night, going undercover almost every waking hour to make meth and weed cases.

But she was right, in the end. It would have been impossible to make a marriage work under those terms. You ask the majority of cops—whether federal, state, or local—and you'll find one constant: Almost all of them have been divorced, separated, or had some very tough times in their marriage.

The demands of the job and the requirements of being an attentive and loving spouse—especially when you're working undercover—just don't go hand in hand.

CHAPTER 5

. . .

THE GOLDEN TRIANGLE

A month after my last major bust in Hawaii, I was back in LA, testifying in the series of trials surrounding the Essell case, when I received an unexpected call from overseas.

On the line was Special Agent Mike Bansmer, a GS-14 over in Thailand. I knew Mike's name and reputation: He was the resident agent in charge in Songkhla, in the south of Thailand, and had been working the Shan United Army over there since 1980.

Mike had done his research. He knew I'd spent about six months making decent cases in Hawaii—all meth and weed. He'd also heard about the scope of the Essell heroin-importation takedown. More importantly, he knew that I'd been in Thailand, albeit briefly, doing the money-courier mission in Bangkok with Rudy Barang that helped bring down Ling Ching Pan, the chief logistician for the Shan United Army.

I was prepping for a long day of direct testimony and cross-examination in what I called the "pantheon" of Essell case trials when the call came in from Thailand in the Group Four office.

"Ed," he said, "this is Mike Bansmer. You know who I am?"

"Yeah, Mike," I said, "I know who you are."

Bansmer already had a wide reputation as a balls-to-the-wall DEA agent.

He told me that he had seen my name on a listing of special agents requesting postings overseas. After the success of the Essell takedown, I'd received a promotion; I'd requested a posting overseas, but I'd been expecting something in the Middle East. Honestly, I wanted to go back to work with Danny Habib, learn Arabic, and be stationed in Cairo. After my month-long stay there during the Berro investigation, the Middle East seemed to be where the real action was.

Now Mike Bansmer was throwing me for a loop.

"Ed, how'd you like to come live in a place where you can't order food without speaking Thai?"

"Come again?"

"How'd you like to live in a place where you have to *constantly* run away from cobras?"

I laughed loudly.

"Well . . . I don't know, Mike."

"Listen, I've asked around about you. Ed, I hear you got *balls*."

"Lately they've been kicked in pretty hard, Mike."

"Don't sweat it," he said. "I'll make it happen. I'll call headquarters, tell them I want you, and you'll come over. I'm living down in the south part of Thailand, in Songkhla. You'll like it down here. But I'm telling you now—we'll be just about the only white guys for miles."

■ ■ ■

I left Desiree behind in Hawaii and relocated to headquarters in Arlington, Virginia, to do the Thai language intensive. Learning

Thai fluently was one of the hardest things I've ever done. It's not like learning a Romance language; you struggle through Spanish or French or Italian, but at least the words are written in our standard Roman alphabet.

To learn written Thai—rather than just some phonetic conversational phrases—you're dealing with characters that are a blend of Pali, Sanskrit, and Cambodian as well as Chinese characters. Then there's the issue of names. Most people in Thailand go by a nickname because formal names there can be virtually unpronounceable: fifty or sixty letters all strung together.

My instructor was a lieutenant in the Thai military: Her name was Boonkock. She was a master Thai linguist, a PhD. Her nickname was Sya, which means tiger.

I would call Sya and tell her I was struggling with the vocabulary. Vocabulary in Thai is called *khamsap*.

"Teacher, I need help."

"What do you want?"

"I'm struggling with our *khamsap*."

"*Mai pen rai*," she would say. "Never mind. I'll help."

She would take time out of her busy schedule and meet me in various coffee shops in Georgetown.

She disciplined me by only allowing immersion in Thai.

"Khun Ed, I will never ever speak to you in English again."

In weeks, my vocabulary improved immensely. True immersion whenever I was with Sya. No English allowed.

Ironically, I became so fluent in Thai that, later, when I was working undercover in Juárez, Mexico, I would inadvertently start speaking in Thai with these Mexican cartel heavyweights.

Luckily the Mexican criminals didn't know shit about Thai. For all they knew, I was just some *loco* gringo speaking in tongues.

The language intensive lasted thirteen months, but I graduated in seven. As tough as the course was, I just desperately wanted to get back onto the street, fly over to Thailand and work with Mike Bansmer to go after Khun Sa.

I flew immediately back to Bangkok to be stationed with Bansmer down in Songkhla.

■ ■ ■

I'd been at Don Mueang Airport before, of course, during that $500,000 money-courier case with Rudy Barang, so when I landed in Bangkok, I recognized the airport from the Ling Ching Pan case. It made me feel slightly less disoriented.

My new boss, Mike Bansmer, was there to pick me up personally in a Land Cruiser. Even at first glance, I realized Mike was everything I thought he was going to be.

He took me straight to our DEA office at the US Embassy in Bangkok, and we met with the country attaché, Don Ferrarone, and the assistant country attaché, Don Sturn. Admin had just purchased a brand-new SUV vehicle for us: a mint Toyota Land Cruiser. But of course, in Thailand, they drive on the other side of the road like the British. The driver's seat was on the right side; Mike was at the wheel.

We had 450 kilometers to drive from Bangkok down south to Songkhla. I was waiting for my trusted .38 Smith & Wesson to arrive from headquarters, and the moment I got in the car, Mike stared at me. He pulled out a 9mm Beretta Model 92 and shoved it in my face.

"You don't go *anywhere* without this—you hear me?"

"Yes, sir."

Suddenly, everything was a bright green blur. We were driving along, moving fast. I soon learned that Mike was a fast and skilled driver. Bangkok driving is mad. The years I was there, thousands would die or be gravely injured in traffic accidents.

They have vehicles in Thailand called *sip-laas*—ten-wheel trucks, like our eighteen-wheelers. Mike explained that almost all the *sip-laa* drivers were on meth, called *jaa-maa*—literally "crazy medicine"—which kept them awake for hours.

As long as I live on this planet, I'll never forget what happened next. Mike was passing one of the *sip-laas* when another *sip-laa* came barreling down the middle of the narrow highway, straddling the center line, straight at us. Mike managed to swerve and avoid a head-on collision, but with a bump and a loud crunch, the driver in the oncoming *sip-laa* knocked our side mirror clean off.

I got quite a glimpse of the oncoming driver's face: sparse goatee, looked about twenty-one, smiling, eyes wide, totally high on crazy medicine.

For his part, Mike didn't even flinch; he'd been in-country for a decade, and already knew that every time you got behind the wheel in Thailand, you were taking your life into your hands.

■ ■ ■

We didn't stop to look at the damage to the Land Cruiser; we were halfway to Hat Yai, and I was nodding off, when Mike pulled up behind two minivans.

"Ed," he said, "these two guys are wrong."

"Huh?"

"That's a *wrong* car."

He meant that one of the vans was loaded up with dope. We followed these two minivans for about one hundred kilometers.

Mike kept insisting that the gray minivan was a load car. As I was to see over the months ahead, Mike had a sixth sense about Thai criminals.

"You wait," he said. "I guarantee you that this guy's wrong."

We didn't do anything further but called the van in to our Thai counterparts from the Office of the Narcotics Control Board (ONCB).

Sure enough, within twenty-four hours, the Thai police made a raid and discovered a hundred units of heroin. Right inside that same little gray minivan Mike said was wrong.

█ █ █

Finally we made it all the way down to Songkhla. Mike often liked to joke that I was "Eddie the Academician." I had read everything I could find about Songkhla. Songkhla is one of the southern provinces—or *changwat*. It's perfect heroin-smuggling territory, right on the ocean; to the south it borders on Kedah and Perlis in Malaysia.

Soon as we got to Songkhla, I went over to find my house. Wiped out, I got undressed and immediately ate a bowl of noodles that my maid whipped up. My living quarters were nice; I was staying in this decent two-story house. As soon as I entered, a green snake slithered across the tiled floor. Nothing to worry about: they're not venomous.

I was jet-lagged, confused, on edge. I fell asleep with Mike's 9mm Beretta pistol in my hand. I had my Cold Steel push knife in my other.

Suddenly, at sunrise, I looked up.

Mike was in my bedroom. I could see his hairy shoulders silhouetted against the sun. Mike's one of those guys whose entire body is covered in thick hair. But I didn't even realize it was Mike at first. I flipped. Sat straight up, bare-chested. I leveled the Beretta and was on the verge of shooting—I was so frightened.

"Eddie, it's *me*—it's Mike."

"What the fuck?" I said, coming out of the haze.

"We're going running," he said. "Get your ass up."

It was bright daylight outside. I threw on my shorts, and we went for a six-mile run on the white-sand beach.

Mike's an accomplished distance runner. He was—and always will be—a stud. At the time he was about fifty years old and I was just thirty-two, but Mike was in absolutely peak physical condition.

He had such stamina, but also a hell of a sense of humor.

One morning, after our run, we went swimming in the ocean off Songkhla. Mike came out of the surf covered in petroleum spillage, which immediately formed tar balls from his neck down. His entire body was covered in apelike fur, and his body hair was now balled up with petroleum.

We went back to Mike's big house, and I watched in astonishment as he began washing his body with undiluted kerosene.

"What the fuck!" I said. "Mike, you're gonna *kill* yourself with that shit."

He shrugged and continued scrubbing.

"Hell, Eddie, you gotta die from *something*."

∎ ∎ ∎

Our offices were located in this huge old house within a secure compound; I immediately saw I had the smallest room in the DEA headquarters—a bare desk and chair—and walked into Mike's office to raise hell.

"Look, Mike, this ain't gonna work. I need a *computer*. I need at least a few hundred bucks. I need to be able to write."

Mike said, "Okay," and it was done that very day.

I saw we had bigger investigative issues, too.

"Michael, the only way we will know what these southern Thailand criminals are up to is if we develop reliable informants. Or else we start invading their electrons. We can't do all this on the street alone."

"I think you're right," Mike said.

I got an inexpensive desktop computer, and we started a brand-new Consolidated Enforcement and Intelligence Program (CEIP)—which over time was to have a major impact on the success of our Shan United Army investigation.

◼ ◼ ◼

A few weeks in-country, and I had become known as the Ghost.

Everywhere I went in the south, every village and farm, every bar in Songkhla and Hat Yai, they shouted "*Pii! Pii!*"—the word for ghost in Thai. And there were days during my three-and-a-half-year stint in the Far East—especially deep in the jungles with Mike—when I started to wonder if I wasn't some kind of walking specter.

Very few other people in Songkhla besides Mike and me spoke a lick of English. It was true immersion. Mike spoke decent-enough Thai—a kind of "street Thai"—but I had become fluent.

I adopted a rigid routine. After doing my six-mile run in the morning with Mike, I'd go to the *wat*—the monastery temple—right down the street, with one agenda: eating a breakfast of fish and rice with the Buddhist monks, conversing with them one hour each day before starting work.

The monks were otherwise healthy and disciplined men, but one thing was odd: They smoked constantly. Almost to a man, they chain-smoked these cheap Asian cigarettes from sunrise to sunset.

I didn't want to be one of those Americans who could only rap a bit about girls. My Thai soon got so proficient that I could talk about politics, world affairs, economics, or religion.

Ironically, when I got in the thick of things, it turned out that the Thai street guys and traffickers wanted to talk *exclusively* about girls.

It cracked me up when the "Ghost" business kicked in. Soon as I'd open my mouth, people would burst into laughter: "*Pii! Pii!*" They couldn't figure out how this pale-faced Irish white boy from St. Louis could be talking about the economy or the king or the corrupt local cops in their local dialect, as if he'd been born in Songkhla.

■ ■ ■

Our undercover roles were those of American criminal heavies—Mike was a New York heroin wholesaler, and I was his protégé from the West Coast. Again, you never have to get specific about your organization—it's all *unspoken*—but it was clear to the Thai traffickers that we were connected to one of the five Mafia families in New York, and had a lot of money to back up our talk.

■ ■ ■

One spring morning I met this sweet-faced, diminutive Thai girl called Noi. She was in her early twenties. Noi was best friends with a woman named Lek-Lek who worked at the main telecommunications company of Thailand.

Back then everything—especially a major heroin transaction—was done with pagers. There were no smartphones, of course—no cell phone industry at all.

The criminals had no other option: They needed to communicate through Thai-language pages.

Customers would call operators at the telecommunications company and leave a message, which Thai girls would type out and then send out by page. At any given time, there were about twenty operators and typists on call, and Lek-Lek was the boss. I got authorization from Mike to pay Noi and Lek-Lek close to $1,000 a month.

As soon as the operators typed the message, they'd transmit it to the criminals' pagers. And guess who *else* got every one of those message pages?

In real time I knew every single thing that the criminals were doing.

I didn't have an eavesdropping or intercept warrant—in Thailand, I didn't do it judicially—but I made sure I gave all the information I was gathering straight to the Thai cops who were our investigative counterparts.

I called it Operation Malacca, after the strait between Thailand and Sumatra—seemed like a fitting name because, like Malacca, our intercept operation became a vital passage for information, much as the dope traffickers moved their heroin through that narrow South Seas waterway.

■ ■ ■

My life in Songkhla was so hectic, the work hours so long and adrenaline-filled, I never had much time for a social life. But within weeks of starting the pager investigation, I found myself falling hopelessly in love with a young Thai girl I'd met while on a brief sojourn in Phuket with Mike.

Her given name was Auwarn Prachoop, but everyone simply called her Gay. In Thailand, as I said, hardly anyone uses his or her actual name: They all use a *chue-len*—the Thai word for nickname.

Gay was special. Like Desiree, Gay was one of the best-looking women I'd ever seen. Her mind was razor-sharp: She was a trained accountant.

But my primary relationship in Songkhla was with Bansmer. Mike and I were also becoming extremely close. As the resident agent in charge in Songkhla, Mike was formally my boss, but in our undercover roles, we were partners. Over the months in Songkhla, Mike and I were to become more than partners. Sounds strange, but working closely with another DEA agent overseas becomes much like a marriage. There are times you want to tear each other to pieces, but you learn to read each other intuitively, to complement each other's strengths and compensate for each other's weaknesses.

I would've given my life in a heartbeat for Mike; he'd have done the same for me. Mike Bansmer is the most fearless man I've ever known—and when he wants to turn it on, some would also call him the most fearsome. Mike was a Special Forces Green Beret assigned to Project Omega (B-50) in Vietnam, went out on nine recon missions along the Ho Chi Minh Trail in 1967. He could find his way out of dense jungles in Burma and the north of Thailand without a compass—I saw this firsthand. The guy was blessed with inconceivable and innate directional skills.

Funny thing: If you were to meet Mike today back home in the States—middle-class guy from Medford, Oregon—you'd pass him in the street without a second thought. Mike's about an inch taller than me, five-foot-nine, a rail-thin marathoner, still does extreme hundred-mile bike rides now that he's in his early seventies. He's a warm, affectionate grandfather. You'd figure he was some retired cop and fitness freak with a lifetime subscription to *Outside* magazine.

■ ■ ■

Long before I came to Thailand, Mike was up in the north, bringing in US Special Forces to train units of the Thai border patrol involved in some of the most intense counter-narcotics interdictions in US law enforcement history. The heroin epidemic created by the Shan United Army was so virulent that higher authorities often turned a blind eye on "extrajudicial actions"—which essentially meant the Thai cops and border patrol officers could take matters into their own hands.

Mike Bansmer had two close DEA partners in Thailand in his previous tour in Chiang Mai, in the far north of the country, an important trading center and way station on the opium pipeline known as the Trail of the Horse, which runs through the dense jungles of Burma down to Bangkok. Ben Yarborough and Jim Matthews were two other DEA special agents going deep into the jungles with their contingents of Thai border patrol officers to eradicate the factories producing heroin for the Shan United Army and independent Thai traffickers. They would drive for hours through the mountainous jungles on Jeep trails, then disembark to be led by an informant into the dense jungle for up to eighteen hours of hiking before finally reaching the secret heroin refinery in the middle of the night. At daybreak, the force would use military raid tactics to attack the refinery, and the entire team would then be extracted by police helicopters.

Due to a death threat against them from the Shan United Army, the agents were evacuated from Chiang Mai to Bangkok, and eventually back to other DEA postings in the States, though by 1990 Mike had returned as the resident agent in charge in Songkhla—that's when he'd put in the call asking me to come join him in the south of Thailand.

Before I'd arrived in-country, Mike and his partners were involved in a lot of heavy engagements and firefights with the insurgents. They had a kind of unique fraternity forged in those jungle raids, and had even designed a gold ring, shared only by the three of them: three Chinese characters that read "The Golden Triangle."

Mike, Ben, and Jim had gone deep into the jungles of Southeast Asia, doing some bold operations, but all those shootings were classified as "actions under the color of law." This wasn't typical DEA work, to be sure: They had done some spine-curdling eradication missions up in the north of the country and in neighboring Burma and Laos.

I'll never forget the night that Mike first showed me a photo album of all the Thai and Burmese drug dealers who were killed during operational raids on refineries. He had a handwritten epigram taken from Hemingway on the cover.

There is no hunting like the hunting of man, and those who have hunted armed men long enough and liked it, never care for anything else thereafter.

I leafed through the album as he showed me all his operational engagements, organized in chronological order: fourteen corpses of drug traffickers.

I've seen my share of gunplay—and been in plenty of morgues—but Mike's photo album was pretty disturbing. In addition to the Hemingway quote, there were those three Chinese characters spelling out "The Golden Triangle."

Late at night, I'd sit flipping through the pages of the book by the open fire, wondering if all those missions into northern Thailand, Laos, and Burma with Yarborough and Matthews had sent Mike over the edge.

Mike was no stone-cold killer, simply a good American cop trying to operate in the crazy-house rules of the Golden Triangle. If the Thai border patrol discovered any jungle-cloaked heroin refineries, they'd simply blow the labs up. It was a different law enforcement mind-set: Nothing would be reported. No probable cause, no warrants, no paper trail.

The minute we had a guy in cuffs, turning him over to our counterparts in the Narcotics Suppression Bureau, I wanted to get out of there as if my hair was on fire. With suspects in custody, Thai cops don't interrogate like cops do in America. They'll beat suspects, threaten them with guns, waterboard them—any kind of torture you can imagine, they've tried it.

Thais would "incentivize" the traffickers like no other cops on earth. They'd take the dealers to their houses so that they could see their wives and kids inside.

"Take a good long look. You're seeing your family for the last time. Your life is going to burn to the fucking ground tonight unless you start cooperating."

Lawyering up? Like you've seen on *Law & Order*? That simply does not exist in places like Thailand. A trafficker falls into the hands of the cops—he gets an offer he can't refuse. Often there's no arraignment, no judges or defense attorneys. The suspect either goes straight to prison or gets coerced into cooperating, shoved back on the street as a police informant. In the years I was in Thailand, whenever I saw the NSB guys get their hands on a drug dealer, there was *always* a confession.

■ ■ ■

During his decadelong stint in Thailand, Mike had become quite an expert in the nuances of corruption in Thai narcotics policing policy. We were almost always working in concert with the Office of the Narcotics Control Board. The ONCB guys are not street cops: They're all well-educated college graduates. Mike told me a story that had transpired in the weeks before I arrived.

"We were expecting forty blocks of morphine in two suitcases," he said. "We're waiting for the arrival via train. A Mercedes comes to pick up the load at the train station. The ONCB guys see the suspects grab the two suitcases, throw them in the Mercedes. The ONCB arrested the delivery guys, but meanwhile the Benz drives off with the dope—scot-free."

Mike told me that one of our DEA special agents, Bob Parks, chased after the Mercedes with the forty blocks of morphine—all the way across Hat Yai, blowing red lights the whole way, finally stopping the car.

There was a regular Thai traffic cop on the corner. But it was Bob Parks—a white American guy—who jumped out with a drawn pistol and arrested the driver with the dope.

He couldn't speak Thai worth a lick, but he managed to convey his meaning:

If you run, you die!

The Thai traffic cops were standing there, watching all this.

When it was time to go to court, the ONCB officers—who weren't eyewitnesses, weren't even on the *scene*, in fact didn't arrive until after Bob made the arrest—took the witness stand.

The defense attorney for the trafficker in the Mercedes was trying to trip them up, catch them in a lie.

"So who was the *white* man who arrested my client?"

The ONCB officer testified calmly:

"*What* white guy? I *personally* arrested your client."

Mike smiled and shook his head as he related the story.

"Ed, that's the ONCB in a nutshell," he said. "Those are the *best* of the best over here. The best of the best lie under oath."

Yet they do have their own "ethical" standards: They don't think it is fair game to frame a guy outright—throw a bag of heroin or morphine into his car. In Thailand there are no conspiracy laws like we have in the United States. You have to catch the dealer red-handed, literally in possession of the bag of dope.

If they do surveillance, listen to the Kel transmission sets, the main dealer may be waiting in a restaurant, not near the dope. But if the Thais make the arrest, they'll force the "clean" guy to pose in an official photograph, pointing at the bricks of heroin—that's their way of making the case stick in court.

Over the next two months, Mike and I started wooing informants, trying to get an introduction to one of the main "logisticians"—or lieutenants—in the Shan United Army.

Mike taught me a hell of a lot about life in Thailand. He couldn't speak educated Thai as fluently as I could, but he could communicate perfectly well—especially to conduct drug deals—in street Thai. Every few days I would drive up from Songkhla in my G-ride—a government-issue compact car—to Hat Yai. In contrast to most other provinces in the nation, the largest city in that province is not its capital, which is Songkhla. The much newer city of Hat Yai, with a population of more than 350,000, is considerably larger: Hat Yai is in fact now the third largest city in Thailand, and the primary economic base in the south.

Provincial capital or not, from a business standpoint—and, most importantly, from a drug-trafficking standpoint—Hat Yai was where all the action in the south happened.

I had to make Hat Yai my backyard. I could negotiate the back streets there better than I could anywhere in the world, better even than in LA or Honolulu.

Mike was in Bangkok, and I went off solo to work another case. DEA agents like me, stationed abroad, will often work symbiotically with spooks on foreign assignments. Over in Thailand the CIA officers were known as the "American liaison" unit. Our "liaisons" would often provide us with "parallel probable cause"—nothing is attributed to an individual, implement, device, or technique.

They *whisper* in your ear—often an invaluable piece of intel—and it's solely on the investigator to go out and develop the case based on that tip-off.

I was assisting the spooks with their own case. I went after this major trafficker named Muy Hein San Tai. That was his Chinese name—in addition to nicknames, almost all Thais in the south have a name too long and unpronounceable for everyday use. Muy Hein San Tai was by far the largest exporter of heroin in southern Thailand.

When working a major trafficking organization, my philosophy was counterintuitive: Always start at the top, not at the bottom of the criminal pyramid. Working your way up from the bottom requires an investment of too much time, too much money; all it takes is one little nod from an underling or minor lieutenant, and the entire case is dead. The boss will be lost in the wind.

Muy Hein San Tai purchased his heroin in volume from the Shan United Army. Virtually everyone in-country got smack from the SUA. He wasn't political, wasn't a separatist insurgent. He was an independent wholesale exporter. He was strictly about his profits. He was all about amassing more of a fortune— so he could lavish it on more of his girlfriends.

Throughout the south of Thailand, local cops constantly told us that he was considered untouchable. His criminal trade-craft was superior to that of everyone else in the region. The Thai cops couldn't build a solid case against him no matter how hard they tried.

I never liked to go outside the DEA fraternity to build a case, but sometimes it was necessary. I asked some of our American intel guys stationed in Thailand to begin monitoring Muy Hein San Tai.

Then, with a crew of our intelligence agents, we laid out an elaborate black ops plan. We had *full* authorization from the Thai authorities. They gave us the green light—every action we took was justified and approved under the Thai legal code—to enter his house by stealth.

As you'd imagine of one of Southeast Asia's leading heroin

kingpins, Muy Hein San Tai lived in a highly secure house. It was no palace, but it was a large and comfortable house by southern Thai standards.

I quickly assessed that the main obstacles to entry were canines. He didn't have trained Dobermans or German shepherds on his property. He didn't need them. His protective ring was a pack of approximately twenty-five mangy dogs in the alley, constantly moving, ferreting, and sniffing around his house. He didn't own them, but he allowed them to live on the entrance to his property, and fed them *minimally*—just enough that they weren't literally starving to death. They were always near ravenous.

Buddhists believe in reincarnation: They don't kill dogs or monkeys—don't even kill any animals they regard as pests—for fear that they may be murdering a reincarnated relative.

We needed to get past those mangy dogs somehow to gain entry to the house in order to monitor the kingpin's movements. The spooks got wind that he was leaving unexpectedly to meet his *feen nit noy*—one of his secondary mistresses.

Muy Hein San Tai was a careful man in all things business-related, but he had one Achilles' heel: womanizing.

To maneuver through the alleyway full of mangy dogs took some thinking. The other flanks all had concrete walls topped off by razor concertina wire. We spent hours strategizing how to create a diversion to draw the dogs to one side long enough for me to gain entry over the fence and make a clean opening in the concertina wire. At that point our intel guys could join me. One of the two spooks was an expert locksmith; the other was a technical surveillance agent. As climbers go, they were both a bit clumsy, but they managed to make it over the wall once I cleared the wire away.

The locksmith showed his true expertise. With a few flicks

and twirls of his tools, he got us in through the front door in a matter of seconds. I stayed outside—entry into the domicile wasn't my job. I stayed out in the darkness, pulling security watch, making sure no one could sneak up on us.

Meanwhile, inside, the technicians took out a table—they snapped a few photos of it for their own purposes, then dragged it out in the yard. Again, they were masterful. The tech guy pulled out a battery-powered drill and made a clean hole up through one of the table legs. He then installed a tiny thin transmitter and closed up the hole with seamless wood putty. The leg wouldn't have passed inspection by a trained expert, but how many people really look closely at the legs of their furniture on a daily basis?

They carried the table back inside, readjusted everything so that it looked normal, then ran a beta test, just to make sure the battery-operated device was transmitting.

"Good to go."

With a bit of a fireman's boost, I helped them back over the concrete wall, then climbed back over myself. The tricky part was repairing the concertina wire. That took a bit of skill so I didn't cut the hell out of my fingers.

We scampered off. I drove away in my G-ride Honda, and our Thai cop counterparts met us at a prearranged rendezvous point.

■ ■ ■

From that point forward, over the following few months, we let the transmitter in the table leg do its job.

Muy Hein San Tai was smart and street-savvy, but even the untouchables always make mistakes—again, it was all due to a connection to one of those mistresses. He left his house to pick up one of his girlfriends and then got on a fishing boat that had

Hill tribe worker harvesting opium sap, north of Chiang Mai, Thailand

Dry opium poppy pods, from which heroin can also be produced

Blocks of Shan United Army heroin seized during a DEA operation in northern Thailand

William Queen

DEA Special Agent Edward Follis (above) and ATF Special Agent William Queen (left), both working undercover, with "armaments flash" in a major heroin sting operation in Los Angeles.

Special Agent Edward Follis (left) in Thailand with a Thai police officer after a seizure of Shan United Army heroin

Edward Follis

A unit of Thai Border Patrol police, trained by the U.S. Special Forces led by DEA Special Agent Michael Bansmer, during a raid on Shan United Army heroin refineries

Hill tribe people of northern Thailand and Burma, a stronghold of the Shan United Army

Special Agent Edward Follis (left) undercover in Songkhla, Thailand, after a seizure of Shan United Army heroin

Edward Follis

Phong, a chief lieutenant in the Shan United Army, forced by the Thai police to point at blocks of seized Shan United Army heroin number-four after being arrested by Special Agents Edward Follis and Michael Bansmer

Edward Follis

Michael Bansmer

THERE IS NO HUNTING LIKE THE HUNTING OF MAN. AND THOSE WHO HAVE HUNTED ARMED MEN LONG ENOUGH AND LIKE IT, NEVER CARE FOR ANYTHING ELSE THEREAFTER.

金三角   ERNEST HEMINGWAY

Cover page of DEA Special Agent Michael Bansmer's photo album of counter-narcotics operations in northern Thailand and Burma

DEA Special Agent
Michael Bansmer
(far right) with fellow
DEA agents Ben
Yarborough (center) and
Jim Matthews (far left) in
an active heroin refinery
during a raid in northern
Thailand

A heroin refinery in
Doi Chiang, Thailand,
after a major raid and seizure
conducted by the DEA and
Thai Border Patrol police

Special Agent Edward
Follis (center) in the
Demilitarized Zone
between North and
South Korea, during
an operation to gain
intelligence on the
industrialized
production of
methamphetamine
within North Korea

Amado Carrillo Fuentes, "Lord of the Skies," godfather of the Juárez Cartel, still ranked by many in law enforcement as the "Richest Gangster of All Time"

Mexican drug cartel cash and weapons seized

Santa Muerte, "Saint of Death," an iconic figure worshipped by drug traffickers at numerous shrines throughout Mexico

The funeral of Amado Carrillo Fuentes, after botched plastic surgery in an attempt to thwart extradition to the United States during a DEA investigation

Edward Follis, while stationed in Kabul, dressed for an undercover operation in traditional Afghan attire

Edward Follis (left), country attaché in Kabul, meets with opium warlord Haji Juma Khan (right).

Taliban financier and opium trafficker Haji Bagcho Sherzai, in DEA custody. Sherzai was convicted on March 13, 2012, and sentenced to twenty years in US federal prison.

Counter-narcotics team in Afghanistan burns a known heroin stash-house.

originated in Burma and was transporting a major amount of heroin. The transmitter gave up all the details, and the Thai cops acted with unbelievable speed.

They stopped the boat, seized the heroin, and had Muy Hein San Tai in shackles.

There's no gray area legally: The penalty for heroin trafficking in Thailand is death. Muy Hein San Tai was convicted at trial and summarily executed.

⬛ ⬛ ⬛

As for Mike's and my own work, the breakthrough against the Shan United Army came after hours and hours of dogged pursuit and negotiations. In all our negotiations Mike was always the alpha dog while I was the beta. Mike played it hard—regardless of the danger—ready to step up and put his ass on the line. My Thai language skills were better, so I was a bit more laid-back, the "talker" in our partnership.

By the summer of 1993, Mike connected me with a character named Lee Shing Yong, a tall, thirty-year-old Chinese heroin smuggler, and we were negotiating a deal for a hundred units of SUA heroin. We first met in the lobby of the Ambassador Hotel in Bangkok. Perhaps it was my conversational Thai skills, but Lee was surprisingly friendly with me, opening up about his childhood in the Yunnan Province of China. His relaxed body language was a good sign; these cagey SUA traffickers were finally beginning to trust Mike and me.

My Thai was now nearly flawless—Mike told me it was almost as good as Ben Yarborough's—but it was the distinctive Songkhla accent that paid off big-time. Lee truly thought I was from the south, which meant I was based eight hundred miles away from his stronghold, not anywhere near SUA territory. That sense of distance gave yet another level of reassurance.

By this time, Lee and his entire circle had all heard rumors about me.

"*Khun pen pii?*" he asked. *Are you the Ghost?*

I laughed. "Some say that—yeah."

Lee insisted that the heroin-for-cash exchange take place near a SUA-held village in the jungle. I nodded, told him in Thai that I couldn't make any promises but that I'd bring the request to my business partner, Mike, who was down conducting business in Songkhla. Lee emphasized the quality and bargain price of the heroin, and then suddenly conceded to possibly making the exchange in southern Thailand, near Songkhla, as long as we'd agree to pay for half the shipment up front before delivery.

I played it nonchalant, noncommittal, always the best bet in negotiations.

"Look, it sounds possible," I said. "I'll *ask*—but I don't know if we should even bother dealing with you guys."

It was mostly a bluff—of course I wanted to consummate the deal—but I was trying to let Lee know that Mike and I had other options, knew other smugglers, had no problems taking our money elsewhere. Lee looked down at the tabletop, frowning. We agreed to talk later after we'd both consulted with our people, and exchanged cell phone numbers.

More than a month went by before Mike's cell phone rang. It was Lee again. He asked for a face-to-face meet. On the afternoon of August 27, we met in the lobby of the Hilton Hotel in Bangkok. But Lee had now backtracked—typical heroin-trafficking gamesmanship—and wanted us to do the deal in the highland jungles of the far north. We refused adamantly. Frustrated, Lee played his trump card.

"You don't understand what I'm offering you," he said. "It's the *best* number four heroin on the market."

Heroin—chemically known as diacetylmorphine—comes in a variety of forms. Heroin number three is a base—not yet brought to pure refinement. It has a lower burning temperature than number four, so it can be easily smoked. But it's not water-soluble and cannot be shot up. Heroin number three was popular with smokers in the Golden Triangle.

Heroin number four is water-soluble, can be cooked in a spoon and shot up intravenously. From a drug trafficker's standpoint, heroin number four is the best, most potent product. And the Shan United Army's heroin number four was even stamped with a trademark—the Double UO Globe Brand—and known as the premier "Cadillac" of smack worldwide.

"Yes, it's the top number four in the world," Lee repeated. "And it comes directly from Mr. Chang."

Mr. Chang? Mike and I glanced at each other, trying not to betray our amazement. "Mr. Chang" was the common street euphemism for Chang Chi Fu—Khun Sa himself.

Mike had been in Thailand years longer than me, and had never, in all his hundreds of dealings with smugglers and traffickers, got an admission that the heroin shipment was coming straight from the infamous chain-smoking Opium Warlord.

■ ■ ■

Weeks passed, and the negotiations had come to an impasse. Typical of smack deals everywhere. I was in a hotel room in

Bangkok trying to jump-start the negotiations with Lee. My girl Gay came along and was staying with me in the hotel. It wasn't exactly a fleabag, but it was no five-star palace either.

Working undercover, I always stayed under the radar, maintained a small footprint. I would never stay in the posh parts of the city, and never near the really high-crime districts. I'd find a place that was nondescript, near a bunch of commercial activity.

I was using the cell to call Lee up north in Chiang Mai. He now claimed his people were willing to sell us one hundred units—or seventy kilos. (Each unit consisted of seven hundred grams of heroin.)

"*Phom ja pai yim khun,*" I said. *Okay, then, I'm going to come visit you.*

"*Maa rew mak,*" he said. *Come quickly.*

I spoke to him for a good twenty minutes in Thai, putting together the details of a meeting. Mike and I needed to book flights on Thai Airways from Bangkok to the city of Chiang Mai in the north.

After the call ended, I set down the cell phone, and Gay stared at me in silence.

I'll never forget the look—the penetrating force of Gay's jet-black eyes—as we were standing by the window.

Below us: the incessant noise of the taxis and *tuk-tuks.*

"Khun Ed," she said softly, hugging me. It's a quite formal way to speak, but in Thailand a woman refers to a man—even her husband or boyfriend—as "Mister." Even though Gay was both my lover and my trusted Thai friend, she always added that honorific when we spoke. Etiquette is so crucial in Thai culture.

She laughed quietly. There was a long silence, broken only by the squealing of the *tuk-tuks* below us in the crowded street.

"Khun Ed," she said, "when I listen to you speak, I wouldn't even know you were white. I know you've *got* them."

■ ■ ■

I quickly got back on the cell phone and called Mike down in Songkhla.

"Better get up here, brother," I said. "We're on for the meet up north."

Bansmer jumped on a plane and was with me in Bangkok that same afternoon.

Because we'd institutionalized our presence with the Thai police, we were now allowed to carry our firearms—had even been issued official permits—on commercial jet airliners. You think the United States would ever allow foreign cops to carry guns in our country on planes? That kind of interagency and international cooperation is unfathomable here.

I would carry my .38 Smith & Wesson snub-nose. As usual, Mike arrived with his Beretta Model 92 with the ported barrel.

■ ■ ■

There was still considerable work to be done in the negotiations once we got to the north of Thailand. On September 16, 1993, Lee asked us to meet him in the Orchid Hotel coffee shop in Chiang Mai. But when Mike and I walked in, we didn't see the familiar smiling face of Lee—it was some other guy, who turned out to be Lee's older brother Phong, already known to us as one of the most powerful heroin traffickers in Khun Sa's organization.

Phong was in his midforties, thick black hair, sinewy muscles, constant hard expression. Clearly not a guy to be toyed with. But, Mike whispered to me, he could already spot the guy's weakness:

There was naked greed in Phong's eyes. He wanted this deal to happen badly—*too* badly.

We sat down, ordered drinks, and began to talk. Bansmer immediately began working Phong, growing angry at times over this incessant demand that we go up into the mountains to make the heroin exchange and that we put 50 percent of the money up front. Every time Phong insisted that we travel alone into Shan United Army territory, Mike looked like he was ready to blow his stack.

There was no safe way for Mike and me to go off into the jungle north of Chiang Mai; without a large contingent of Thai border patrol, we'd be inviting an ambush and almost certain death. The DEA would never allow half our cash—$180,000 in US dollars—to fall into the hands of the SUA.

The negotiations ping-ponged for more than an hour—tense one moment, then relaxed, then even tenser. But Mike never relinquished control of the room. I watched, impressed, as Bansmer used his fluctuating anger the way a matador waves a cape. He moved in and out during the negotiations, arguing that our New York Mob backers did not want to risk losing the money in the jungle. He insisted the entire transfer be done right here in Chiang Mai.

Phong sat stone-faced, adamant in his refusal. We were at loggerheads. Whenever they reached an impasse, they'd sit silently for a moment, sipping their drinks. I'd hear Mike's heavy, frustrated exhalations. I'd try to use my Thai language skills as a mediator. Each man was proud, willful, and had his own reasons for not walking away; after a couple of minutes, one of them would find another angle, another reason to keep the discussions alive.

"Let's be honest, confidence has been lost on both sides," Mike said finally in Thai. Phong nodded, looking plenty pissed off.

"You sound like a cop," he said with a sneer.

"How about this?" Mike said. "Let's do a deal—it can be a small one, and maybe we can restore that confidence."

"What kind of deal?"

"Say we buy two units now. If that goes through without a hitch, we can talk to our people in New York about buying the rest of the hundred units."

"I don't like the sound of it."

Mike pressed forward. "Just get the two units and bring it here."

Phong drew back, looking insulted, then finally agreed.

"Okay," he said. "I'll call you in a few hours when I have it."

We shook on the deal, and Phong split.

As he exited the hotel, Bansmer blew out a hot exhale and sat down.

I could see that Mike was pissed off. Two units—1.4 kilograms of smack for $7,000—was not a big bust, certainly not the hundred units we'd been angling for. Still, I reassured Bansmer, a two-unit deal was big enough. Phong could get the death penalty for selling that quantity of heroin. Mike nodded, knowing a looming death sentence would give us more than enough leverage once we had Phong in cuffs.

Eight hours later, at nine p.m., Phong called Mike's cell and told him he was in the lobby of the Phucome Hotel, about a twenty-minute drive away. Nothing to be too alarmed about: That was typical for Thai drug deals—switching up the meeting place at the last moment. Mike and I quickly drove over to the Phucome Hotel.

Phong was there with his assistant as backup. But now Phong tried to move the goalposts again, saying we needed to drive to one of his cousins' houses, where we could make the two-unit deal.

Mike and I looked at Phong with contempt. Mike's face went bright red, and he laughed aloud. Switching up hotels was one thing, but we weren't going to go to some unknown house where they could possibly whack us.

Mike insisted that Phong go get the smack and then meet us in the lobby. This is what made Mike such a great undercover negotiator—he never wavered on matters of security, and he always maintained his position of power and control. Phong agreed, and I handed him my empty gray backpack for the heroin.

Nearly two hours later, Phong and his assistant returned. They greeted us in the lobby, and Phong handed me back the now dope-laden backpack.

I took it outside to our car and tested the heroin with my Marquis reagent kit. When I came back into the lobby, I nodded to Mike—definitely heroin number four, and nearly pure. Mike told me it was now cool to get the money. I went back to the car and got a plastic bag. Bansmer took an envelope from the bag and handed it to Phong, who opened it, studied the $7,000 cash intently for a few moments, and then nodded.

"We can now all trust each other," Phong said, finally.

Mike and I smiled back.

Phong now let his guard down and explained the intricacies of how a significant heroin deal worked within the Shan United Army. A broker had to travel deep into the jungle, crossing the Thai border into Burma, and actually place a written order for the heroin at an SUA camp. Shortly thereafter, a contingent of

SUA soldiers would take the heroin to a controlled area and release it to the broker only after the broker had paid the entire amount owed. It was all to be done in the open, under the guns of the SUA soldiers, in a clearing in the jungle, hours from the nearest non-SUA village.

Mike and I glanced at each other. It was important for us to understand the logistics, but there was no way in hell we were going into the jungles of Burma—into Shan United Army stronghold villages—on our own, carrying hundreds of thousands in cash.

Phong could see we were ready to walk away.

Mike's temper flared again, and Phong immediately sweetened the pot.

"I will put in one-fourth of the money myself," he said.

Mike came at him again, hard: "Look, enough games, I want to meet the refinery owner," he said.

"Maybe, after the deal is done."

Mike and I exchanged knowing glances. We'd hit our roadblock; we couldn't push Phong any further.

■ ■ ■

Mike told Phong he wanted to talk to him in private about making the bigger deal. Phong was still relaxed after the successful two-unit deal, and let his guard down enough to meet us in the back of our four-door Toyota sedan.

Phong inched over to the middle of the backseat, and Mike and I squeezed in on either side of him. Two Thai cops, posing as drivers, were sitting up front. Phong's look of icy menace had now melted; he was smiling.

The time was right: I felt for my little .38 snub-nose in my waistband.

I glanced warily at Mike. Bansmer nodded, and like veteran partners, in unison, we pounced.

We each grabbed Phong by one of his thickly muscled arms.

"Phong, you're under arrest," Mike barked.

"We're DEA, and those are police officers in the front seat," I said in Thai.

A sudden look of fear shot across Phong's face, and he immediately began to struggle. Mike and I were shocked at his strength. He knew he was facing the death penalty and fought like a wild beast. Mike and I grappled with him, but it was difficult getting a proper choke hold on him in the backseat. At least Phong could not reach his pistol, though he was struggling mightily to do so.

Phong was in a total panic, kicking the front seats, desperately trying to wrest his arms free to get to his gun. He fought quietly and with wild eyes. The three of us struggled violently before Mike had enough. Mike relinquished his grip and calmly pulled out his 9mm Beretta and stuck it hard into Phong's ear.

"I don't want to shoot you—but by God, I will!" he shouted.

Phong froze. The power drained from his arms, and he seemed to crumple in on himself. I used all my own strength to wrest him away from Mike's gun—almost pulling his head into my lap. I knew Mike was ready to shoot if Phong didn't stop kicking and struggling, and I didn't want him to die there in my arms.

We handed Phong over to the Thai cops to make the arrest, and in short order they'd flipped him. Phong became our principal informant in the case we developed in northern Thailand—ultimately known as Operation Tiger Trap—that would lead to the demise of the Shan United Army.

Phong soon led us to a lychee farm three hours north of Chiang Mai, right on the border of Burma, near a stronghold village of the SUA. On that lychee farm the DEA bagged more than three hundred kilograms of pure number four heroin. Shortly thereafter, the DEA and Thai authorities seized an even bigger haul of Shan United Army heroin from a trawler in the Gulf of Thailand.

■ ■ ■

With those massive seizures we were able to bring down sweeping indictments in New York's Eastern District against thirteen senior Shan United Army traffickers, all major figures who were known to be the linchpins of Khun Sa's operation.

But now the Opium Warlord's wrath was intense.

Catherine Palmer, assistant US attorney in the Eastern District, received multiple death threats—and an explosive device was sent to the prosecutor's office.

■ ■ ■

Our case was rock solid. But Khun Sa had not risen to his position of power by chance; he was no fool, and realized that he didn't want to spend the rest of his life in a US penitentiary. He worked out an arrangement with corrupt Burmese officials to avoid extradition to the United States, even as I was preparing to testify against him in federal court.

In 1996 Khun Sa officially "surrendered" to the country's military junta but, instead of being sent to prison, was allowed to live in seclusion in Yangon, reportedly still running an array of business ventures in secret. He ultimately died on October 25, 2007. The official cause remains unknown, but the formerly untouchable, chain-smoking Opium Warlord—the "Prince of Death"—had long suffered from diabetes, heart disease, partial paralysis, and high blood pressure.

CHAPTER 6

I I I

THE LORD OF THE SKIES

They called him the Lord of the Skies: Amado Carrillo Fuentes, godfather of the Juárez Cartel. A man so feared, so wily, and so wealthy that even today—long after his gruesome demise—he's still ranked number one on many unofficial lists of the "richest gangsters of all time."

He earned the name "Lord of the Skies" due to his private fleet of planes, including nearly two dozen private Boeing 727 jet aircraft, which he used to import cocaine from Colombia to Mexico, where it was later smuggled into the United States. As the de facto CEO of a sprawling cocaine empire, Carrillo Fuentes had an estimated net worth of $25 billion. In the mid-1990s, we in the Drug Enforcement Administration ranked him as the most powerful cocaine trafficker in the world.

Still in his thirties then, Amado was known as a criminal mastermind, one of those audacious—and utterly brilliant—businessmen who come around once in a generation.

Through the 1970s and '80s, of course, it was Colombian

kingpins like Pablo Escobar and the Ochoa brothers who dominated the cocaine trade. They used Mexico only as a transshipment point: perfectly situated, with its broad and pervious border to the US markets.

Amado had been there as a young narco-trafficker at the founding of the Federation, a cooperative conglomerate of previously competing local Mexican bosses, put together by Miguel Ángel Félix Gallardo, known as El Padrino, the original Guadalajara-based godfather of the Mexican cartels.

But Amado Carrillo Fuentes, bright and enormously ambitious, wasn't satisfied with the status quo. He determined that, for all the tens of millions coming into their coffers, the Mexicans were little more than glorified mules; they were being used by the Colombians to advance the trade but not receiving what Amado deemed due compensation.

Amado developed a new vision under the tutelage of Félix Gallardo, reshaping the transshipment of cocaine to American locations, mostly along the West Coast of the United States.

Previously, the Mexicans had been paid in cash per kilogram of pure cocaine. But with one stroke of genius, Amado Carrillo Fuentes changed the entire game. He said to the Colombians:

"Forget the cash—just pay me in product."

He offered to fly his own 727 jets into Colombia, pick up the cocaine, and guarantee safe delivery to the vast wholesale and retail markets in the United States.

To the Colombian cartel bosses, it made little difference: After all, it was just processed coca. Rather than compensating their middlemen in cash—pesos or US dollars—they'd simply pay them in product.

Around this same time, the most powerful drug traffickers in Colombia were starting to come under indictment by US federal prosecutors. After decades of seeming impotence, the Colombian government had finally stepped up and begun to extradite cocaine traffickers to US jurisdictions. Many of the Colombian cartels' coca loads were being seized and destroyed, and they were losing fortunes.

It was much safer for them to simply move the coca from Bolivia, process it into raw product in Colombia, then let the Mexicans take over the rest of the operation. True, this meant a smaller profit to the Colombians, but also much less risk. The Mexican mobsters already had an established network of soldiers, workers, and gang affiliates in California willing to assume the risk of transportation and distribution.

In retrospect, it was absolutely *brilliant* mercantilism. Now Amado Carrillo Fuentes could sell the exact same product—the same quality of pure cocaine—in California and across the United States at a much lower price point. After all, the cocaine had cost the Mexicans *nothing*—their only investment was risk.

Within a very short time, Amado and his confederates had completely undermined the Colombian cartels, selling the cocaine wholesale at a cheaper rate. Indeed, this became the business model that all the modern Mexican cartels follow today, set in motion by that dark visionary Amado Carrillo Fuentes—a complete shift in the financial paradigm.

Today, the only remaining Colombian cocaine trade is to Europe, transported via container ships to the coast of Africa, smuggled in with the collusion of corrupt African officials and then overland up to the waiting markets of Western Europe.

I first got involved in Mexican cartel investigations immediately after our successful takedown of Khun Sa and the Shan United Army. Don Ferrarone—the country attaché in Bangkok—was in the process of being transferred back to Houston, Texas.

Ferrarone called me into his Bangkok office and asked me if I'd relocate to Texas with him. I respected Don immensely. He stood six-one, strong features, receding hairline, and he had decades already on the job: When I was still a kid in St. Louis, Don had worked the famous Nicky Barnes case, taking down Harlem's "Mr. Untouchable."

Don convinced me to apply for the job in Houston, but his real plan was to send me to El Paso, the hot spot in the Southwest for the Mexican cartel crisis. He wanted me in El Paso because it was, as he put it, "across the street" from Ciudad Juárez, which had earned an ugly reputation as the murder capital of the world.

Don arranged for me to be stationed in El Paso on what's known as "temporary-duty basis." The basis soon became quite permanent. I never even made it to Houston.

Honestly, it was a steep learning curve. I knew virtually *nothing* about cocaine. Mike Bansmer had given me a thorough education in Golden Triangle heroin, in the corruption, politics, and counter-narcotics policing of Southeast Asia—but the Mexican cocaine cartels were brand-new ground for me.

I was immediately assigned to working the Amado Carrillo Fuentes and Juárez Cartel investigation. Formally, we were designated the Organized Crime Drug Enforcement Task Force, but we all referred to it simply as the Amado Task Force.

I spent hours reading intel reports, learning everything I could about Amado Carrillo Fuentes and his second-in-command, his brother Vicente Carrillo Fuentes—also known as El Viceroy.

█ █ █

For decades, the Drug Enforcement Administration had been trying to infiltrate the increasingly powerful Mexican cocaine cartels. It was all too often a deadly proposition. In 1985, while on assignment in Mexico investigating drug trafficking, DEA Special Agent Enrique "Kiki" Camarena was abducted. Shortly after leaving the US Consulate in Guadalajara, Kiki was kidnapped—went missing, without a trace. His corpse was found several weeks later, partially decomposed and wrapped in a plastic bag, buried in a shallow grave seventy miles north of the Mexican city.

His death had been particularly gruesome. Kiki had been tortured—sodomized with a broom handle—and kept alive, wide awake, through the vicious interrogations by a physician injecting him with amphetamines, before ultimately being buried while still alive and breathing.

Kiki Camarena's disappearance became an international incident, briefly straining relations between the United States and Mexico. The case featured as *Time* magazine's cover story, "Death of a Narc," on November 7, 1988, and the Drug Enforcement Administration launched Operation Leyenda, the largest homicide investigation in DEA history.

Investigators soon identified the Federation's boss, Miguel Ángel Félix Gallardo, and his two closest associates, Ernesto Fonseca Carrillo and Rafael Caro Quintero, as the primary suspects in the kidnapping. Fonseca Carrillo and Caro Quintero were quickly apprehended and imprisoned; Félix Gallardo initially remained free, but was later convicted of the murder.

The Mexican physician Humberto Álvarez Machain, who allegedly prolonged Camarena's life so the interrogation and torture could continue, was brought to the United States to face justice. Álvarez was tried in US District Court in Los Angeles, but acquitted. Four other suspects—Javier Vásquez Velasco, Juan Ramon Matta Ballesteros, Juan José Bernabé Ramirez, and Rubén Zuno Arce—were ultimately found guilty of the kidnapping.*

Nine years after Kiki Camarena's murder, the task of trying to infiltrate and take down Amado Carrillo Fuentes and the Juárez Cartel seemed no less daunting than it had been in Kiki's day, but within two months of my arrival in El Paso, I was fortunate enough to partner up with the foremost expert on drug-investigation wiretapping in the Southwest United States.

When I arrived in El Paso, Special Agent Steve Whipple—today he is the special agent in charge for all of Texas, based out of Houston—had been pursuing and wiretapping a group of Juárez Cartel gangsters engaged in overland transshipment.

Steve's a born-and-bred Texan, six-two, imposing, always impeccably dressed in cowboy boots, crisp blue jeans, and snap-button cowboy shirts. He took me under his wing and gave me

---

* In October 2013, three retired federal agents told Fox News and various newspaper reporters that the Central Intelligence Agency participated in the kidnapping, torture, and murder of Kiki Camarena because the agency was supposedly involved in drug trafficking from Latin America to Mexico during the 1980s to raise money to aid Nicaraguan Contra rebels. The Central Intelligence Agency promptly released a statement to the media claiming that "it's ridiculous to suggest that the CIA had anything to do with the murder of a U.S. federal agent."

my education on wiretaps, cocaine, and the tremendous—often capricious—violence of the Mexican cartels.

Amado Carrillo Fuentes may have been the mastermind of his criminal empire, but he'd more than met his match in Steve Whipple. Everyone in law enforcement knew that if you were a drug trafficker anywhere near a phone—on *either* side of the border—you were never safe from Special Agent Steve Whipple.

I was only a week into my new posting when I saw the cartels' ruthlessness firsthand. We got a tip from the Hotel-Motel Group of the DEA El Paso office. The Hotel-Motel Group was often a vital source of intel about the activities of cocaine traffickers crossing over from Ciudad Juárez to transact business in El Paso.

We quickly acted upon the intel: We found a suspected stash house that had been leased in the name of Caroline Morrison, and soon determined that she was a stripper whose dancing name was Tammy.

Tammy was part of a group of migratory exotic dancers who travel back and forth, in an arc—sticking to the I-10 Corridor. From Santa Monica to Jacksonville, from Southern California to North Florida, these young women bounce from club to club. Some of them—especially the young, attractive ones like Tammy, those billed as "featured dancers"—do very well financially, pulling in undeclared, untaxed cash working that I-10 Corridor.

Tammy had the look of a West Texas cheerleader, but in reality she was a blonde, blue-eyed California girl. She danced a few nights a week in El Paso, at a club called the Prince Machiavelli

Lounge. The girls working there often danced for the Mexican cartel traffickers who'd crossed the border.

The lure would start off innocently enough: The Mexican gangsters would approach one of the strippers, pay for a few lap dances, buy a round of drinks or a bottle of champagne. After a few nights of that, the girls would be approached about making some "extra" money. The cartel was moving so much product, they were *always* in need of stash houses.

But a Mexican national taking out a lease would instantly bring heat from the El Paso cops. In our DEA office, the Hotel-Motel Group agents were experts at developing informants who knew the locations of stash houses.

The gangsters would routinely target these innocent-looking white girls like Tammy, throw them $1,000 cash per month just to lease a house. The girls wouldn't even have to *live* there, just open the garage door, switch on the lights, and make the place look like someone was actually home—not storing hundreds of bricks of pure cocaine.

■ ■ ■

It was the middle of a cloudless Texas night, and I was rolling with a DEA agent named Ricky Farrell. We arrived at the stash house, made a warrantless entry: coming into Tammy's place under exigent circumstances.

We found eight hundred kilograms of pure cocaine.

Stash house?

The cocaine wasn't even *stashed*. All eight hundred kilos were stacked right out in the open. The house had no furniture. No appliances. No signs that anyone had ever lived there.

We seized all the cocaine and, from documentary evidence,

established that the lease was in the name of Caroline "Tammy" Morrison—a featured dancer at Prince Machiavelli.

Ricky Farrell and I drove straight to the club, located at 533 Executive Center Boulevard, just off Interstate 10. The Prince Machiavelli Lounge looked like an upscale joint—one of those places that style themselves "gentlemen's clubs" rather than "titty bars," catering to visiting businessmen and professional ball players—but it had a long history of criminal activity.

A few years later, after I'd left El Paso, the club's liquor license was revoked after a dancer allegedly sold cocaine to undercover state narcotics agents. In 2001, federal officials accused a University of Texas at El Paso research assistant and his wife of smuggling women from Russia—essentially "white slave trading"—and making them work as topless dancers at the club.

We pulled into the nearly full parking lot of Prince Machiavelli and assessed the security situation: There was one bouncer outside and another inside the corridor.

The first bouncer I ran into was towering: six-foot-six, heavy build, light-skinned, but with strong Aztec features. Even though he could see we were cops, at first he wanted to deny us entry. I reached into my pocket and badged him—showed him my DEA credentials. He took a step back. Then Ricky and I made our way inside.

The place had that unmistakable smell of strip clubs everywhere: too much body spray and inexpensive perfume barely masking the more tart odors of sweat and sex.

Two girls were writhing on poles, their lithe limbs reflecting bits of multicolor glitter sweat-glued to their thighs and hips and chests. Ricky Farrell and I started grilling the manager and some of the strippers.

"Where's Tammy tonight?" I said.

"Who's Tammy?"

"Don't give me that shit. *Tammy*. Your dancer. Blonde, about twenty-four years old."

The manager, a middle-aged Mexican-American, tried to play it tough, cold, steely-eyed. We were in plainclothes, so again I flashed my DEA credentials.

"Stop with the fucking games."

"Oh, Tammy. *That* Tammy. She didn't come in tonight."

"Where you think she is?"

I pressed into the manager while Ricky went off talking to the other strippers.

"Look, honestly, I don't want no problems. I really don't know where she's at."

"Does she meet with any Mexican guys here?"

"I mean, she dances for everyone. White guys, black guys, Mexican dudes—"

"Not lap dances. Has she ever met with Mexican guys? Private conversations, I mean. *Business* conversations."

The manager was clearly afraid. He didn't want to answer. But I had him under pressure now. Only took a few seconds before he buckled.

"Yeah, she does."

Then he rattled off the names of a bunch of other strip clubs she could be dancing at that very night.

■ ■ ■

We had no time to lose. While the rest of the DEA team were loading the seized kilos of coke into trucks to be taken to the evidence locker, Ricky and I scoured the places we'd learned that Tammy would frequent in El Paso: restaurants, bars, other strip clubs like the Red Parrot, Nero's, Jaguars Gold Club, Kayak, Ecstasy Palace, the Players Sports Bar and Grill.

From spot to spot, I was speeding, muttering at Ricky, "Dude, we've got to find this chick."

"You're right—we gotta find her before *they* find her."

"If we don't find her, she'll be in Juárez tonight."

We ran around all over El Paso that night till the sun came up, asking questions, scouring dozens of locations—to no avail.

The following day, through our intel sources and informants in Mexico, we learned that Tammy had indeed been taken across the border from El Paso into Juárez.

She had suffered the grisly fate meted out by the cartels. They ruthlessly killed her, then dismembered her body. The cartel gangsters refer to it as making *sopa*.

They place the dismembered corpse into a fifty-five-gallon metal drum and pour battery acid over it. Within hours, there is no corpse, just a grim sludge of former human remains. All that's left to dispose of are a few vestiges of bone and teeth.

Tammy's death haunted me through many sleepless, sweaty El Paso nights.

It was a stark awakening to the twisted rules the cartels were playing by.

The Juárez Cartel blamed her personally for the seizure. Didn't matter that she hadn't been an informant, didn't matter that she hadn't been flipped by us, didn't matter that she hadn't pocketed some of the cocaine for herself.

She'd made only *one* mistake: being reckless or greedy enough to put the lease in her name—assuming responsibility for anything that happened to the product stashed inside. For that mistake she'd paid with her life.

It was an execution committed out of revenge—but it was also a clear message to all the other exotic dancers willing to try to make some extra cash leasing houses for the cartel: *Don't fuck up with our product, or you'll suffer the same fate as Tammy.*

▪ ▪ ▪

The next week another routine—and seemingly inconsequential—blip came across our radar. I'd been working my confidential sources in El Paso and managed to flip an informant: a twenty-four-year-old Mexican gangster named Palomo. Palomo told us about a young apprentice of Amado named Guzmán.

He was arriving in El Paso to purchase sets of stainless steel kitchen sinks. Guzmán was supposedly some up-and-coming trafficker, known for his capacity for violence, but he was still only a low-scale lieutenant in the Amado organization.

Nothing special. We had him under surveillance, tracked the movements of this young Guzmán. I tailed him into downtown El Paso, where I watched him visiting a bunch of Mexican hardware places and kitchen supply outlets.

Turned out this trip had nothing to do with cocaine. Guzmán was simply buying stainless steel kitchen sets—he purchased close to fifty—putting them in a flatbed truck, then taking them back into Juárez, where he could sell them on the black market, untaxed, at a profit.

As usual, I took note of the kid's name—Guzmán. Even jotted down his nickname, El Chapo, slang for Shorty. But didn't give him much more thought until about a decade later.

By then he'd made a meteoric rise through the Mexican underworld. Unbelievably, El Chapo Guzmán—the same kid I'd tailed as he bought kitchen sinks—would be ranked by *Forbes* magazine as the eighty-sixth richest man on earth. *Forbes* also deemed the diminutive billionaire the forty-first "most powerful person" in the world. No other Mexican, not even the president, made the list. Considering his estimated net worth of more than a billion dollars, *Forbes* referred to El Chapo, perhaps with a dash of hyperbole, as the "biggest drug lord ever."

▪ ▪ ▪

Even before I arrived on the scene, Steve Whipple had achieved great success disrupting the cocaine smuggling of one of the Juárez Cartel's more dangerous crews. There are five major ports of entry in El Paso, and the Juárez Cartel would pay off various officials, oftentimes Mexicans but also corrupt US border patrol, drive their truckloads across, and place the cocaine in stash houses, where it would be prepared for transshipment across the United States.

The principal young border-crossers for the Juárez Cartel were the Espinozas, a tight-knit group of brothers and cousins based in El Paso but answering to their masters in Ciudad Juárez. They were moneymakers for Amado and his brother Vicente, but they'd recently run afoul of their bosses, largely due to the ingenious work of Steve Whipple and his wiretapping team.

Before I came to Texas, Steve had made several significant stop and seizures, including one instance where he apprehended seven hundred kilograms of the Juárez Cartel's purest cocaine. Steve came up with the idea of executing the first legal "staged carjacking"—formally called a delayed-notice search warrant—which would prove to be an outstanding investigative tool to generate confusion and chatter on our wiretaps.

When the task force received reliable intel about a major land transshipment, a group of three or four agents would make a vehicle stop: hyperaggressive, shouting only in Spanish, identified by generic police markings, black balaclavas covering their faces.

I went on a few of the missions with Steve. We'd do a thorough vehicle search—never arresting anyone or leaving a copy of a search warrant. These Mexican gangsters were so conditioned to dealing with dirty cops—or even rival crews of gangsters *pretending* to be cops—that most times they fell to their knees, certain we'd come to kill them.

From a legal standpoint, we were operating under the Carroll Doctrine, a US Supreme Court decision from the Prohibition Era that upholds the validity of warrantless automobile searches—often called the "automobile exception."*

We'd make the drug seizures: Technically all the cocaine moving across the border is *already* the possession of the US government as a controlled substance under Title 21. Then we'd leave the transporters terrified, loosely bound in flex-cuffs, muttering prayers in Spanish, but *always* still holding on to their cell phones.

---

* *Carroll v. United States*, 267 U.S. 132 (1925), holds that a vehicle can be searched without a search warrant if there is probable cause to believe that evidence is present in the vehicle, coupled with exigent circumstances to believe that the vehicle could be removed from the area before a warrant could be obtained.

The delayed-notice warrant tactic generated invaluable calls within the crew, as well as to the network of defense lawyers and up the chain of command to the bosses of the cartel. Among ourselves, we called it "tickling the wire."

I knew we had to get inside the Juárez Cartel's Espinoza crew before they ultimately got whacked by their mercurial bosses; losing a significant stash of cocaine—as we'd seen with Tammy— earned a summary death sentence. Something intuitively told me that they would be our entry into the inner circle of Amado, Vicente, and the other high-ranking Juárez Cartel gangsters.

The key would be me going undercover to infiltrate this group of what we termed "narco-juniors": young border-crossers of the Espinoza crew. As the frontline troops and lieutenants for the Juárez Cartel, these men were young and ruthless.

This Espinoza gang always wore a distinctive—and deceptively innocuous—trademark: T-shirts and jackets emblazoned with the yellow cartoon image of Tweety Bird. Their cars were also adorned with Tweety Bird decals. Bodies inked with Tweety tattoos.

Among the Mexican drug cartels, Tweety Bird has a coded and malign meaning, making him one of the pantheon of patron saints of the Mexican Mafia. Tweety is viewed by the Mexican gangsters as a young *pollo*—a baby chicken—which is also Mexican slang for an illegal border-crosser. *Pollero* is slang for a smuggler.

Many Mexican narcotics traffickers worship dark "patron saints" such as Santa Muerte and Jesús Malverde, a legendary bandit killed in Sinaloa in 1909. Malverde is viewed as a Latin-American version of Robin Hood, and smugglers bringing drugs across the border pray to him to deliver them safely across and often carry icons and images of Malverde with them.

Although Santa Muerte is not recognized by the Roman Catholic Church, the name literally translates as "Saint of Death" and she is a deity or iconic figure worshipped at shrines throughout Mexico; drug traffickers pay homage to her and pray to her for the safe passage of their drug loads, as well as prior to executions.

For years now, many Mexicans have been shot dead at her shrines or their decapitated heads left as a grisly offering to her.

Several other traditionally recognized saints, such as Saint Jude, patron saint of hopeless cases, are also worshipped as deities by narcotics traffickers.

As for the Looney Tunes cartoon image of the trickster canary, many drug traffickers place Tweety Bird stickers on their trucks or Tweety air fresheners on their rearview mirrors: The drug dealers and transporters like to see themselves as the invincible little bird that can never be caught.

■ ■ ■

The Juárez Cartel had learned through regular, often brutal interrogations—as well as via leaks from a corrupt defense attorney on their payroll in Texas—that Steve Whipple was the author of the wiretaps and the case agent on these various investigations. They acted swiftly and ruthlessly. They targeted Steve for a hit—knowing full well that he was a DEA special agent.

Over weeks of careful cultivation, we convinced my informant Palomo to introduce me to members of the Espinoza crew who were operating a window-tinting and stereo-customizing business in El Paso.

Two of the Espinoza cousins were managing the office, and I was introduced to them by my informant as a man called Fast Eddie who could take care of "difficult work." I looked the part, had my ponytail down to the middle of my back, was wearing dress slacks, a button-down shirt, and simple black loafers. I was ostensibly a private eye from LA.

Before I got there, we had an FBI break-and-enter team come down in the middle of the night; with surveillance cover from the DEA task force, the B&E team installed video and audio bugs in the auto-tinting shop prior to my first undercover meet.

■ ■ ■

On a blindingly bright February morning on the East Side of El Paso, Palomo took me to meet the Espinoza crew in their auto-tint and customizing shop.

They were all kids in their early twenties, but they were speaking directly on behalf of older Juárez Cartel family members and associates who'd recently been arrested, convicted, and imprisoned based on Steve Whipple's wiretap work.

The leaders of the crew were Ivan Espinoza and his younger brother Julio Cesar Espinoza. In a prior meeting we'd secretly surveilled and recorded, Palomo had prepped them about my impending arrival.

Palomo told them that I was a corrupt PI who now had a personal vendetta against Steve Whipple because he'd arrested some of my clients, costing me many thousands of dollars.

"Great shop you've got—I hear you do nice work," I said, turning to admire some of the luxury cars and SUVs they were kitting out.

The Juárez Cartel bosses—who live in the secure Campestre

section of Ciudad Juárez—all drove black Chevrolet Suburbans with fully tinted bulletproof glass, booming state-of-the-art sound systems, and Level 3 armor plating. They traveled around Mexico like invincible warlords in those tanklike vehicles whose interiors resembled the most opulent limousines.

"Yeah," Ivan Espinoza said, stroking his sparse goatee.

"I also do *nice* work," I said, offering a half-smile.

"That's what we hear."

Wasn't the first time I'd played the role of a hit man. When you're selling yourself as a killer for hire, you never start off saying anything too direct—"I can body that guy" or even "I can do him." That'll raise the bad guys up instantly.

You speak in an understood criminal code: innocuous-sounding phrases, half-finished statements, and knowing glances.

"I hear you have some *issues* here," I said. "Heard you have an infestation."

They nodded, warily.

I kept glancing around the tinting shop. "I'm the kind of guy— Well, I know how to *eradicate* disease."

"Yeah?"

Now I leaned in close, lowering my voice to a half-whisper.

"Look, I can *do* the job. But I'll need ten large. I'm not using my own ride. I'll need a clean car. And I'll need something to scatter the disease to the winds."

They understood. Having gained their confidence, I showed them pictures of Steve Whipple taken on "surveillance" to confirm his identity.

"Yeah, that's the cop—that's him," Ivan Espinoza said.

Cognizant of the risk of being accused of entrapment, I gave the Espinozas several clear opportunities to back out of the hit.

To seal the deal, I took them outside the shop to show them my beat-up, rust-flecked gray Ford LTD. I opened the trunk, and they could see that it was entirely covered in sheets of heavy-duty transparent plastic—evidence that I knew what I was doing when it came to the disposal of "messy" work.

"The car you get me should be— Well, I don't care what kind of car it is, as long as it's got a trunk at least this big."

They nodded, understanding. Steve Whipple's a very hefty guy, so the size and depth of the trunk was important.

We took a brief ride around El Paso in that Ford LTD.

What they didn't realize, of course, was that the car had been kitted out in its own way—wired up for audio and visual so that we captured all of our conversations.

The Espinozas agreed to all the terms: to pay me ten large, and to provide me with a clean four-door car and a shotgun, preferably a Remington.

After the first meet, back at the task force, we strategized and mulled it over:

What would be our next move?

Suddenly, Steve Whipple himself came up with an audacious plan to provide the Juárez gangsters with irrefutable "proof" that I'd completed the hit on him.

■ ■ ■

Working in tandem with the coroner's office in El Paso, we went out into the desert to photograph the "murder" scene. Steve had recruited two El Paso Police Department homicide detectives, Max Zimmerly and Mickey Wilhite.

We drove my big gray four-door Ford LTD out to the desert so that it was also visible in the background of the photos. Max

Zimmerly combined fake blood—as professional as any Holly-wood studio makeup man—with regular supermarket-bought Heinz ketchup to make the job look real. They duct-taped Steve's hands and feet. They slipped a plastic bag over his head, then duct-taped the bag around his neck.

Then they created the effect of a head shot as if he'd been blasted at close range by my 12 gauge. They dragged Steve around in the dirt, put dusty boot prints on his back and rear end, and made him look like he'd taken a righteous ass-whipping before my Remington had administered the coup de grâce.

Then they took a dozen Polaroids of the "corpse."

The pictures were so disturbing that when I first saw them, I was pretty shaken up. It actually looked like Steve had been shot point-blank in the head. They were extremely graphic. Even today, I wouldn't want Steve's children to see those Polaroids, because it looked like I really did him.

But the staged hit on Steve took an unexpected twist. Through a jailhouse snitch, the Espinoza crew got spooked. They became so worried about the wiretaps, and the possibility of a leak within their organization, that they wouldn't agree to the last meet to pay me the $10,000 for the completed hit.

But that didn't make much difference to the federal prose-cutors. We still had the entire Espinoza crew on conspiracy to commit murder, so we bagged every last one.

▪ ▪ ▪

Two months after my arrival in El Paso, I'd furthered my rap-port with my informant Palomo, who was able to cross over into Juárez for personal contact with the Carrillo Fuentes brothers; an introduction had been made through a trusted associate—a

Chinese-Mexican restaurant owner—and we'd even been able to arrange face-to-face meetings at the Carrillo Fuentes homes.

As with any confidential informant, you only trust what you can corroborate, but over the course of months, Palomo became my surrogate eyes and ears. I would send Palomo across the border many times to do work, because for me to go under-cover in Ciudad Juárez and try to engage Amado or Vicente was unfeasible.

In this respect, the Juárez Cartel gangsters weren't like other major narcotics figures I've worked undercover during my career. This wasn't like Mike Bansmer and me meeting face-to-face with Thai traffickers, or my solo interactions with a Nige-rian like Sam Essell or a Lebanese like Kayed Berro. The rules are different south of the border. The Carrillo Fuentes brothers, like the other major Mexican cartel bosses, had a strict policy of meeting directly only with other Mexicans.

Nonetheless, through my confidential informant Palomo, I managed to get nine audiotapes; eight were of the younger brother, Vicente, and one was solely with Amado. For the first time, we had two bosses of the Juárez Cartel implicating them-selves on crystal clear tape recordings.

Then, suddenly, things turned extremely tense back at DEA headquarters in Arlington; there were senior DEA officials who could not believe we'd actually got close enough to Amado to capture his voice, or even that we'd developed an informant who could gain such intimate access as we did.

Days after we filed the twenty-nine-count complaint against Amado and Vicente, along with their chief operations officer, Javier Herrera, we learned of a power play among the competing brass within DEA, specifically the Special Operations Division.

The internecine wrangling erupted into an internal investigation calling into question the origin and authenticity of the tapes.

Steve Whipple and I had to fly to DEA headquarters to be grilled as to how we obtained the intelligence. At one point—much to my chagrin—the tapes were accused of being staged, complete with fabricated voices.

Fortunately, after a full week in Arlington, all nine of the tapes were proven to be the real deal, corroborated by other intelligence sources as being the authentic voices of Amado and Vicente Carrillo Fuentes.

■ ■ ■

With the veracity of our tapes vindicated, we could begin to close the legal snare. In the American judicial system, there are four forms of charging offenses: a complaint, an indictment, a grand jury indictment, and information from the US Attorney's Office leading to prosecution.

Things were proceeding at breakneck pace: I'd obtained a complaint against Amado Carrillo Fuentes in conjunction with the US Attorney's Office in the Fifth District.

We were entering uncharted waters: on the verge of charging, and ultimately getting an extradition against, both Amado and Vicente Carrillo Fuentes. There would be considerable legal hurdles ahead, but we were finally beginning the process of trying the untouchable Lord of the Skies himself in a US federal court.

Of course, Amado Carrillo Fuentes didn't rise to his position of power without having a wide network of spies and informants, both on the streets and within the Mexican government. Knowing how close we were to getting an indictment that could lead to his extradition, Amado began to take dramatic evasive measures—much like Pablo Escobar and other Colombian drug lords had done a decade earlier when under threat of extradition to the United States.

Through our excellent intel sources in both the United States and Mexico, we knew that he had started on a secretive tour to find a place he could stash his ill-gotten billions.

We knew he had traveled to Cuba, then down to Bolivia, then on to Buenos Aires and Santiago. The pressure within Mexico was getting too intense. Amado would only move around Ciudad Juárez in ambulances: The insides were kitted out in opulence like a limousine, but the exteriors resembled functional ambulances to thwart law enforcement surveillance.

In those frantic days we were pursuing the indictment against Amado, I found myself speeding down a slick black strip of highway. I had a new motorcycle that my stepfather had purchased for me—a Harley-Davidson Softail. I'd decided to do a marathon ride from the eastern border of Texas to El Paso—about 883 miles all told.

I would ride for three or four hours, pull over for fifteen minutes to drink some water and gas up, but I wasn't lingering anyplace for too long; I wanted to make it across the state of Texas in one day.

As I was riding along like a madman, somewhere near Odessa, I pulled over. I'd received an urgent message from one of my supervisors in El Paso, Dennis Clark.

By now the Texas heat had given way to a sudden thunderstorm; I stopped the Harley under a little bridge where I could escape the violently pelting rain.

I noticed a rusted-out, dilapidated, and abandoned Pontiac parked under the bridge. I put my Softail on its kickstand, slid into the driver's seat of the dilapidated car, and called Dennis on my cell.

"What's up, Dennis?"

"Amado's fuckin' dead."

"I know. We're about to bring the hammer down on his ass—"

"No, Eddie. He's *dead*."

"Dead?" I repeated it twice—not a question, just stunned, disbelieving. "Amado Carrillo Fuentes is dead . . ."

"Dead."

I looked over, and there was a thin emerald-green-and-black snake slithering around the backseat.

"*Murdered?*" I said, finally.

"He died after surgery. Don't know all the details yet. Too much anesthesia."

I was so frustrated, so pissed off. I glanced back and saw that emerald-green snake squirming up the backseat and actually thought—for an instant—about pulling out my piece and blasting the snake's head clean off.

"Fuck!"

The entire chassis of that beat-up Pontiac reverberated from my shout.

■ ■ ■

When I got back to the El Paso task force office, the pieces of the story began to fall into place. On the verge of fleeing Mexico to escape our indictment, Amado Carrillo Fuentes had arranged for massive liposuction and facial reconstruction.

Four Mexican doctors performed the surgery, which lasted

hours. Amado came out of surgery and grabbed the anesthesiologist at his side. Slowly regaining consciousness, moaning in pain, Amado complained: *Look, I need more.*

The anesthesiologist was reluctant—this physician was no quack; he was a veteran of countless plastic surgeries for Latin America's wealthiest and most powerful citizens. But he nonetheless administered more oral painkillers.

Amado, still in great pain, demanded even *more* painkillers.

Amado died of respiratory arrest on July 4. The surgeons had completely reconstructed his facial features and removed thirty pounds of fat from his midsection.

I kept mulling over the information in my mind. Dead on a coroner's table, his body bloated and distorted from the surgery: the richest drug trafficker on the planet—gone.

■ ■ ■

After Amado's death, for thirty days there was an unholy bloodletting in Juárez. Anyone who owed Amado any money, or was in some way indentured to him, went out and butchered all the Carrillo Fuentes people he could find: street soldiers, lieutenants, even high-ranking officers in the cartel organizational structure.

Better to kill now, in the interregnum, while there was no boss.

In those thirty days there were ninety-four murders, an average of more than three murders a day.

■ ■ ■

The Mexican cocaine cartels maintain a complex, incestuous structure unlike any other drug empires on the planet. Sometimes they come together to behave like a criminal cooperative— as in the case of the original Federation.

Other times, especially in a power vacuum, they wage vicious war among themselves, on a scale that dwarfs the Capone-era gangland wars of Prohibition. Just since 2006, more than 66,000 have been killed in the Mexican drug wars, a figure far exceeding the total number of US servicemen killed in the entire Vietnam War.

And unlike the American Mafia—as we'd seen with the attempted contract killing of Steve Whipple—the Mexican cartels observe no boundaries about killing lawmen, judges, politicians, or one another's closest family members.

There's a famous story, told throughout the Mexican drug world.

When El Chapo Guzmán's son, twenty-two-year-old Édgar Guzmán López, was publicly murdered in a shopping center parking lot by at least fifteen gunmen using assault rifles and grenade launchers, El Chapo made a chilling vow:

"If my son can't have a life, then neither can yours."

Though it's never been proven, it's widely believed that Guzmán ordered the hit on one of the sons of the rival drug lord who Chapo blamed for the death.

It's still often heard in barrios of Ciudad Juárez:

"Chapo wanted his pound of flesh and, yes, he got it."

◼ ◼ ◼

I drove down into Ciudad undercover one day during the thirty-day bloodletting in the wake of the death of Amado Carrillo Fuentes. As you drive south through El Paso on Interstate 10 and look to your right, you see the sprawling barrios of Mexico's most violent city: Ciudad Juárez.

In the wintertime, you smell the burning tires throughout

the barrios. I looked over, picturing the stark contrast between the abject poverty of those Juárez slums and the opulence in which Amado and Vicente had lived—untouchable lords—in their secure Campestre section of the city.

Amado may have been dead, but one of my primary targets, named in the charging document, was Javier Herrera, the operations officer and chief enforcer for Amado and Vicente Carrillo Fuentes.

Immediately after Amado's death, Herrera was publicly executed outside of the Juárez bullfighting stadium.

Like the Taliban in Afghanistan, the Mexican drug cartels have a particular weapon of choice: the AK-47 assault rifle, gas-powered, firing 7.62×39mm rounds from a curving magazine they refer to as the *cuerno de chivo*—the goat's horn.

Outside the bullfighting arena, in front of dozens of witnesses, Javier Herrera was shot more than thirty times in the face. They unloaded the entire *cuerno de chivo* magazine at point-blank range. Even among the cartel, that's a particularly sadistic brand of execution.

When you tear up a man's face with thirty rounds, the flesh and features are destroyed. It's an act of sheer sadism, preventing the mother or widow from having an open-casket funeral.

■ ■ ■

As for Amado himself, we knew we could not trust any of the information we were getting out of Mexico. We had to be certain that the Lord of the Skies had not cleverly staged his own death—used a bit of Hollywood-style trickery, in an eerie replication of what we'd done with Steve Whipple out in the desert.

Immediately after Independence Day weekend, we went down

to Mexico to get eyeballs on his corpse. Amazingly, the family *did* have an open-casket funeral. It was enough to shock even a hardened lawman.

Amado's face was grotesquely distorted, almost charred-looking: a bluish-gray ghoul. I had to match his fingerprints to an existing print we had—we had one on file because Amado had once applied for a visa to enter the United States.

Sure enough, the prints were a match. Steve Whipple and I had lost our quarry; the richest gangster of all time was dead.

■　■　■

And the plastic surgeons? They paid the ultimate price for their dance with the Juárez devil.

The retribution was swift. One vanished without a trace. Rumors continue to swirl about him—he somehow escaped, or perhaps became a cooperating witness.

The other three doctors are known to have been murdered by the Juárez Cartel in the most grisly manner. Just like poor Tammy Morrison, the stripper we'd tried desperately to rescue, the doctors were torture-murdered. All three corpses were dismembered, the body parts placed into those fifty-five-gallon metal drums and drenched in acid. No remains were ever found.

■　■　■

The fate of Amado's brother Vicente, meanwhile, remains baffling to this day. Perhaps murdered, perhaps hiding under another identity—Vicente has simply vanished from the face of the earth.

No one in the DEA believes he's dead, but he has successfully disappeared; from 1997, all the way to 2014, there has not been a single verifiable piece of intelligence that Vicente is still alive. And despite all our advancements in surveillance techniques, we haven't got a single voiceprint of Vicente in decades.

Perhaps he made it to Cuba, Bolivia, Chile, or Argentina—we just don't know.

According to some sources, Vicente is still handling about a fifth of Mexico's $40-billion-a-year narcotics trade as the Juárez Cartel's godfather in absentia. Right now, the Carrillo Fuentes drug-trafficking organization, using fleets of tractor trailers, is still regularly moving multihundred kilograms of cocaine, as well as multiton amounts of marijuana, through the Ciudad Juárez–El Paso corridor for distribution to cells in Texas, California, and Illinois.

The US Department of State is currently offering an award of $5 million (US) for information leading to the arrest and/or conviction of Vicente Carrillo Fuentes.

◼ ◼ ◼

On February 22, 2014, Mexican authorities finally captured Joaquin "El Chapo" Guzmán, now fifty-six years old—ranked on the DEA's Wanted List as the world's most powerful cocaine kingpin—in the resort city of Mazatlán. Amado Carrillo Fuentes's one-time lowly lieutenant—who I'd followed through the streets of El Paso as he bought stainless steel kitchen appliances—had risen to billionaire status and the *Forbes* list of the "World's Most Powerful People." He was ignominiously nabbed by the Mexican marines at 6:40 a.m. in a high-rise condominium fronting the Pacific in Mazatlán.

US officials announced that the Drug Enforcement Administration, as well as the Department of Homeland Security, had been instrumental in providing the intelligence that led to the capture of El Chapo. US Attorney General Eric Holder called the capture a "victory for the citizens of both Mexico and the United States."

PART THREE

CHAPTER 7

■ ■ ■

THE GREAT GAME

Now I shall go far and far into the North playing
the Great Game.   RUDYARD KIPLING, *KIM*

Since our takedown of Khun Sa and the Shan United Army
in the 1990s, worldwide heroin production had shifted its axis,
from Southeast Asia to Southwest Asia. With the downfall of
the SUA, the traffickers of the Golden Triangle switched almost
exclusively to manufacturing methamphetamine.

Today, Afghanistan has a virtual monopoly on the world's
heroin trade: Approximately 92 percent of the illegal heroin
sold globally is Afghan in origin.

But how did the shift from east to west happen? Few
Americans—few Westerners—understand the full story of how
Afghanistan, under the Taliban, cornered the global market in
opium production.

A landmark report from the United Nations Office on
Drugs and Crime (UNODC) details the massive and profoundly
negative impact of the Afghan poppy trade:

The world's deadliest drug has created a market worth
$65 billion, catering to 15 million addicts, causing up to
100,000 deaths per year, spreading HIV at an unprecedented rate and, not least, funding criminal groups, insurgents and terrorists.*

In 1999 Afghanistan saw a bumper opium crop of 4,500
metric tons. But in July 2000, Mullah Omar issued a surprising
judicial ruling under Sharia law.

Mullah Omar was the spiritual head of the Taliban, but
also Afghanistan's de facto head of state from 1996 to late
2001, under the official title Head of the Supreme Council.
His word was law. He announced that, according to the Holy
Koran, the use of any kind of psychotropic substance was strictly
forbidden.

Taliban signs began to appear around the country reading:
"The Islamic Emirate of Afghanistan not only engenders [sic]
illegal things forbidden but launches effective struggles against
illicit drugs as these drugs are a great threat to personality, wis-
dom, life, health, economy, and morality."

The ban was so effective that, officially at least, Helmand
Province recorded no poppy cultivation during next season.

Early in 2001, the Bush administration made a $43 million
"eradication" reward payment to the Taliban regime. At the time
this was billed as one of the most successful antidrug campaigns
in history.

---

* "Addiction, Crime and Insurgency: The Transnational Threat of Afghan
Opium," a report by the United Nations Office on Drugs and Crime, 2009.

But was it? Prior to the September 11 attacks, Mullah Omar called a historic meeting of dignitaries in the Pakistani city of Quetta. The conference has come to be known as the Quetta Shura. All accounts indicate that those in attendance at this first sit-down included Haji Bashir Noorzai, Haji Bagcho Sherzai, Haji Baz Mohammad, and Haji Juma Khan (or HJK, as I would later come to call him).

"Haji" is the honorific title given to any Muslim man who has made the pilgrimage, or hajj, to the holy city of Mecca. But every one of these "Hajis" at the conference in Quetta was known to us as a major opium and heroin trafficker in Afghanistan and Pakistan. It was reportedly Noorzai and Juma Khan who masterminded the meeting.

Time magazine reporting would later suggest that the Taliban's ban on the cultivation of poppies and production of opium was the idea of Al Qaeda's financial experts working with HJK and other top Afghan drug traffickers. According to *Time*, the ban "meant huge profits for the Taliban and their trafficker friends who were sitting on large stockpiles when prices soared."

Mullah Omar had reportedly told them: *Yes, we've issued the fatwa that drug dealing is forbidden under Koranic law, but privately, we'll keep stockpiling opium base.*

There are four stages in the production of heroin: poppy flowers, which are refined into opium paste, which is refined into morphine base, which is refined into heroin. While morphine base and heroin will deteriorate rather quickly, the brownish-black jellylike opium paste, unlike most agricultural products, can easily be stored for many years without refrigeration. Secreted away in warehouses, mass quantities of opium paste have a shelf life of at least ten years.

Right after our Coalition forces invaded Afghanistan in the fall of 2001, the Taliban reversed its religious position. Mullah Omar issued a second fatwa saying, in effect, that the cultivation of poppies and heroin production—though not *consumption*—were not only approved but encouraged, because now opium traffickers were funding and facilitating the campaign against the foreign invaders and infidels.

In warehouses all over the country, men like Noorzai, Bagcho, and HJK had stockpiled tons of opium paste. The Taliban was now able to virtually corner the worldwide market; for several years, we now know, the Taliban had set aside half of their annual opium harvest. By lifting the ban, Mullah Omar sent their profits shooting up nearly tenfold: A kilogram of opium had sold for $44 wholesale before the ban, but one year later the price had risen to $400.

Drug lords like Haji Juma Khan became overnight billionaires. Worst of all, from an American perspective, these opium billions were funneled into the insurgency and Al Qaeda cells. The DEA came to believe HJK alone was providing more than $100 million a year to jihadist terror groups.

Those of us in the counter-narcotics business saw Mullah Omar's first fatwa for what it was: a shell game, a clever con—a piece of dogma-cloaked PR for foreign consumption. Really, it was just a traditional price-fixing scam. Mullah Omar had announced a religious ban on opium production, but had his intimate consort of traffickers secretly stockpile a decade's worth of product. It was a classic case of market manipulation carried out by a small cabal of Afghan drug lords.

The stark reality is that the heroin production crisis in Southwest Asia is getting even worse as the US military completes its final drawdown from Afghanistan in 2016. Due to the widespread collusion between the Afghan government, police and intelligence operatives, and tribal drug kingpins, the heroin-terror connection is certain to increase—with disturbing repercussions for Americans both abroad and at home.

Although Afghanistan is ostensibly our ally—and counter-narcotics partner—many of us within the counter-narcotics community have come to refer to the nation as the "Narco-terrorist Islamic Republic of Afghanistan," a national security threat posed by the confluence of endemic political corruption, highly structured drug cartels, and extreme terrorist organizations.

■ ■ ■

Everything changed for me on September 11, 2001. On the morning of the attacks, I'd been at the DEA headquarters in Arlington, Virginia, and had seen the American Airlines Flight 77 jetliner hit the Pentagon, roughly two hundred yards from my office window.

I watched the fireball in real time. I saw that grisly "pie slice" crater, first flaming and then smoldering . . . After recovering from shock, I rushed over to the Pentagon to pull out bodies—but there were no bodies to pull out.

In the following weeks, I desperately wanted to get into the fight overseas. Over and over, I told my friends and family:

"I want a shot at Bin Laden."

Then, in 2006, the position of assistant regional director and country attaché to Afghanistan opened up—the two jobs were being consolidated into one. It was, to say the least, an unpleasant posting.

Back then, we had scant military support for our counter-narcotics efforts in Afghanistan. And making matters worse, other intelligence entities were undermining *everything* that DEA was trying to accomplish from a counter-narcotics standpoint. Still, I remained gung-ho.

"If I want to go after Bin Laden," I told my family, "this is the way to do it. If I take this job, I'll be right there, going after the traffickers who finance his whole terror network."

Everybody in my family—my mother and stepfather, Ray; my younger brother; all my friends at work—said the same thing:

"Eddie, don't take it. You've got a promising future in the DEA—don't throw it away in Afghanistan."

Finally, one Tuesday morning, I awoke with the answer clear in my mind.

You know what you need to do. If you have any chance to do this guy, Ed, if you think you can help bring down UBL, you've got to do this. Everyone else wants you to put your career first, but you've got to go to Kabul.

I applied for the position and the DEA administrator, Karen Tandy, thought I was the right guy. Like that old saying "It takes a thief to catch a thief," my own variation spun through my thoughts: *It might take a zealot to catch a zealot.*

Almost as soon as I arrived as country attaché, stationed in the US Embassy compound in Kabul, I assessed that we had serious problems—in terms of both morale and tradecraft.

Before arriving in-country, I'd read all the existing DEA files. We had myriad major Taliban-linked opium warlords to contend with. The primary three "Hajis" on our radar were Bagcho Sher-zai, Khan Mohammad (not to be confused with Muhammad Khan), and HJK.

There was no way to target these opium lords using traditional—military-style—operational methodology. At some point soon, I knew, we'd need to go undercover, just as street cops would, into the hinterlands of that untamed war zone.

But before I could even think about going undercover myself, my primary task was to change the mind-set of our DEA staff in Kabul. It was only my fifth day in-country; I brought all thirty of my people into the big conference room of the embassy, both my permanent agents and all our support staff.

I was dressed in an open-necked shirt, intentionally casual, no spit and polish. Even before speaking, I could see—just glancing around my group—that my men were disheartened and disenchanted; they'd spent months—some of them years—fighting a battle they felt we could never fully win.

A lot of the DEA special agents who'd volunteered for the Kabul posting wanted to put on military fatigues and strap on heavy weapons; they wanted to go up in the Super Stallion and Cobra helicopters; they wanted to engage the Taliban drug traf-fickers as the military would. True, they'd been trained in law enforcement techniques, but they'd also volunteered for service overseas.

It was understandable: *Nobody* volunteers for duty in Afghan-istan to work as an undercover narc. They all signed up to see *action*.

But trying to take down this massive, sprawling world of her-oin and opium kingpins—scattered across a vast, often unnaviga-ble country—was impossible using a paramilitary mind-set. My men were being beaten down: depressed, fatigued, and frustrated on a daily basis.

We needed to go from behaving like soldiers to using the techniques of street agents—the mentality and tradecraft I'd first learned in LA Division Group Four—and applying them to a combat zone. No one had yet brought undercover skills to play in Afghanistan.

There were a few nods around the room, but mostly blank stares. Only a couple of the guys had ever worked undercover. And if they had, they'd been in urban areas like Detroit, New York, or LA. But working as a UC in the States, whether in the inner city or the suburbs, is nothing like being undercover in a place like Kabul.

First order of business: I told them to get out of their BDUs— battle dress uniforms, the basic fatigues that are used by the armed forces as their standard uniform for combat situations— and start dressing like the DEA special agents they were. When necessary, I knew, we'd be donning the garb of various Afghan ethnic groups to go undercover, so around the embassy, I did not want to see any of my people wearing BDUs.

I had one DEA special agent—actually a valuable investigator—who walked into the embassy carrying a live grenade. He was strolling around the embassy compound, in those damn battle fatigues, strapped with an M67—the standard 6.5-ounce fragmentation hand grenade used by the US military.

I took him aside and, without hesitation, gave him a private tongue-lashing.

"What're you *doing*? Get that grenade *out* of here. Christ! You're a DEA agent—not a Marine!"

There was certainly no need for any of us to be armed inside the secured embassy compound. In addition to the intense perimeter security of Gurkhas, I had the members of the DEA's Foreign-Deployed Advisory and Support Teams (FAST). In the early 1990s, as part of the Drug Enforcement Administration's global counter-narcotics strategy, DEA formed five elite Foreign-Deployed Advisory and Support Teams. One of the FAST teams is permanently stationed in Afghanistan; the other four are based out of Marine Corps Base Quantico and are dispatched to various hot zones around the globe.

A typical FAST team is comprised of eight special agents, an intelligence specialist, and a team leader. Much of their equipment is supplied by the Pentagon.

I met with Jeff Higgins—a GS-14—who was overall commander of the FAST team members. A lot of my FAST guys had been tacticians, shooters, raid agents. They'd been the "hard men"—worn the DEA windbreakers and Teflon vests, carried the battering rams—the first guys through the door during raids.

I had to turn them into what Rogelio Guevara and José Martinez had taught me to be when I was still a kid in LA: premier investigators and undercover operatives.

"We are *not* doing military-style eradications," I told Higgins. "We are developing cases for prosecution, here and in other competent authorities: England and Germany and Turkey—but especially back home in the USA. Understand that. When we go out on operations, we are doing so strictly from a law enforcement mind-set."

A lot of my FAST team guys would only be working on the periphery of our upcoming missions. They were going to be "tacticians," as I liked to call them, but I still had to show them adequate respect. I'd need them to take care of business when the bullets started flying. My first week of briefings around the embassy was essentially an attempt to hit a reset button on our operational techniques. There'd been a clear demarcation of duties when I arrived, but I now, with a sense of relief, was confident that I'd melded the tactical FAST guys with my core investigators and molded them into a single and cohesive law enforcement team.

■ ■ ■

The principal law we were operating under was US Code Title 21, 960a, the 2006 narco-terrorism statute that afforded the Drug Enforcement Administration greater latitude to operate abroad, targeting and arresting these Taliban-linked opium kingpins and extraditing them to the Southern and Eastern Districts of New York, as well as the federal court in Washington, DC. The new statute also gave us federal budgetary consideration and access right up the chain of command, even a seat at the table with the National Security Council.

Under my watch, the first major trafficker we targeted was Bagcho Sherzai, against whom I would later testify in court as a subject-matter expert. In terms of sheer income from illicit drugs, Bagcho is ranked—even today—as perhaps the most successful heroin trafficker in history. Through surveillance and informants, we developed solid intel that Bagcho was exporting heroin to more than twenty different countries, including the United States. He lived in Marco Khune, a village in Nangarhar Province, but also kept a fortified compound in Hayatabad, outside of Peshawar, Pakistan.

In order to get near Bagcho we had no choice: We'd have to go down to Jalalabad—which was one of the most dangerous places on earth, even deadlier to an American than Ciudad Juárez. Even our US Marines would only go down to Jalalabad in numbers: at least two or three platoons driving Humvees, armed with M50 machine guns.

To clear the operation, I went into the office of Ambassador Ronald Neumann; he was a veteran State Department official, and as savvy a diplomat as I've ever worked with. Neumann had formerly been a deputy assistant secretary of state, and knew the intricacies of the Middle East far better than me. He'd already served as ambassador to Algeria and Bahrain and was most recently stationed in Baghdad with the Coalition Provisional Authority.

During his swearing-in ceremony at the State Department, Ambassador Neumann had announced that his priorities in Kabul were "fighting narcotics, establishing rule of law, and enhancing security." He'd argued that only by fighting the narcotics barons in Afghanistan would we "ensure that the country will never again be a safe haven for terrorists." Ambassador Neumann often told me that he'd inherited his commitment to diplomacy and to the nation of Afghanistan from his father, who was US ambassador to Afghanistan in the 1960s.

I sat down at the ambassador's desk, laying out an undercover op against Bagcho.

"Haji Bagcho Sherzai?" he said, incredulous. "Ed, can we actually *get* this guy down there in Jalalabad?"

"Yes, sir. I believe we can bag him. But we can't lure him

here to Kabul. We have no other option. We're going to have to go get him down there in his stronghold."

The ambassador was no shrinking violet, and he was the only US State Department official with whom I'd entrust our UC activities.

"Okay, Ed," he said. "You've got my support. Just promise me you'll come back here *alive*."

In effect, as he well knew, this was our first high-risk test to see how the DEA could function under our new rules of law enforcement engagement in a war zone.

■ ■ ■

I little realized, when I took the position of DEA country attaché and assistant regional director, managing fifty special agents and scores of support staff, that it would be an unceasing battle with the corruption of the Karzai government and our own recalcitrant intelligence agencies.

Desperately in need of an Afghan ally, in my official capacity as the country attaché, I began to meet regularly with General Mohammad Daud Daud, the deputy minister for counter-narcotics, and he quickly became one of my dear friends.

Together we put in countless hours to develop Afghanistan's first dedicated counter-narcotics police agency. Within weeks of my arrival in Kabul, General Daud was telling me, over jasmine tea at his humble residence, his stories of having fought the Soviet Red Army as a mujahideen. He'd lived in a cave, like a prehistoric man, for more than *seven* years. He knew the austerity under which the typical Afghan was prepared to live.

"Ed, most of you Americans don't understand this," he said.

"They truly want *nothing* you have. They do not want to live a Western lifestyle. They've lived like this, and will continue to live like this, for centuries."

When the Soviet Union invaded, rival warlords had banded together in ranks of mujahideen: warriors in a jihad for Allah. Demonstrating asceticism beyond Western comprehension, the mujahideen drove the great Soviet military machine out of Afghanistan.

With General Daud's help, we also had to train the prosecutors in the newly formed Afghan system to manage actual drug courts—with due process, cross-examination of witnesses, adequately trained defense counsel—rather than the previous draconian Sharia laws. We also crafted a version of a controlled-substances act modeled on our own in the United States—a team of assistant US attorneys had come to Afghanistan to help local prosecutors write those statutory requirements.

■ ■ ■

I needed five guys, including myself, for the Jalalabad undercover operation. For a month, all five of us had grown out our facial hair. We were going down to Jalalabad in full "Haji" mode: dressed in linen *shalwar kameez* with black scarves around our faces. I had a Pashtun-speaking tailor come into the embassy and make us each our own *shalwar kameez*. On our heads, we'd all wear Massoud caps.

As with our outfits, the authenticity of our vehicles was paramount to the mission. We clearly couldn't drive our government Land Cruisers. It would be like having a bull's-eye on our backs for any suicide bomber. I acquired the money to buy four old Toyota Corollas—rust-flecked, dented, six or seven years old. I lined the floors of the Toyotas with ballistic blankets to protect us from IEDs and hand grenades.

Some of the agents were frankly alarmed by the sight of those fragile-looking Japanese compact cars.

"Look, I told you: We're *not* military," I said. "We're undercover cops. We're pursuing these traffickers in their own environment. That means using their own vehicles."

"What the hell?"

They all—to a man—looked at me like I'd become unhinged.

"We're not gonna get within miles of Jalalabad driving a bunch of armored Land Cruisers or Suburbans," I said. "And we're gonna carry AK-47s. We're not carrying any American guns."

Carrying an M4—toting a US military weapon—would have instantly blown our cover, so we were armed only with those AK-47s, the weapon most favored by the Taliban and Al Qaeda—and by the foot soldiers of heroin kingpins like Haji Bagcho Sherzai and Haji Juma Khan.

▪ ▪ ▪

For the Jalalabad mission to succeed, I needed to go into the field personally. In order to enter Jalalabad—as a GS-15 and the DEA's country attaché, undercover—I needed written authorization from headquarters.

Luckily, by the time of the mission, the approval had come through from the administration back in Arlington.

There was no way, other than firsthand observation, to grasp the scope of the drug-trafficking problem. No one—neither the Afghan intel services nor our own spooks at Langley—had a handle on the details of the heroin pipeline, from the cultivation of the poppy crop to its refinement into opium paste, morphine base, and ultimately processed heroin. Our lofted high-resolution optics surveillance can only do so much.

The mission was going to be high-risk, and I knew I couldn't rely solely on my FAST team guys. In order to go down to a place as violent as Jalalabad and capture actual prosecutorial evidence, I needed further backup.

The ops plan was to infiltrate the biggest opium bazaar in Afghanistan. It was located right in the heart of Jalalabad. There was no way I could accomplish that with my DEA guys alone— even with the FAST team on the periphery.

By now I had befriended a military colonel named Greg Pate, USMC. There were various branches of the armed services I could have turned to, but I only trusted the Marines. There's a strong, lifelong sense of brotherhood among us.

I met with Colonel Pate in my embassy office.

"I need peripheral support," I told him. "I may need a quick reaction force. I may need medevac. I may need Humvees with 50-cals."

Colonel Pate almost laughed in my face.

"Jalalabad? We don't go down there unless we're in company strength. You're taking a handful of your guys and Afghan nationals in some Corollas?"

"Yeah, this is what we're doing. Get ready."

"Are you fucking crazy?"

"I don't know if I'm fucking crazy, but it's what we're doing."

We had the full support of the USMC, but I also managed to convince this young Marine colonel to have his men operating under DEA rules of engagement: no *hoo-rah*, no M4s drawn, no BDUs—no hard-core jarhead shit.

Of all the remote and desolate regions of Afghanistan, *nothing* is more sobering than traveling through the Khyber Pass. Since the Coalition invasion of Afghanistan in 2001, few Americans have gone through the Khyber Pass unscathed.

Along the drive, we hit all kinds of checkpoints, and sharp-eyed Taliban guards would mistake us for actual fundamentalists, asking us in Pashtun:

"Are you Talib?"

We returned hard stares—not a word of English to give us away.

We'd always let Aziz, our Afghan investigative assistant, answer the questions.

The Talibs could only see our eyes behind our sand-flecked scarves. We drove those rattling Corollas up into the Khyber Pass, following the thousand-year-old opium smuggling route into the Kush.

The Khyber Pass, at an altitude of 3,500 feet, connects Afghanistan and Pakistan. Once a crucial part of the ancient Silk Road, it's considered one of the oldest trade passages in the world. Throughout history it has been an important trade route between Central Asia and South Asia as well as a strategic military location.

When you first encounter the Khyber Pass, you feel the presence of all the would-be invaders, from Alexander the Great through the Brits and the Soviets. Even today, monuments left by British Army units, as well as hillside forts, can be viewed from the highway.

The Khyber is essentially a massive cavern. Today—and for

generations—it's been known as outlaw country. You wander off that road and you're very quickly in the barely controlled Federally Administered Tribal Areas (FATAs).

Life is worth pennies down there. From those towering cave-pocked cliffs, any Afghan sniper can take you out with a rifle without you even seeing it coming.

While driving my Corolla, I was looking up at the cliffs, thinking of the Sean Connery character, Danny, in *The Man Who Would Be King*—the British mercenary overtaken by his own hubris, ultimately killed by Afghan tribesmen on this same desolate terrain:

> *A glorious band, the chosen few*
> *On whom the Spirit came;*
> *Twelve valiant saints, their hope they knew,*
> *And mocked the cross and flame.*
> *They met the tyrant's brandished steel,*
> *The lion's gory mane;*
> *They bowed their heads the death to feel:*
> *Who follows in their train?*

We made it safely through the Khyber Pass, rumbling through the Northwest Frontier, skirting the Federally Administered Tribal Areas, the barrels of our AKs bobbing in the backseat, but I knew we were still constantly being watched . . .

Somehow—miraculously—our cover held.

Jalalabad was inarguably the most dangerous city in the region. There was no corner of that swarming city where a Westerner could feel safe. I've been in some scary locations—Thailand,

Burma, Ciudad Juárez—but Jalalabad was like no place I'd ever been in my life.

And the opium bazaar was like no other drug location on the planet. It almost resembled a flea market, but instead of a bunch of costume jewelry and old furniture and bicycles, there were dozens of stands selling different brands of pure opium and refined heroin and morphine base.

The place was huge and carnival-like; the atmosphere is actually convivial.

To do the actual drug buy, I sent two of my Afghan guys in—most crucially our indigenous Pashtun-speaking informant Aziz. The opium bazaar was so brazen, you could openly buy kilos, or even make a consignment order for a larger purchase.

Before I sent Aziz on the set, I'd secured a "hawk" around his neck.

The hawk is a covert recorder—not US government–made but produced by a private-sector company and state-of-the-art. The hawk records clear video as well as audio. It's undetectable. The downside is that, unlike a Kel device, it doesn't transmit: It simply records, so the backup team can't rush on the set if shit goes bad.

At this time the hawk was so new—so minute, so sophisticated—that even if the Taliban drug lords were to examine it, they would never even know what they were looking at.

I was hanging back, dressed in my Talib disguise, watching as Aziz met face-to-face with Haji Bagcho Sherzai. Bagcho was surprisingly small, about five-foot-two, with a friendly-looking face and snow-white beard. The first bombshell piece of evidence was the moment we got him admitting to his opium production and heroin sales on the hawk videotape.

Then Aziz purchased two kilograms of pure heroin from

Bagcho's stall in the bazaar. That was all we needed from that raucous opium marketplace.

Immediately after the heroin purchase, I called in the FAST boys. I got Jeff Higgins on the radio.

"All right, Higgins. Unleash your dogs."

Now the FAST team members could go in and do what they'd been trained to. They stormed into the bazaar and kicked ass.

The entire bazaar went berserk. At any time one of these Talibs could have whipped out an AK. But we were lucky: We acted so quickly, we avoided a gunfight.

Higgins and our FAST team tore the place apart, seized all the ledgers, all the evidence that we'd need from Bagcho's booth in the bazaar.

Shortly thereafter, we executed raids on Bagcho's various residences in and around Jalalabad. We seized one ledger that was a treasure trove of records of all his narcotics deals and finances.

His workers had written everything down—old-school. They didn't even use calculators. Every single major opium transaction was handwritten in those kinds of ledger books that haven't been used by accountants in the States in decades.

One ledger, cataloguing Bagcho's activities during 2006, reflected heroin transactions of more than 123,000 kilograms. The evidence was incontrovertible that Bagcho used a portion of his drug proceeds to provide the Taliban governor of Nangarhar Province and two Taliban commanders responsible for insurgent activity in eastern Afghanistan with cash, weapons, and other supplies so that they could continue their jihad against US and other Coalition troops.

We later learned perhaps the most stunning statistic of all: Based on heroin production statistics compiled by the United Nations Office on Drugs and Crime, in 2006, Haji Bagcho conducted heroin transactions worth more than $250 million, approximately 20 percent of the world's total production for that year.

In Nangarhar, Bagcho was not only the biggest drug warlord; he was sending millions of dollars to Japan, importing vehicles. In fact, ironically, as I later found out, the very Toyota Corollas I had purchased turned out to be ones that Bagcho's organization had imported from Japan.

Once we garnered all the evidence against Bagcho, we had to take it to the US prosecutors. We first took the case to the Southern District of New York. They weren't interested; for a variety of political reasons, they balked.

So we went to the Narcotics and Dangerous Drugs Section (NDDS) within the Department of Justice.

NDDS gladly took the case and indicted Haji Bagcho Sherzai. He was "rendered"—but only after the president of Afghanistan had, reluctantly, given us authorization. Despite what you hear in the press, rendering a wanted criminal to the United States is not *extralegal*—it's not in violation of international law: It's just an atypical way of doing an extradition. There was no extradition treaty between the United States and Afghanistan, so we had no other option but to render Bagcho.

Most of the times when we render an Afghan opium kingpin, we get him across the border into Pakistan, load him onto a military helicopter, then onto a long-range transport aircraft, which flies nonstop to Dulles Airport. As soon as he lands in the United States, he is formally charged and locked up in the US federal system.

After a high-profile trial in Washington, DC, Bagcho Sherzai became only the second person to be convicted under the Title 21, 960a, narco-terrorism statute.

He received a sentence of life in prison.*

■ ■ ■

Only hours after we had successfully rendered Bagcho, we received an even more alarming piece of intel, again through one of our highly reliable Pashtun-speaking informants in Jalalabad.

Yet another Taliban-linked opium warlord was planning an attack on our troops. Though he wasn't as big as Bagcho in terms of annual opium and heroin sales, this warlord proved a greater risk to our armed forces in the region.

Haji Khan Mohammad was a diminutive, black-bearded Taliban—who looked, frankly, like a pint-sized version of Bin Laden. At first glance, we thought Mohammad was simply another opium trafficker. We targeted him, and I decided to send down one of our most capable Pashtun-speaking informants.

I briefed the informant in my office.

"Make sure you get inside his underwear," I said.

He stared at me, uncomprehending.

Within the embassy walls, I was known for that phrase, but it meant nothing to Pashtun-speakers.

"I just mean, get right *next* to him," I said.

---

* I was the sole subject-matter expert witness on the stand in the three-week-long trial of Haji Bagcho Sherzai. He was convicted by a jury on March 13, 2012, of one count of conspiracy to distribute one kilogram or more of heroin, knowing and intending that it would be unlawfully imported into the United States; one count of distribution of one kilogram or more of heroin, knowing and intending that it would be unlawfully imported into the United States; and one count of narco-terrorism.

We sent our informant in, wearing the hawk, for a face-to-face meeting with Mohammad—we often also referred to him as HKM. He bought a few kilos of dope from Mohammad. From that initial meeting, the informant spent weeks gradually gaining HKM's trust and actually befriended him. Of all the major traffickers in the region, HKM was the most extreme Taliban supporter and financier. Through the informant, we learned about a Taliban rally scheduled to take place just outside Jalalabad in Nangarhar Province.

It was a nighttime rally, visibility would be low, so we could now assume the calculated risk of sending in actual DEA agents—white American faces thoroughly obscured by Afghan head wraps and scarves—to observe the Taliban rally undercover.

Now we weren't dealing strictly with opium and heroin merchants but with actual frothing fundamentalists, and those rallies—all recorded on our hawk devices—were an invaluable intel source. At these rallies, Taliban fanatics would go into a state of reverie: They had no governors on their mouths. All their screaming, their hatred, their threats against Americans came out unfiltered. They named names, shouted accolades and praises about all the local Taliban cohorts and traffickers in Nangarhar Province who supported them.

All our people inside the rally were wired up with hawks, and besides Mohammad, we identified additional traffickers operating in Nangarhar. It was rather like the FBI back home, when Mafia families have a wedding or christening; all the feds will aggregate on surveillance, using long-range lenses to take pictures of the attendees and the cars' license plates.

From this rally, we learned that Mohammad was not only

selling heroin; he also was stockpiling a cache of weapons, including Russian rockets.

And it was more than just foaming at the mouth. HKM directly told two of our informants, all recorded on our hawks, that he was going to use those weapons against our military forces in Jalalabad at our forward operating base.

When the intel came to me, I went straight back to Ambassador Neumann's office.

"This is even more pressing than heroin," I told the ambassador. "They're about to drop rockets on our boys."

"How imminent is the threat?" he asked.

"I think they're going to attack Jalalabad within a matter of days."

Ambassador Neumann questioned me on our sources of intel. I told him how we'd made the initial purchase of dope from HKM, which in turn had led to us infiltrating the Taliban rally.

"What are you going to do, Ed?"

"We're going to arrest him."

That was one of the ambassador's main diplomatic agendas. He always stressed the need to teach Afghans good governance, to lead by example: show them that we abided by the rule of law—not just in principle but also in practice. Ambassador Neumann was an unyielding proponent of that. He didn't like the so-called "kinetic" list—by which the Department of Defense often targeted these opium warlords, without arrests or trials, simply using stealth drone strikes.

He truly believed, as an idealist, that we were there to rebuild the country. We were not there to have our FAST teams out on paramilitary raids; we were there to inspire the local Afghan police into developing a functioning state. Jeffersonian democracy may not have been feasible, given the complexities of the tribal and regional history, but the ambassador believed that we were there to serve as a model, to inspire an Afghan variation of our Western democratic rule of law.

■ ■ ■

We knew now that Mohammad was unequivocally a Taliban financier, but he was also known to be extremely elusive. We targeted him and other Nangarhar-based traffickers we'd learned about during the rally. They all lived near Jalalabad, but more in the outlying province south of the city, near Tora Bora—the remote cave complex where we nearly caught Bin Laden in 2001.

This was more than a typical Drug Enforcement Administration operation. We had to run it the way the spooks would—as a black op. We used optical surveillance to follow Mohammad's people. Sure enough, the information from the rally wasn't idle talk: He had stockpiled a cache of Russian rockets, mostly Type 63 or Type 81 Russian-made 107mm.

I made one of those executive decisions that never get documented in the official reports. "We're not making any arrests at this point," I said. "We'll just go *take* the missiles."

And that's what we did. Jeff Higgins led the FAST team out there, and in the middle of the night, in some remote desert patch, they started digging with spades. They found Stingers, MANPADS, and those Soviet-era surface-to-air rockets.

We loaded them up in our vehicles and disappeared into the Afghan night.

It was, again, a classic strategy for creating internal dissension. I was applying the street-policing technique that Steve

Whipple had taught me of "tickling the wire" back in El Paso and Ciudad Juárez. Soon enough, the theft of the rockets caused major dissension within Mohammad's group.

We were up on all their cell phones, of course, and we quickly heard all the chatter: They thought that someone was betraying them from inside; that one of them had turned informant or, worse, was selling the rockets for his own personal profit.

It crushed all internal cohesiveness and trust. One by one, they began to turn on one another. And through that dissension, flipping informants, we lured Mohammad out.

We didn't even charge him with the potential attacks on our forward operating base; we simply made the drug-trafficking case stick. Got him across the border into Pakistan, rendered him on charges of violating the 960a statute, and like Bagcho he was immediately on a Dulles-bound C-130 military jet.

Also like Bagcho, the Taliban opium lord ultimately got life in a US federal prison. My strategy of taking the street-policing techniques I'd first learned under Rogelio Guevara and José Martinez, then furthered working with Mike Bansmer in Thailand and Steve Whipple in El Paso, was paying impressive and immediate dividends.

■ ■ ■

The opium bazaar takedown of Bagcho Sherzai and the seizure of Mohammad's cache of rockets were major successes, to be sure, but of the three Afghan opium lords—the three Hajis—I worked with during my time as country attaché in Kabul, I little realized that it would be with the most enigmatic of the trio that I would become most intimate; that indeed we would start to think of—and even to refer to—each other as brothers.

CHAPTER 8

I I I

SHIRAZ

He was a lumbering mountain of a man, standing six-foot-five, weighing more than 370 pounds—a billionaire narco-trafficker with the build of an NFL lineman. None of our intel photos had done HJK justice: When I first met him, he was so massive, he could scarcely fit through the doorway of my apartment at the US Embassy.

His full tribal name was Haji Juma Khan Mohammadhasni—that's how he was listed in our DEA files—but I never heard anyone call him that. Among Afghans in the street, he'd be spoken of, reverentially, in half-whispers, by other aliases: Haji Abdullah and Haji Juma Khan Baluch.

To me he was simply HJK.

The name itself is a string of lofty titles: "Juma Khan" translates as "Mr. Friday." And "Haji," again, is the honorific bestowed on a man who's made pilgrimages to Mecca—Islam's holiest site. Being a Haji afforded HJK enormous respect in the Afghan streets, but also—as I would later see when I lured him into coming to

Jakarta in 2006—from millions of Muslims, even members of law enforcement, around the world.

Like many major traffickers, Haji Juma Khan was no fundamentalist. He was first and foremost a savvy businessman, a man who knew how to save his own skin—along with his billions of dollars—navigating the murderous years of Soviet invasion, civil war, the rise of the Taliban, and the 2001 invasion by our Coalition forces.

He was an ethnic Baluch—one of the country's smaller minority tribes—so his power was centered in the Baluchistan region, but his organization spread over swaths of eastern Iran, western Pakistan, and southern Afghanistan. He'd seized control of the desert province of Nimruz in late 2001 and turned it into his personal fiefdom. The Nimruz region is dotted with labs producing opium paste and morphine base: simple shacks where turbaned men use chemicals and vats of boiling water to refine bars of sticky brown opium into bags of powdery white or brown heroin.

Haji Juma Khan's personal wealth was staggering, his profits calculated in the billions. The DEA believed that several hundred million of his narco-dollars went straight to the Taliban and Al Qaeda, as well as to other jihadist and Baluch insurgent groups.

HJK was known to be a close confidant of Usama Bin Laden and Mullah Omar. He'd been a founding member of the Quetta Shura—the elite council composed of top leadership of the Afghan Taliban, known to be directing the military insurgency against our US and Coalition forces.

But Haji Juma Khan also had friends and relatives within

the highest ranks of government. Within the Karzai administration, his cousin was minister of tourism and tribal affairs. I personally saw HJK coming to stay in the minister's residence whenever he visited Kabul. Indeed, the British intelligence agents at MI6 reported that HJK had allegedly used Ahmed Wali Karzai—the president's own half-brother, who has since been assassinated—as "a conduit to bribe both governors to allow narcotics to be processed and transported through their provinces without impediment."

■ ■ ■

One warm Thursday night in Kabul, I found HJK holding court at his favorite Persian restaurant, Shiraz, where he sat in his usual corner table, back to the wall, eyes on the door. The restaurant staff treated him like royalty. Shiraz was no dive; it was the equivalent of a five-star restaurant, though a fine meal there would only cost us a few US dollars.

The restaurant was dim, mostly candlelit, with a few shaded bulbs, the carpets a deep shade of maroon. All around us, the walls were decorated with wooden-framed pictures of young Persian women draped in their classical dress; the intent was lurid, but the only flesh you could see was the two inches around their eyes. But such eyes! Almond-shaped, jet-black, piercing, all-knowing eyes. A hundred of the most gorgeous, heavily lashed Persian eyes watching you from every wall and corner of the restaurant. It was the closest you'd ever see to a sexually explicit image in Afghanistan.

As usual, HJK was dressed simply in a *shalwar kameez*, all white, with inexpensive leather sandals. He sat upright, confidently, huge black beard flecked with gray, a simple flip cell phone clutched in one massive hand and in the other a *misbaha*—the string of Muslim prayer beads, ninety-nine smooth round gemstones for reciting the ninety-nine names of Allah. Nothing to distinguish him from any other Afghan businessman. It made you wonder: Could the stories of his immense wealth be true? Was this massive man really one of the oligarchs of Southwest Asia and the Middle East?

We gave each other a hug in greeting; he held my shoulders firmly for a long time after the embrace. He liked when I referred to him as "the Great" Haji Juma Khan—one thing he was certainly not lacking was vanity. For his part, he preferred to call me "Mister Ed"—he felt it lent a formality to our relationship.

He was a man of enormous appetites. Over the months ahead, I ate with him many times, and always marveled at his capacity. He would never glance at a menu. The waitstaff all knew the Great Haji Juma Khan, and they would keep bringing an endless stream of his favorite dishes.

I've never been a big eater; in the course of a long night I'd pick at a couple of chicken kebobs. HJK would always order twenty to twenty-four chicken and lamb kebobs, devouring them without so much as a hiccup. The waiters were constantly rushing back and forth to our table: plate after plate of chicken and lamb kebobs with tomatoes, onions, potatoes, and cauliflower—that's the staple vegetable of their diet. The average Afghan must eat his own body weight in cauliflower every week. I'm told they've been eating the same meals, virtually unchanged, since Genghis Khan's armies overran the country.

Haji Juma Khan and I are almost exactly the same age. He grew up in rural poverty, a child of the Soviet occupation. When I was finishing up college, enlisting in the Marine Corps, he was a kid in the trenches: The USSR military machine was laying waste to his land.

Back home, I'd been through months of expert training, read more than a hundred books on the region, but here was how I *truly* learned about Afghanistan, through HJK's eyes—the eyes of a boy and teenager in Baluchistan, near the Iranian frontier, during the years of great bloodshed and upheaval. As we sat in that back table of the Persian restaurant, HJK gave me a full-time course in Afghan history and austerity.

There was *one* thing I needed to understand about his country, he stressed as the steaming plates of kebobs and vegetables arrived. The various tribes and peoples—Pashtun, Tajik, Hazara, Aimak, Turkmen, Baluch—had been forged by the winds of history into an extraordinarily *intuitive* nation. These were the people who had survived conquest by four great empires. They fought fiercely and fearlessly—but also knew how to fall back, to blend in with the conquerors whenever they needed to.

Haji Juma Khan told me—echoing Faulkner's famous remarks about the American South—these ancient conquests are not history. They're not even the *past*.

"We survived Alexander—and we then survived Attila," he said.

Genghis Khan, too, and his hordes of horsemen—the Mongols found the terrain impossible to control. And then, the greatest empire of all, he told me: the British, with their disciplined ranks of redcoats. Even with nineteenth-century technological advancements, Afghanistan was too inhospitable; like the Mongols, the Brits realized they could *occupy* Afghanistan but they could never govern it. When the Afghan tribes finally rose up in rebellion, it was carnage. Some 16,500 British were killed—butchered—when they were already in full retreat from Kabul during the Battle of Gandamak, in 1842.

It struck me as telling, and strange: Here we were, living in an age of GPS and ever-present cell phones (Afghanistan has the best cell coverage anywhere on earth, much better than Los Angeles or New York; our spooks, for their own intel-gathering purposes, have made damn sure of that), and a man like HJK would drop a reference to that centuries-old massacre.

Gandamak.

Said proudly—defiantly—proof of the indomitable national character.

"That's something you Americans don't understand. *Time.* Yes, time passes differently in Afghanistan. As a boy, I heard this all the time in the years of the mujahideen: 'Young one, be patient. We can always *wait.*'"

He told me about those adolescent years during the Soviet occupation, watching the survival skills of the older Afghan tribesmen, graybeards who knew every hidden underground aquifer, every piece of arable land, every possible escape route into the high hinterlands and ice-bound mountain passes.

■ ■ ■

Today, traveling the vast stretches of that country, you see millions of Afghans living like they did at the time of Alexander: no electricity, no flowing water. More than 90 percent of Afghans still do not have access to electricity. Those living in Kabul have access to electricity only four hours per day, every other day. My first days in-country, I visited major Afghan government officials in their homes: With just one simple electric heater for personal warmth, they'd drape their windows with homemade rugs to hold in the heat; at night they'd cover themselves with rugs and blankets.

Driving out of the embassy compound, you saw that 90 percent everywhere: average Afghans living as they have for centuries. My friend General Daud was right: *We have nothing they want.*

Especially in the winter, without electricity, without natural gas, everything is cooked on open wood fires. They often defecate outside their hovels, and the human waste vaporizes. Westerners are perpetually sick in Kabul. Just breathing the air will do you in. Everybody in the embassy was stricken with dysentery.

During the winter months, most people just hunker down, some living in caves, subsisting on sparse rations of mutton and chicken but mostly cauliflower and rice: the same rudimentary meal every single goddamn day.

In my mind, they were mirror images of each other: No two men were more emblematic of the Afghan instinct for survival than my friends General Mohammad Daud Daud and Haji Juma Khan. This hulking tribal drug lord had survived for thirty years, transshipped metric tons of opium and heroin around the globe, by blending in, cooperating, co-opting, constantly maneuvering—an uncanny ability to shape-shift.*

But more than just adapting, he found ways to manipulate whoever took the reins of power. He played the Soviet conquerors to his advantage; he'd used the tribal warlords; he'd used

---

* Indeed, in 2001, after the Coalition invasion of Afghanistan, Haji Juma Khan had been briefly detained by US authorities, but—for reasons that remain somewhat mysterious even today—he was almost immediately released.

the Taliban; he'd used the Coalition, used his high-ranking contacts in the Karzai government. Now—of course, no one was being naïve—he was trying to use me every bit as much as I was using him.

HJK was tearing into another one of the chicken kebobs, proudly telling me about his fourteen wives and the twenty-nine children he had scattered around the region. He had sixteen sons by the various wives and mistresses. The lists of names washed over me; reminded me of sitting in the pews of St. Gabriel's, in St. Louis, as a kid and hearing those Jesuits rattle off the progeny of the patriarchs in the Old Testament.

I could never wrap my head around one thing: For some reason, HJK loved his nephew Abu Aziz more than he loved his own kids. He said it often and openly: He cherished this one nephew more than any of his sons. He shook his head and called his eldest son a word in Dari that roughly translates as "miscreant."

He cherished his nephew Abu Aziz so much that it was clear that he was grooming the young man—not any of his sons—to step in as successor to his sprawling "business" empire.

* * *

Strange as it sounds, the hours I spent undercover with HJK were becoming a source of solace: an escape from the stress of embassy politics, the constant infighting and war of wills with our CIA agents and the British SAS and SBS (Special Air Service and Special Boat Service) officers.

On a daily basis, I was never sure who I was going to have more friction with: the spooks or the Brits. Reading the newspapers back home, you'd hear about the united front of the Coalition—

sure, we may have done joint operations together, but as in the days of Patton and Montgomery, more often than not we hated each other's guts.

Still, what our own spooks had done that very week with this kid Goldie went beyond the standard internecine bullshit. It was, in my eyes, criminal negligence.

It had cost me one of my best men. Any cop will tell you that he's only as good as his informants. "The worst men often give the best advice," as Sir Francis Bacon famously wrote.

Informants have put their lives in your hands. You've got to woo them, nurture them, care for them, and provide them with a sense of security and protection. In Kabul it was next to impossible to protect my informants. Unlike the rest of us—DEA, CIA and FBI, State Department staffers—they weren't living in the secure fortified embassy.

Obviously, Afghanistan doesn't have anything like our domestic witness protection program. Every time one of these young Afghans cooperated with us, they weren't only risking their lives; they were jeopardizing the safety of their entire families. The Taliban and Al Qaeda often practiced "collective" vengeance for those they considered traitors and infidels.

Once word got out that an informant had helped us, there was no safe haven: I had to immediately get him out of the country. Even today, I've got at least a dozen guys who worked our cases who can *never* return to Afghanistan. Not even for their parents' funerals.

You can't imagine how many fast-track immigration visas I had to get through just to save my informants' lives because their names had been leaked to jihadists in the Taliban or Al Qaeda operatives. I had to race through some form of visa—usually student—and get them out of Afghanistan before they got whacked.

In fact, though I was doing my damnedest to keep a poker face throughout dinner, I'd taken a body blow: I'd just lost my first informant in my entire career. This twenty-seven-year-old, Goldie, who'd been working with the US government since we first came in to liberate Afghanistan from the Taliban in 2001. Sure, he was an opportunist. All informants are mercenaries: some motivated by revenge, some by money, and some by idealistic or nationalistic concerns.

Goldie's motives were financial, but he was an educated kid, and ultimately he wanted to come to the United States, attend college—I was already processing the paperwork to get him a student visa to come to the United States. For some reason he had his heart set on going to a university in Wyoming, though I think he just liked the way those syllables sounded on his tongue . . . or maybe he'd seen a few too many cowboy movies . . .

I'd sent Goldie undercover pursuing several Taliban associates trafficking in heroin. He was out on a meet; then we lost contact. He went missing for three days. We were looking everywhere for him. Even the FBI said they'd help—but we all knew the Feebs couldn't find their asses in the dark with two hands.

As for the spooks, they were no help. It turned out to have been their egregious fuckup. We had to share information about our DEA informants with them because oftentimes informants would work both sides of the fence. I doubt it was a malicious act—probably just incompetence, sloppiness—but within a matter of days Goldie was gone.

The CIA told their counterparts in the NDS that Goldie was

working undercover for us—the NDS was a notorious intelligence sieve.

When we finally found Goldie, our worst fears were confirmed: He'd been butchered like a lamb, dumped in front of a mosque, strangled to death with wire. They'd pulled the wire so tight that his throat was sliced open ear to ear.

The executioners believe that there's Koranic justification—they're going to be rewarded in heaven for taking care of a "traitor" to Islam. They don't see themselves as cold-blooded murderers but as Allah's avenging warriors.

As soon as my cell rang, I jumped in my Land Cruiser and raced over to the mosque. Goldie was lying in the back of a pickup truck, face drained white. I cradled the boy's body in my arms. His blood soaked through my shirtfront. What gave me such enormous guilt was that I was just a few days short of securing the visa and passport to get Goldie out of the country. In the last conversation we had, I told him he'd better prepare for the bitter winters in Wyoming . . .

Then I'd had to notify the family. Goldie's mother was wailing like a banshee. Inconsolable. I stepped out of legal boundaries, reached into my DEA operations account, and gave the family $10,000 in cash. Completely against department rules, but I thought, *Fuck it, this kid gave up his* life *to help us.* The average household income in Afghanistan was between $300 and $500 in US dollars, so my little extralegal death annuity of $10K would, hopefully, set Goldie's family up for twenty years.

From that week on—for the rest of my DEA career—I kept a picture of Goldie slipped in with my own DEA identification creds, always in the lanyard around my neck. Not a day would pass when I didn't look at him. I wanted to stare back at Goldie's eyes every single day and remind myself of how we'd lost him, and what the stakes of my work as a counter-narcotics leader were really all about.

"Look at yourself," HJK said, breaking the long silence. "Your plate is cold. What's the matter? You have the weight of the world."

"Yeah," I said, letting out a sigh between clenched teeth. "Honestly, I've been getting my ass kicked all week. I could use a . . ."

All alcohol consumption is *haraam*—strictly forbidden in Islam. Talking to believers, you'll get different justifications for the prohibition, but most give you a famous sura of the Prophet:

O, you who believe! Intoxicants and gambling, sacrific-
ing to stones,
    And divination by arrows, are an abomination of
Satan's handiwork.
    Eschew such abomination, that you may prosper!

But let me tell you how it *really* is: In Shiraz—and virtually every other restaurant and kebob joint we frequented—the staff always keeps a bottle of Johnnie Walker Black hidden in a cupboard in the back.

I can't count how many times I watched these guys—Afghan politicians, cops, military officers, even the highest-ranking government officials—getting blind drunk on Johnnie Black and then staggering to mosque the first thing the next morning to bow down on their pristine prayer rugs before Allah . . . I've been to many parties in Afghanistan where the cops and the NDS guys were eating pork—tantamount to blasphemy. And I still have no idea how they got it into the country. I never saw a *pig* in all my years living there.

But I did want a stiff shot of spirits right then.

HJK nodded at me, offered a wry smile. "Listen, Ed, you're not a Muslim. I will allow you to have a glass of wine."

He gestured to one of the waiters with a flick of his massive right hand. Instantly, I had a simple drinking glass of red wine placed in front of me.

We touched our glasses, his filled with water, mine red wine.

"Our Lord's first miracle was turning water into wine," I said, softly, more for my benefit than his.

He didn't know the exact details of the Gospels, but he smiled.

"Yes, Jesus is a disciple in Islam."

"A disciple?"

"A great prophet, a righteous messenger of Allah. We, too, believe Isa will return one day—as a man, to serve Allah's will . . ."

■ ■ ■

Perhaps it was Allah's will. Who can say? But it was the cancer that cemented our friendship. Cancer—his and mine—formed the final, immutable bond of trust. On that hot July morning, we literally stripped ourselves naked to the waist in my sweltering office in the embassy compound . . .

For all his well-honed survival skills, his ruthlessness in attacking external threats to his power, Haji Juma Khan couldn't beat one enemy through sheer cunning: the virulent, rapid cell mutation attacking his hulking body from within.

On that morning there was an unmistakable note of hesitancy, almost a tremble, when he spoke. HJK was one of the most confident, controlling, dominant men I've ever met. Now something had changed. Why was he calling my cell sounding positively frightened?

"Mister Ed," he said, "I have to see you."

"What's wrong?"

"I need to see you to explain," he said.

HJK came to my office in the embassy compound—accompanied by his beloved nephew, Abu Aziz—and, from the moment he sat down, started telling me about his recent health concerns. He wasn't feeling his normal bull-like strength. He was worried about the strange red splotches that had developed slowly, mysteriously, over the course of months. He'd been to see some local tribal doctor in Baluchistan, but he didn't have the medical knowledge, let alone the technology, to tell HJK whether or not it was cancer.

I watched as he methodically unbuttoned the top of his *shalwar kameez*. I immediately saw the four large growths on his chest. Huge external skin tumors. They were bad. In fact, it was amazing to me that he had let the situation go on as long as he had. These were five-inch tumors: raised and asymmetrical, a deep shade of scarlet.

Sitting next to him, I held his gaze.

I told him this was nothing to take lightly.

"How do you know?" he said.

I pulled up my own button-down shirt, made a half-turn, and showed him my torso. In the center of my back, just above the lumbar region, I have an enormous raised white-and-pink scar that forms a near-perfect cross.

"What happened to you?" Haji Juma Khan seemed genuinely concerned.

"Malignant melanoma," I said.

Now I told him the story: how I'd been snorkeling off Kona in Hawaii, back in the summer of '94, diving down deeper and deeper into the clear azure water . . . and when I surfaced, pulled myself out onto the boat, my old boss Don Carstensen noticed something strange on my wet back.

Don was still the head of the Organized Crime Strike Force for the Honolulu prosecutor's office, and we'd kept in touch for years, since I was a young USMC military policeman. Don told me he'd recently watched a TV documentary detailing the ABC's of skin cancer. Squarely in the center of my back, he said, was a growth that was asymmetrical, colored in weird hues of blue, red, and orange.

"Eddie," Don said, "this is no joke. We need to get you in to see a specialist."

Next day, we flew back to Oahu—but I was in denial or being unbelievably stubborn, because there was *no way* I was going to see a doctor. I didn't want to believe I had skin cancer.

Thankfully, Don Carstensen is such a powerful guy, physically and emotionally, that through brute force he dragged me to an Oahu dermatologist. The dermatologist said: "No time to wait—we're doing a biopsy."

The next morning, he said grimly: "I'm sorry to tell you, Mr. Follis. You have malignant melanoma."

After a second biopsy, the surgeons cut the tumor out: a four-inch-diameter incision that went almost all the way down to the spine. We'd caught the malignancy early, but we had to make sure it hadn't spread. The surgeons felt they had clean margins. That's why they cut out four full inches of rectangular-shaped tissue. But only time would tell: If you can make it four years cancer free, they said, it means you're a survivor.

"That's the only reason I'm sitting here and talking to you today," I told HJK. "The only reason I'm not lying someplace in a cemetery. We acted fast—decisively and aggressively."

But being a complete madman, with this stuff still oozing out of my back—a catheter draining the red and pink fluid—I checked myself out of the recovery room and was on a flight back to Thailand, where I'd been working deep cover with Mike Bansmer, constantly trying to advance the Shan United Army case.

I didn't dare tell HJK about the complications that resulted from medical error. Wrapping up the procedure, the surgeon had left a suture inside when he sealed me back up. Over time, I developed a ridge-like hump on my back that people used to teasingly call my dorsal fin. I thought it was scar tissue—turned out to be an accumulation of white blood cells and body fat forming a benign growth called a lipoma, shaped into this long, hard, raised ridge. You could see it through my summer shirts and my sports coats. My DEA buddies would constantly bust my balls about it. "Yo, Eddie, what's the *deal* with your dorsal fin?"

▌ ▌ ▌

In my sweltering office at the US Embassy in Kabul, I didn't tell HJK about the complications or my dorsal fin, didn't tell him anything other than how my buddy Don Carstensen had been so vigilant, so persistent, that he'd saved my life.

Now I wanted to do the same for him.

The opium king sat there, watching me speak, all the while tracing one finger along his jawline, through the thick black bristles of his holy man's beard.

"Listen," I said, "I don't know if your tumors are malignant—could be a benign growth—but this shit is nothing to mess with. You need to take care of business here. You don't want it spreading to your organs or your lymph nodes."

We were speaking half in English, but mostly our words were being translated by Tariq, my primary Afghan investigative assistant. For the first time, as Tariq relayed my meaning about the cancer possibly metastasizing, HJK seemed genuinely upset. He didn't understand it on a cellular level, but the very thought of some mysterious disease spreading, multiplying, taking over his vital organs, clearly terrified him.

"Mister Ed," he said, softly, "what do I do now?"

The scheme hit me, in a flash.

"Look," I said. "You can't deal with this shit here. Afghanistan doesn't have the proper facilities . . . What if I arranged for you to come to DC with me?"

"Come to United States?" He looked incredulous.

"Yeah, come with me to Washington. We can have some competent doctors examine you. I don't think you're going to find anyone here in Kabul who knows what he's doing. And you damn sure can't rely on some kind of goddamn tribal medicine."

He glanced at his bodyguard, eyeing me warily.

"While you're there in DC," I said, "we can talk to you about a few things . . ."

HJK nodded. He understood the unspoken: that we would debrief him about whatever he knew about Islamic terrorist activity and its symbiotic relationship with the opium and heroin trade.

Up to that point in our relationship, I would casually, tangentially broach the subject of Al Qaeda and Taliban terror activities—but *never* heroin.

It was highly ironic, of course. HJK was integral to the global drug trade—a man whose personal armies were responsible for a large percentage of Asia's opium and heroin production—but his *own* involvement was always unspoken.

Again the subtle dance, this implicit understanding between us. He was playing me for what he could get, in terms of American protection and influence, and I was playing him for whatever actionable intel I might glean down the road . . .

Seeing his fear about his skin cancer, I saw that I had the opportunity to engage him on a deeper, more profound level.

That's the thing most people don't get about undercover work. It's not enough to be able to improvise on the fly. You also need to use what's real. You can't *fake* a cancer scare. No one is that good a fucking actor.

We had been sitting there and staring at each other a long time, both seeing that ineffable glimpse of death burning like the black pinpoints in our irises.

"Then we're agreed? I'll fly you to DC, get you in to see a decent dermatologist," I said. "If necessary, we'll get some other specialists to examine you."

He held my gaze, unflinching. But he wouldn't articulate the questions evidently burning behind those jet-black eyes: How could he be sure that this wasn't some trap? How could he really trust me if he put his safety in my hands and flew to America?

I tried to contain my excitement, not betray any emotion.

But I knew that, in that simple nod, I had the Great Haji Juma Khan in my hands.

■ ■ ■

The months of having gone into the field with him, traveling on my own, without security, now began to pay dividends. Indeed, HJK said that he trusted me enough to vouchsafe his security. I arranged to get him a false passport and visa—so he could travel under an assumed name—and put him and one of my interpreters on the same flight.

It wouldn't be an American military transport; he'd never agree to that. I told him he could fly covertly, undercover, as if on his own personal business. I would purchase a first-class ticket for him on a commercial Emirates flight from Kabul to Dubai.

■ ■ ■

When he arrived from Heathrow at Dulles Airport, we met him at the arrivals gate like he was a traveling head of state. We had a Lincoln limousine, with diplomatic plates, and put him up in a comfortable—if relatively discreet—hotel in Chantilly, Virginia. First, the spooks wanted to debrief him; they had their own long-standing, if highly controversial, relationship with HJK dating back to 2001.

In fact, it was the CIA that provided the doctor to come do an assessment of HJK's skin cancer, right there in his hotel room. The doctor was ex-military, apparently a well-regarded Washington dermatologist. The doctor had a look at the tumors, made a preliminary diagnosis of squamous cell carcinoma—treatable, to be sure, and not the aggressive malignant melanoma I'd been diagnosed with.*

The dermatologist set up an appointment for three days later and recommended a course of treatment for HJK. We did debriefings with him in the hotel, and we took him out for a good time on the town every night.

I brought in various people to speak to him, all representing themselves as major Department of Defense figures—full-bird colonels and one-star generals. They were actually all DEA special agents working undercover for me. They didn't come in uniformed, of course, but wearing business suits and ties. No one outside of the Pentagon would ever have guessed these guys weren't high-ranking DoD brass.

We were constantly stroking his ego. HJK's narcissism was boundless. Since I always referred to him as "the Great Haji Juma Khan," as if that were an official title, now our undercover DEA agents followed suit. These were supposedly Pentagon brass, kissing the ass of a tribal drug lord from the badlands of Nimruz.

On our second afternoon, I finally broached the subject of the drug trade. There was a long and uncomfortable pause. HJK denied even remotely being involved in drugs. He was cagey enough not to make any personal admissions. Of course, he knew *everything* there was to know about *other* people's operations. He talked freely about Bagcho and Noorzai and Mohammad. He could quote us chapter and verse on all his rivals and competitors, every other major trafficker underpinning the Taliban, but would never admit to his own massive operations in Baluchistan.

---

* In 1998, after four years without any regrowth, my doctors in St. Louis told me my cancer was in full remission.

As the conversation unfolded, HJK leaned back on the off-white sofa and sipped his cup of jasmine tea. He'd already polished off three plates of the halal chicken kebobs we'd provided from a Middle Eastern takeout joint called Sahara.

His was a cunning shadow dance. HJK moved like the most skilled boxer, sticking and moving, never getting pinned in the corner. Sure, he'd cooperate—be very forthcoming—about *other* major narco-terrorists, Taliban leaders, and command-and-control figures in Al Qaeda, both in Afghanistan and Pakistan.

Now, like some ancient caliph, he laid out the three overland smuggling routes: There was the venerable Silk Route to Iran and up through Turkey, then onward to cities of Western Europe; the northern route up through Uzbekistan and Tajikistan into the heart of Russia (which now has an astronomical rate of heroin addiction); and the route straight down through Nimruz Province to the great Pakistani port of Karachi, where the opium base and heroin can be smuggled onto container ships to travel anywhere on the globe, primarily up through the Suez Canal and into the Mediterranean.

I already knew—from our satellite surveillance and from the weeks I'd spent traveling undercover through Afghanistan—that HJK had his tentacles reaching down all three heroin-smuggling routes, but the bulk of his drugs were smuggled through his Iranian crime associates and down into Karachi. Once again, though, he would admit absolutely nothing about his own involvement in the opium and heroin trade.

CHAPTER 9

THE PASSION

When I arrived back in Afghanistan with HJK, working the Kabul streets again undercover, things began to heat up. The undercover case with HJK now went into its second phase, yielding surprising and unprecedented results. This is one of the least-understood aspects of undercover work.

Sun Tzu delineates it explicitly in *The Art of War*:

> Spies cannot be usefully employed without a certain intuitive sagacity. They cannot be properly managed without benevolence and straightforwardness. Without subtle ingenuity of mind, one cannot make certain of the truth of their reports. Be subtle! be subtle! and use your spies for every kind of business . . .

In the weeks and months ahead, I did manage HJK with "benevolence and straightforwardness." I'm not sure I was always so *subtle*. But HJK would prove to be one of the United States' most valuable counterterrorism assets. Indeed, it wasn't until we sent him back from DC to work with me undercover in his native country that we would see how valuable indeed.

■ ■ ■

Ramadan was quickly approaching, and the entire US Embassy was on edge. The holiest month in the Muslim calendar was set to begin in the evening of Saturday, September 23. There was an overwhelming dread that this particular Ramadan could turn into a contemporary version of the Tet Offensive, the massive uprising and counteroffensive begun on the Vietnamese New Year's celebration in 1968.

I'd been battling various bugs and infections, on and off, ever since I got to Afghanistan. As soon as I arrived back in Kabul, I had walking pneumonia for ten days. That's nothing to play around with, and I reluctantly went to see our embassy doctor. His name was Dr. Jordan—technically a physician's assistant—a sixty-five-year-old former Army field medic who lost half a finger in Vietnam. He laid me up for a day or so, gave me antibiotics on an IV drip.

And it was in the clinic, in the days leading up to Ramadan, as I was drifting in and out of fever, that Dr. Jordan gave me the truth. He told me that many of our spooks and the FBI guys were coming in suffering from anxiety disorders. Every single morning they woke up fixating on those same five words that had haunted me back in LA.

You want to die today?

Virtually everyone else in the embassy compound—CIA, DEA, FBI, and State Department staff—was under unbearable stress and many were taking medication to handle it.

I long ago got out of the judgment business. "Whatever gets

you through the night," like John Lennon said. Guys were doing what they had to to keep functioning. I suppose it was better than self-medicating with booze. But how are you meant to get through the night—or the day, for that matter—when the place you work, your supposed safe haven, has repeatedly been shot up by fanatics with AK-47s? It's all you heard about in the hallways and at dinner: the perils of living with PTSD.

Everyone within the embassy compound was freaking out over getting post-traumatic stress disorder before it was even *post*.

I knew what they'd be dealing with as soon as they returned to the States: Waking in the middle of the night in a cold sweat. Consumed by nightmares. Paranoia. Seeing in every face on the street corner a looming threat, thinking the harmless Middle Eastern checkout kid at the local Costco is a potential suicide bomber . . .

It had already started its creep into my unconscious. From my desk at the embassy, I'd been keeping in touch with my family back home, of course, but couldn't tell them directly about the daily dangers I was facing—though some were too high-profile to keep hidden.

I'd been on the cell phone with my mom live—Kabul to St. Louis—when a three-hundred-pound Semtex bomb nearly took out the entire embassy compound.

It was perhaps the most sophisticated VBIED seen in Kabul since the arrival of the Coalition forces in 2001. The jihadists had packed the front end of a Volvo sedan with ball bearings—they'd devised an elaborate detonation system involving the air bags—and set their sights on the US Embassy as the direct target.

The damage zone resembled a fuming meteor's impact crater: The bomb tore a hole some three hundred yards wide in the street, killing twenty-eight, wounding more than fifty. I was dashing around outside the walls not long after the explosion, as a first responder and then as a street cop reconstructing the crime scene. After a few hours, we found the foot of the suicide bomber some fifty yards away from the blast site.

At the precise moment of the Semtex explosion, I'd been having a routine conversation with my mom back in St. Louis. When the explosion hit, I heard my mother gasp, then a truncated half-scream—and our phones went totally dead. They first evacuated us all into the embassy bunkers, but within ten minutes a crew from Fox News was on the scene; my mom and my stepfather, Ray, were watching the shrieking and mutilation and mayhem live on TV, not sure if I'd been blown to bits in that blast . . .

Some nights, half in delirium, I flashed back to the first time I ever heard the term "PTSD." It was in our local church, St. Gabriel the Archangel, on Nottingham Avenue, St. Louis, where I met one of the most inspirational figures in my life: James Fuller.

Mr. Fuller was a US Army veteran; he'd been hit by a rocket-propelled grenade (RPG) in Vietnam on August 8, 1969. He returned home to St. Louis, returned to our own St. Gabriel's, missing half his left arm and the index finger on his right hand.

I was eight years old when we met in the church pews.

He became my godfather, though in everyday speech I usually called him "Uncle Jim." He was a remarkable man; even with all his disabilities, he made no complaints, still managed to learn how to do air-conditioning and heating repair, stained glass window repair, carpentry, plumbing. He worked as the handyman and jack-of-all-trades at St. Gabriel's.

I lived most of my life from the age of eight through twenty-two at St. Gabriel the Archangel, graduating from altar boy and becoming the church custodian in high school. I probably spent three or four hours each day in those pews.

By the time I was about thirteen, I started to call Uncle Jim the "Unexpected Warrior." He didn't want to be a soldier. He didn't want to go to war, certainly never imagined he'd be thrown into the maelstrom of vicious jungle combat. All he ever wanted to be was a motorcycle cop like his father. Jim's dad, Big Joe Fuller, was a motorcycle police officer in St. Louis, dead from a heart attack at age fifty—long before I was born.

But Jim never fulfilled his dream, though he later told me he still had spectral images of himself tearing down the open highway on a Harley. No, by the time he came of age, the Vietnam War was heating up. Jim was drafted into the Marine Corps; with no real educational or occupational specialty, he simply became a grunt.

Grunts are a different breed; more than anyone else, they bear the brunt of any battle. They're the guys right on the ground. Right at the front. They're literally what the politicians and generals mean when they talk about needing to put "boots on the ground." And no matter how technologically advanced we've become with our satellite surveillance and UAVs (unmanned aerial vehicles), short of an all-out thermonuclear strike, there's always going to be the need to have boots on the ground.

I was his little helper around the church, and he would constantly tell me stories. In 1967, Jim was drafted, went into the Marine Corps; after boot camp, he served briefly in Chicago, worked on the pallbearer patrol as all the corpses came back from Vietnam. He was on the Marine detail of escorting the dead to the burial sites. He told me that had quite a profound impact on him psychologically, seeing all those young men killed in action, going to their final resting places in flag-draped coffins, before he'd even left for his tour of Vietnam.

Then he got his orders, shipped out, and was immediately in the Central Highlands of Vietnam. He did eighty-eight days before he was hit. He vividly described it to me: rising at dawn, humping throughout the day to find an adequate ambush site. The quarry would eventually walk through a gauntlet, and Jim and his fellow grunts would blow them to pieces.

On the night of August 8, 1969, they were set up as usual when a whole company of North Vietnamese regulars over-whelmed them. Jim got hit with the RPG, which blew off his biceps as well as his index finger. Of the twelve guys in his squad, only three survived. Jim, nearly bleeding to death, was medevaced out from Saigon to Guam.

Uncle Jim was a constant source of inspiration during my years in Afghanistan. He overcame all of his physical hardship, although the events of that night never left him: He remained in almost constant pain. Never had full use of his arm or remaining hand again, but still learned how to do just about any task that St. Gabriel's had need for. He could climb sixty feet in the air on a ladder to paint, spackle, sand, and do cement replacement.

Jim had three daughters of his own but no sons, and we would talk for hours as I assisted him with his work, sometimes in the half-shadows of the pews, or the shimmering beams from those towering stained glass windows. To this day, I can remember in great detail every story he told me about Vietnam; how, after hours of being unconscious, he came to in a hospital bed in Guam, confused, pumped full of morphine, missing his bicep and finger, to the sounds of "Jumpin' Jack Flash" from a nearby transistor radio.

Jim was going through his battles with post-traumatic stress disorder, but he never bitched and moaned. Got up at dawn and did his work. He was a typical south St. Louis guy who'd been drafted into the military, came back physically and mentally damaged, but never let that slow him down.

Jim Fuller was constantly teaching me without even realizing it. Every little thing—even routine horseplay—became an opportunity for a life lesson. At Bishop DuBourg High School I played varsity basketball; despite being only five-foot-eight I was our starting point guard. What I lacked in size, I made up for in quickness. Senior year, I even made All-City. And though I wasn't on the wrestling team, Uncle Jim and I used to wrestle constantly.

I came into the church one day after school, had to put in four hours of work as his handyman assistant before a big basketball game that night. He was extremely focused on his work. I was bouncing around, full of energy and testosterone.

"Come on," I said. "Uncle Jim, take a break. Uncle Jim. Let's wrestle."

"Nah."

"Come on!"

Uncle Jim was about five-nine and 210 pounds. Despite the disabilities—or maybe compensating for them—he was strong as a bull. For a few minutes, I watched him assembling wood paneling on one of the stages in the church. I was wound up, getting ready for the basketball game that night, and for some reason, shadowboxing in place, I punched the paneling and knocked it everywhere.

His expression instantly changed. He didn't want to play around. Jim stood up, grabbed me, spun me, and tossed me on the floor. In a flash, he dropped to a knee and had me in a leg lock, pushing down hard on my toes. I was squirming, tapping my free hand on the polished wood floor to say, *I give!*

"You give? My ass! Eddie, you just destroyed *two* days of my work." He pushed down so hard on my foot that I could hear my knee popping out of the socket. He didn't mean to injure me; he was just pissed off and didn't know his own strength.

After the tussle, I was flinching, but the pain wasn't that bad and together we popped the knee back into the socket. That night I played in the big game with my leg taped up so tight that I had to run up and down the court stiff-legged. Lesson learned: Never mess with a guy putting in an honest day's work.

■ ■ ■

As for my own honest day's work, there were times when my friction with our CIA agents and our Brit counterparts got so intense that I used to indulge in a little middle-of-the-night reverie. Half waking, half dreaming, in my single bed at the embassy, I could see myself running away to live the rest of my life with HJK.

Of course, I wasn't going to become a drug trafficker, but every night in Kabul I would feel this intense unconscious desire to take off with Haji Juma Khan, become part of his circle, his self-contained empire in the wilds of Nimruz Province.

Almost everywhere in the world I worked, I had static with the CIA. We're often working the same terrain, but with different legal and moral parameters. Not being a law enforcement agency, they have no requirements of evidentiary discovery. They care solely about intel—not assembling the building blocks of a case, establishing probable cause, ensuring a chain of custody. They exist completely in the shadows. Nobody ever testifies. You really want to scare the shit out of a CIA agent? Put him on the *stand*.

In the late summer of 2007, my beef with Thad "Tex" Saget, one of the CIA's top-ranking agents in all of Southwest Asia, nearly erupted into a brawl.

On nine occasions since I'd been appointed country attaché, the embassy had taken direct hits from enemy rockets. Through our DEA intel—particularly some sixty informants we'd developed within Pakistan—we'd been able to predict seven of the nine attacks. And because of my intimacy with HJK, the singular confidence we shared, the spooks began accusing me of knowing all about the attacks in advance—for some *irrational* reason, supposedly so that I'd have higher standing as an intel source with Ambassador Neumann.

That morning, Tex got into a screaming match with me in the ambassador's office.

"I think Ed may have had *prior* knowledge of these attacks, Ambassador," Saget said.

"That I've had *what*? *Prior* knowledge? What are you saying, Tex? You're saying I've been *consenting*?"

Finally, the ambassador stepped between us, physically separated us, and got Tex to shut his mouth. Good thing, too. Accusing me of conspiring to have my own government—my own *people*—attacked and killed? Man, I was ready to go toe-to-toe with Tex right there in the embassy.

Little wonder then that I'd lie there in my Spartan bedroom almost every night, dreaming of running away with HJK, lost in clouds of desert dust, rolling through those badlands in caravans of SUVs. Sounds strange but—compared to the amorality and treachery of these spooks—I felt more at ease in the world of guys like HJK.

I got so intimate with this guy that, even though I couldn't speak Dari or Baluchi properly and his English was very basic, I felt I could occasionally open up to him.

There was warmth to his manner, openness in his laughter, a sophisticated charm. A skeptic could stay it was *all* charm—a master manipulator at work. But I'd like to believe there was something deeper at play.

Most important to me, on a personal level, was the fact that he was respectful of me as a Christian. I reciprocated by always showing him the utmost respect for his Islamic faith. I know all the tricks and ploys of undercover work; this wasn't a mask, a persona, something either of us was faking. He carried those iridescent stone prayer beads—the Arabic translation is actually "worry beads"—and was always fingering them, silently reciting the names of Allah.

I'd inwardly smile as he did it, too, thinking, *This guy is just a version of me.* I remembered the countless hours I'd spent fingering my own rosary, growing up with the Jesuits in St. Louis.

One thing made HJK unusual, especially among devout Muslims: He was constantly inquisitive. He did not judge. Though he understood next to nothing about Christianity, he was always asking me to explain more about what I believed. Again, going back to one of those principles I'd learned in Honolulu with Don Carstensen, I was finding that area within HJK's personality that was still malleable, with which I could connect using genuine empathy.

It was a cloudy and moonless Saturday night when I came to find him again at Shiraz. At his request, I brought my laptop—there was a copy of *The Passion of the Christ* on the hard drive. We took our place in the usual back table—we'd always stay in these restaurants for three or four hours at one sitting—surrounded by the paintings of those beautiful black Persian eyes . . .

Before leaving for Kabul, I'd done some intensive prepping of my own, studied all the suras in the Koran. I'd gone with the Egyptian edition that is considered by many authorities the most faithful English-language version. I'd read and reread the passage that specifically calls for the destruction and enslavement of non-Muslims—Jews and Christians.

But when I asked him about it, HJK would shrug and smile, never venturing into the darker interpretations of his religion. He'd always talk about the goodness of the Koran—to him it was all about the love of Allah. He never wanted me to ask him about the extreme beliefs of the Taliban, or what I saw as the religion's intolerant or violent side.

We were eating our seemingly endless courses of kebobs, vegetables, and naan. Every few minutes, he felt the need to offer up a reassurance.

"I do believe in Isa—in Jesus," he'd say.

We were at the Garden of Gethsemane scene—the temptation was starting in earnest—and he asked me to stop. I hit the pause button on the laptop.

"I don't understand," he said.

"I've been there," I told him.

"Jerusalem?"

"The Garden of Gethsemane."

"It's still there?"

"Sure. On the Mount of Olives. Right on that very spot—I fell to my knees and prayed."

I didn't tell him that the first time had been while I'd been deep cover, working the Kayed Berro heroin case that had taken me from Paris to Cairo and on to Jerusalem.

"Daud's city," Haji Juma Khan said.

"Daud?" At first I thought he meant my dear friend the general . . . Took me a moment to realize he was talking about the psalmist.

"We revere Daud," he added. "In the Koran, he is both *nabi* and *rasul*: prophet and messenger of Allah. So is his son, King Suleiman."

As he said it, my mind flashed back—back to St. Louis, through wind-whipped clouds of fine snow, back to the brick church on Nottingham Avenue. I was eight years old, sitting in the pews of St. Gabriel's, bathed in the turquoise and amber and red beams from the stained glass windows that my godfather, Jim, had recently repaired.

Mr. Fuller was straightening the hymnals in the next pew. He saw me struggling with the pages of First Samuel, smiled, walked over, and told me that David—long before becoming king—was the first undercover agent.

"Undercover? King David?" I said, incredulous.

"Yes," he said. "First undercover in history. Read that verse again, Eddie."

Sure enough, it was there: David, guileful as Odysseus, adopting a false persona, pretending to be insane, in order to infiltrate the court of the king of Gath.

> And David laid up these words in his heart, and was sore afraid of Achish the king of Gath. And he changed his behavior before them, and feigned himself mad in their hands, and scrabbled on the doors of the gate, and let his spittle fall down upon his beard. Then said Achish unto his servants, Lo, ye see the man is mad: wherefore then have ye brought him to me? Have I need of mad men, that ye have brought this fellow to play the mad man in my presence? Shall this fellow come into my house?

The passage had lodged in my brain like a shard of brilliant, iridescent stained glass—the idea of putting on a persona, infiltrating the inner sanctum of a foreign king.

Or *kingpin*. I laughed now under my breath.

I felt surrounded by all the hundreds of painted Persian eyes in Shiraz. Eyes that seemed to be laughing, too. "Have I need of mad men, that ye have brought this fellow to play the mad man in my presence?"

   ■ ■ ■

"Yes, the City of David," I said.

Haji Juma Khan was still squinting at the laptop screen; he cleared his throat, coughed quietly into his fist. The scene, he told me, troubled him. In fact, it made no sense to him, no sense at all.

Jesus looks forlorn and abandoned and asks:

"Father, is there no other way?" That phrase knocked HJK

off guard, rattling around as he shook his head. He wouldn't let me unpause the DVD. My version of *The Passion* was Farsi overdubbed, and HJK stared at me, repeating the phrase.

"My Father, if it is possible, let this cup pass from me."

"I know," I told him. "It's hard—a lot of Christians can't wrap their heads around it either. The battle was not won at Calvary on the cross. The battle was won in Gethsemane. You see, at that moment, he could still easily have escaped into the desert, then circled up to Galilee and been safe. He could have escaped. But in the Garden, he asks his Father, three times, 'Are you sure? Is there any other way?' Because he knew what he would have to endure. Three times, he's asking his Father, 'Is there no other way?' That's what he means by saying, 'If it is possible, let this cup pass from me.'"

Haji Juma Khan kept squinting at me.

"We do not accept his godliness—Allah is one," he said. "But for you, he is the King of the Universe?"

"He is."

He tore into another piece of naan—fresh and puffy and lightly fragrant of olive oil—mulling over his thoughts carefully before speaking.

"But if this is the *Son* of God," he said, "why would his Father put him through this ordeal?"

He couldn't fathom the concept of God sending his Son to earth to be tortured and butchered for mankind's salvation.

"Tell me: Does God not love his Son?"

I shut my mouth—and let him talk. The questions and commentary flowed from his mouth in a stream: some Dari, some English. One more cardinal rule when you're undercover: Never enter into an unnecessary debate. You nod, you listen, and you draw out your subjects' thoughts. You don't need to hear your *own* views. You need to understand how their brains operate.

"No, it does not make sense," he kept saying. "If God did love his Son, why make him suffer such an agony?"

I sipped the dregs of my red wine, hoping the waiter would notice and discreetly top off my glass.

I stared back at Haji Juma Khan for a long time. The restaurant was silent but for the sounds of chewing, forks and knives scraping on plates. Now those hundreds of Persian eyes on the walls around me seemed to be squinting, questioning, judging. I couldn't answer him. Without realizing it, HJK had asked the most crucial question of all—one that has led to countless believers doubting their faith. Why would the Father put his Son through such physical and mental torture?

Why was there no *other* way?

■ ■ ■

That Monday morning—in fact, as soon as I got off the IV drip—I'd been called into a private meeting with Ambassador Neumann to discuss our strategy.

"Ed," he said, "we're seriously worried that this is going to be another Tet Offensive. You've read the intel—all the reports about these foreign fighters coming into Kabul, stockpiling weapons and detonators for IEDs."

The ambassador made a special request—a highly unusual assignment.

Since I'd become so tight with HJK, I had unprecedented access: With him at my side, I could go out, undercover, unaccompanied by any other DEA agents, and visit various mosques throughout Afghanistan. I was the only American who could travel freely to the dozens and dozens of mosques in Kabul and get an eyeball assessment: Were there foreign fighters amassing in the mosques before Ramadan? If so, that would be strong evidence of a coordinated attack on the embassy.

I didn't mind the mission. Dressing as a Haji was something I'd done often enough, and working undercover with HJK was becoming second nature to me now. What made all the difference in the world—at least for Haji Juma Khan—is that I had to do it by myself, without any other Americans. No bodyguards, no other agents, no translators. Together we went from mosque to mosque—sometimes more than six or seven in one day; I was always looking for signs of unrest. Groups of jihadists stashed inside the mosques. I was always looking for the typical foreign fighter: Saudis, Iraqis, Yemenis, Syrians, Egyptians, Lebanese.

Why would a young Arab even be in Kabul? They damn sure weren't there to enlist in the Taliban. The Taliban wouldn't even *accept* them. Though an asymmetrical counterinsurgency, the Talibs fight more or less like a conventional army—albeit one with morals, and tactics, from the Bronze Age. The Taliban is proud, in its own way, of engaging in a homegrown war against the invading infidels. They don't want the help of these Arabic-speaking outsiders.

No, these smuggled-in Arabs—almost all young men between the ages of eighteen and twenty-six—were there for one mission, brainwashed into believing they must martyr themselves as suicide bombers. Of the dozens of suicide bombings, mostly VBIEDs, I witnessed in Afghanistan, I can't remember a single occasion when the suicide bomber was a native-born Afghan; they were almost all carried out by these Arabs who'd been smuggled into Afghanistan.

In tandem with our counter-narcotics work, my friend General Daud and I had spent hours studying maps and classified intel reports to work out the logistics. The Arab jihadists were being smuggled by Al Qaeda in an elaborate pipeline: through Iran, then across the border into Pakistan. They gathered and got mission assignments in the Pakistani city of Quetta—the hotbed of radical jihadists—then traveled via caravan down into Kandahar Province, and were finally stashed in safe houses in Kabul. During our counter-narcotics operations in Afghanistan, we raided dozens of these safe houses, arrested many Arabs for possession of detonators—rigged cell phones that would ignite a massive suicide explosion the minute the phone was engaged.

This, far more than the Taliban insurgency, was the gravest threat we faced in Kabul. General Daud had given me a primer on how to spot these foreign-born fighters. The Arabs hiding in Kabul tended to be lighter-skinned, with distinctively Semitic facial structure, but there was also a discernible difference in deportment and disposition.

Typical Afghan men don't carry prayer beads unless they've made the pilgrimage to Mecca—like Haji Juma Khan. But *most* Arab men carry prayer beads and are constantly fingering them. Though the Arab men would dress in the "Haji pajamas," as we irreverently called the *shalwar kameez*, they always looked rather awkward, pulling down and adjusting that knee-length shirt, like an American kid chafing at the tight collar and tie of his First Communion suit.

Inside the mosques, unlike the native Afghans, the young Arab men were uptight and fidgety before worship. While the regular worshippers were relaxing, making casual conversation, the Arabs would keep to themselves and make no eye contact.

But the most important distinction, Daud told me, was the *intensity* of worship. During prayers many Afghans simply go through the motions, reciting the suras, bowing down on their prayer rugs, no more enraptured than a typical American at his local Sunday church service. The Arabs were infinitely more intense in their worship: five times each day, facing Mecca, heaving upward, and throwing themselves down again with the fervor of Christian Holy Rollers at a revival. Down on those prayer mats, in a psychological state approaching possession, they would bang their heads penitently into the ground—*thud, thud, thud*—over and over again. It was a wonder that they didn't knock themselves out cold.

It was the telltale stigmata, General Daud taught me: "After prayer service, always look for anyone who has bruised his forehead by smashing it on the ground.

"Trust me, Ed," Daud said. "If you see anyone with a dark bruise in the middle of his forehead, he will *not* be an Afghan. He will most surely be an Arab."

■ ■ ■

The hardest part for me wasn't working undercover in a war zone, dressing in traditional Afghan attire, or pretending to be someone I'm not—I'd done that my whole career. The toughest moment was that when I entered one of the mosques with HJK, I'd immediately have to give up my weapons.

I had no backup, no surveillance, no one with me but Haji Juma Khan. But I usually kept four weapons on my person. I had my Glock 9mm tucked on my right hip. The 9 was adequate for a shoot-out, but the trouble with the Glock—or any plastic-based semiautomatic for that matter—is that if you get in a close-range fight, tussling and struggling, and you press the gun against someone, the cycling of the slide will often jam—what's called a condition-three failure. Nothing more useless than a jammed piece. That's why I'd also brought my personal Smith & Wesson .38 revolver to Kabul; worn on my ankle, it was the ideal "contact weapon." With that two-inch barrel, you can shove the .38 into somebody's ribs and it will never jam.

I also carried two knives, strapping them on me from the moment I got out of bed in the morning. I've been a knife fighter since I was a kid in St. Louis. A close friend of mine, Lynn Thompson, is the owner of a company called Cold Steel, and when I was about to leave for Kabul, Lynn gave me a handmade Laredo bowie knife, which I always carried on my back. I also had one of Lynn's five-inch push knives in a special scabbard on my left side.

Legal? Depends who you asked. In Afghanistan, honestly, we did whatever we wanted—whatever we felt was warranted—in terms of our own protection. Working in Mexico was a different story; DEA Special Agent Victor Cortez was once arrested by the *federales* down there for carrying an automatic weapon.

For me, law enforcement duty in Kabul was like being a federal marshal in 1880s Tombstone. Everywhere you looked, people were packing heat, openly toting AK-47s: security guards at offices, bodyguards of government ministers and diplomats, even ordinary citizens strolling down a crowded street. Everyone was openly carrying. There wasn't a place in Afghanistan—and I covered the entire sprawling country—that I didn't see someone toting a Kalashnikov.

Still, despite the outlaw frontier ethic, there's one place where strict rules *do* apply: You cannot dishonor a mosque. You have to take your shoes off. All you can bring inside is your prayer rug.

Before we left the car, I looked at HJK, he glanced back at me, and I disarmed. Secreted away my Glock, my Smith & Wesson snub-nose, and my two Cold Steel knives.

I walked in the front door, shoulder to shoulder with HJK. The only things I did manage to smuggle in were my tiny gold cross and my pocket Bible. I never went anywhere without the Bible, gray leather and small enough to fit in the palm of my hand.

It had been given to me by Terrence, one of my close Marine buddies while I was an MP stationed in Hawaii. "Promise me you'll carry this every day, Ed," he'd said before he left the USMC to become a minister.

I kept that promise—still do—despite the fact that bringing a Christian Bible into a mosque is considered by most Muslims a sign of disrespect. Like most things in my Kabul life, I had to do it slyly, surreptitiously.

The mosques were always packed—especially on Friday *Jumu'ah* services. There were at least three or four hundred worshippers, segregated by sex, jamming the mosque to capacity.

Barefoot and solemn—while the muezzin was still making his wailing *adhan* calling the faithful to the noontime Friday service—we'd proceed to the tables with the small cisterns of water and the tempered silver bowls. Like a gentle schoolmaster, HJK would guide me through the ritual purification—cleansing our hands and our hearts—before we found our places, side by side, unfurling our rugs and facing in the direction of Mecca for the *Jumu'ah* service.

■ ■ ■

I'd never underestimated him; I always had a healthy respect for his intellect. Some reports had him listed as illiterate, but you don't rise from abject poverty in the badlands of Baluchistan to a position of wealth and international influence by being any-body's fool.

In hindsight, I can say HJK was probably the smartest man I've ever worked. But it was only inside the mosques that I realized how intelligent he really was.

The man does not understand Arabic; cannot speak it con-versationally beyond simple greetings like "*as salaamu alay-kum*." In conversation, he was most comfortable in Dari—the Afghan variation of Farsi—and Baluchi, a distinct northwest-ern Iranian dialect.

Yet he could recite the Koran—the entirety of the 114 suras—syllable for syllable. Never pausing, never stopping to think: He had the entirety of the Koran committed to memory. I know my Old and New Testament pretty well—the Jesuits back at St. Gabriel's made sure of that—but I certainly can't unfurl a prayer rug and recite every verse from Genesis to Reve-lation.

That's one of the most intimate acts two men can share—bowing on their knees and praying side by side. Despite not being a Muslim, I would get down on my knees, too. In fact, I had my own personal prayer rug—a beautifully woven red-and-black rug that General Daud had given me as a gift.

I wasn't reciting the Koran, of course. I was praying to Jesus. Ever since I'd worked undercover in Israel on the Kayed Berro case, at the very start of my DEA career, I've always used the Aramaic name, the one spoken by the disciples in Galilee and Jerusalem. *Yeshua Ha'Mashiach.*

Bowed low on that prayer rug, surrounded by several hun-dred Muslims, I murmured silently:

"I'm no longer simply *working* this man. It's not just another *case*. Look at us: I am becoming this man's brother. What am I supposed to do when the time comes to arrest him? I'm not sure I'm prepared—not sure that I'm strong enough—to handle that day. So I'm asking you—and you asked it yourself in the Garden—'Is there no other way?'"

■ ■ ■

We knelt and bowed in prayer, side by side, for more than an hour. After forty-five minutes my knees were burning like I'd been stung by wasps—and the answer came to me. There was *no* other way.

I did the only thing left to do—prayed for strength.

Prayed for the strength to do what I needed to do. For the strength to bring down a man who had opened up his heart to me. For the strength to betray a man who . . .

Just then, I glanced up and spotted, about thirty feet away, rising from his prayer rug, a fair-skinned Arab with a well-trimmed dark-brown beard who bore a striking resemblance to the young Pacino. Definitely not Afghan: Syrian, possibly Lebanese, maybe Saudi . . .

And just as General Daud had told me, there it was: the telltale bruise of the fanatic—bluish-black, almost rectangular, dead center in the middle of his forehead.

This young Arab kid was not averting his gaze. Had he made me for an American? Singled me out? He was clocking me hard, taking my measure.

Instinctively, I felt for the Laredo bowie knife at the small of my back, then for the push knife on my left waist—the scabbard was empty. Except for my tiny cross and handheld Bible, I was naked in the mosque.

My mind was racing. The Arab fighters always traveled in numbers. And despite the prohibition against weapons in the mosque, with these foreign-born jihadists, all bets were off. In fact, we knew they often stockpiled AK-47s and other automatic guns and explosives in mosques—under the religious justification that they were tools in a holy war against the invaders and infidels.

What was my next play? What would I do if I was surrounded in the mosque? What if someone had sold me out?

As I rose from my knees, I felt a heavy weight pressing down on me. I started back, feeling a cold tremor shoot up my spine, then realized it was simply HJK resting one of his massive arms around my shoulder.

"Grant me the strength," I said again silently.

His own strength was astonishing. As he pulled me face-to-face, smothering me in a bear hug, his long black beard scraped down my face and throat like coarse sandpaper. I'm pretty solidly built, but as he hugged me tighter, he lifted me off the ground like I was some six-year-old boy.

Then he kissed me quickly, four times, on both cheeks—traditional among Afghan friends and family at the end of the *Jumu'ah* service.

Seeing that I was with Haji Juma Khan—unequivocally my protector—the young Arab averted his gaze back to the pale-blue tiled floor.

HJK pressed his hand firmly into my shoulder; with prayer rugs rolled tightly under our arms, we walked together to the front of the mosque.

In my right ear I felt the kiss-like warmth, his breath faintly scented with roasted cauliflower and jasmine tea. For the first time he used the Dari word to address me.

Baradar.

Even today, I can feel the wiry barbs of his black beard pressing into my cheeks.

"You're more than a friend, Ed," he said. "I love you today as my brother . . ."

CHAPTER 10

▍ ▍ ▍

THE LAST CALL

I loved being a street agent. But it was inevitable—with recognition comes rank.

I'd taken a routine fall. We were out in the field near Kabul, looking for one of the myriad illicit heroin labs hidden in caves all over the country, and I slipped on some jagged shale, busted up my knee badly. For weeks I was limping around the embassy compound with my leg wrapped up in a brace and bandages—just like the day Uncle Jim had popped my knee out of its socket.

Eventually, the pain got so bad that I had to return to the States to have an MRI, saw an orthopedic surgeon and then underwent meniscus surgery.

While I was recovering in DC, Karen Tandy, the DEA's administrator, announced that I was getting a bump up to SES, a member of the DEA's Senior Executive Service, no longer in the typical chain of command of the DEA but serving at the "pleasure of the President of the United States."

I told her that I wanted to return to Kabul, but as an SES, I could no longer serve there as country attaché. My new posting meant I was stationed in the United States, briefly in Nevada and then permanently back in the LA headquarters.

I was the associate agent in charge of the Los Angeles Division, overseeing and directing some 850 agents, analysts, and support staff in Southern California, Nevada, and the entire Pacific Basin—all our special agents stationed in US territories like Guam as well as Indonesia, Malaysia, and the Commonwealth of the Northern Mariana Islands. I did an awful lot of traveling and even more writing. I authored the DEA's global heroin strategy as a budgetary submission to the US Senate, and was a primary contributor to the DEA's post–9/11 global heroin enforcement strategy for Central Asia.

I also went to work developing the DEA's Financial Investigations Unit, which was assigned the Bin Laden money trail. In conjunction with the FBI, I led the investigation into the cash from the various *halawas*—traditional Arabic banking exchanges—that paid for the 9/11 attacks. All told, we identified $300,000 originating in Middle Eastern *halawas* and channeled through Thailand, purportedly for the 9/11 plot.

But writing up reports for Congress and chasing money trails wasn't enough. Again, even as a member of the DEA's Senior Executive Service, the equivalent of a brigadier general in the US Army, I kept going undercover, kept hitting the street.

Didn't always make my bosses happy—in fact, I was held in contempt by a lot of my peers in the DEA—but that's the only way I knew how to do my job. Like all the good bosses I've known—from Rogelio Guevara through Don Carstensen—I'd never ask my guys to do something I was leery of doing myself.

The odd thing was—and I still don't quite know why—throughout my career, I always have seemed to be saving drug traffickers' lives. Especially during the course of my years overseeing the Pacific region at SES, in countries like Indonesia, where there's an automatic death sentence for drug trafficking. Several times I called major dealers—in Thailand, in Malaysia, in Indonesia—and told them that their best bet was to go directly to the local authorities and try to work out a deal:

"Listen, you're in danger. Don't go home tonight. If you want to stay alive, your best bet is to start cooperating *now*."

I didn't care if it had the government's stamp of approval— maybe it's the old Jesuit in me. I never wanted these traffickers or their families to get killed.

From my office in LA I ran the investigation to bring to justice the Ecstasy kingpin Yitzhak Abergil, known as the "Mr. Untouchable" of Israel.

For decades, Israel had an internal Mob crisis, internecine wars among violent clans of the Mizrahi—Jews originally from the Middle East: Egypt, Syria, Iraq, Morocco. With the advent of the Internet and inexpensive international travel, Israeli mobsters began looking outside the borders of their country for potential markets.

Virtually overnight, they created the Ecstasy market. Just as Colombian kingpins like Pablo Escobar were able to dominate the importation of cocaine into the United States by making use of long-standing marijuana smuggling routes, the new Israeli Ecstasy kingpins had a unique advantage over competing global mafiosi.

They owned most of the underground drug labs in the Netherlands and Belgium and already had an infrastructure in place for smuggling diamonds, often employing strippers and ultra-Orthodox Jewish teenagers as mules on flights to New York and Los Angeles. No one played the E smuggling game more shrewdly than Yitzhak and Meir Abergil, two feared young brothers based in the coastal resort town of Netanya.

Don't be fooled by the reputation of 3,4-methylenedioxy-*N*-methamphetamine, or MDMA, as a harmless "party" drug: The global Ecstasy market is monstrous. In 2005, the UN Office on Drugs and Crime valued it at more than $16 billion. Within Israeli society, control of the trade soon led to bloodbaths. Daring daylight assassinations carried out by car bombings and ex–Special Forces hit men weaving through the streets of Tel Aviv on motorcycles.

As long as they held to Bugsy Siegel's famous line about gangland murders—"We only kill each other"—the mayhem of the Israeli Mob was confined to blaring Hebrew tabloid headlines and lurid TV newsmagazines. But then innocent bystanders started to get whacked, and the general public said: "Enough!" The turning point came in July 2008, on the beachfront in Bat Yam, just south of Tel Aviv, when Margarita Lautin, a thirty-one-year-old social worker, was mistakenly assassinated in front of her husband and two young children.

The Abergil case predated me, but I got personally invested when I was named SES of our LA Division. Around the same time, the Abergil crime family was bringing its murderous methods right onto our doorstep. The Abergils were major suppliers looking for a distribution network; they decided to partner up with the Vineland Boyz, one of LA's deadly Latino street gangs. A clever smuggling marriage was made—including such ingenious flourishes as stuffing the Ecstasy pills into toy tigers—and business was booming. But in the drug game, murder *always* follows money. Their first California hit happened when Abergil gangsters assassinated Sami Atlas, an Israeli drug dealer living in Sherman Oaks, who they accused of ripping off a large drug shipment.

Realizing the multinational scope of the Abergils' enterprise and the increasing risk it posed here in the United States, we launched an investigation—logging hundreds of hours of wire-taps, interviews with witnesses and accomplices—to bring down the Abergils.

We'd indicted them through Beverly Hills and Hollywood informants; in addition to the murder of Atlas, they were responsible for major importation of Ecstasy obtained from Amsterdam.

As SES, I was often running into friction with the attorneys in the Central District of Los Angeles. They brag of having one of the highest conviction rates of all the US federal courts, but in my opinion, that's because they only take cases that are virtually prosecuted *before* they go to court.

I traveled to Israel and worked closely with the newly established anti–organized crime unit of the Israeli police. As soon as I got to Tel Aviv, I met with the brigadier general in charge.

"Do you know how important this is to us?" he told me. "This guy is our John Gotti. But we will never get a fair trial here. Abergil is still running everything from prison here."

It was tough negotiating, but in the end the stakes were high enough that we hammered out a compromise with the Israeli Supreme Court.

On January 12, 2011, Yitzhak and Meir Abergil, together

with three other crime family members, were extradited to the United States, arriving in Los Angeles, and were charged in a seventy-seven-page, thirty-two-count federal indictment with murder, massive embezzlement, money-laundering, racketeering, and running the largest Ecstasy ring in the United States.

Facing a life sentence in prison, in May 2012, Yitzhak Abergil pleaded guilty in a Los Angeles federal court to being part of a racketeering enterprise that distributed Ecstasy and whose members employed murder as a routine tool of enforcement. On May 21, 2012, in a landmark plea agreement, the formerly "untouchable" kingpin was sentenced to ten years in prison.

◼ ◼ ◼

We were also in the midst of developing cutting-edge technology and social networking to take down some of the world's most notorious narco-terrorists. No one had done this before, certainly not in American law enforcement. I established the Special Investigations Unit, a dedicated narco-terrorism investigative team based in the LA Division office. I loaded it up with my best investigators interested in developing narco-terrorism cases, going exclusively after the big guns: Al Qaeda, Hamas, Hezbollah.

As with any Internet start-up, it took months to work out the kinks, but we finally began to establish undercover personas—or avatars—in the online world of narco-terrorists. These virtual personas would enter forums to discuss radical politics, fundamentalist Islam, all in pursuit of dangerous narco-terrorists.

The Special Investigations Unit quickly became a beehive of high-speed modems and tapping keyboards and a gaggle of languages: I had to bring in translators expert in Pashtun, Baluchi,

Farsi, Dari, and Arabic. Our work in the unit led to one of the first drug-related investigations of Hezbollah in the United States. To my mind, this unit represents the investigative future, the leading edge in our fight against the global threat of narco-terrorism on both the real-life and virtual fronts.

■ ■ ■

Even after I'd left Afghanistan, in a sense I was *always* there with HJK.

It was by far the biggest case of my life, the culmination of a lifelong career working undercover, cultivating informants, gathering actionable intel. Some twenty-seven years of law enforcement training, every instinct and trick of the trade, came into play as I engaged and befriended the wealthiest heroin trafficker on earth.

After my return to Los Angeles, I went to Walmart and bought a Samsung flip phone solely for calls from HJK. He'd sometimes call me three times in one night. There's more than eleven hours' time-zone difference between Kabul and LA, so it was the middle of the day for him. Routine questions, checking in—occasionally more serious information he had on some major Taliban figure that he hoped would buy him some capital with me.

■ ■ ■

But by the summer of 2008, there'd been a dramatic policy shift in Washington. In mid-July, I learned—from Jimmy Soiles, the same Boston-born agent who'd been my undercover tutor in Paris—that the Department of Defense had placed Haji Juma Khan on the "kinetic" list.

An innocuous-sounding euphemism—more palatable, I suppose, than "targeted for elimination via unmanned aerial vehicle."

Placing HJK on the kinetic list meant that the DoD was going to call in a strike to take him out.

They didn't want to "eliminate" Haji Juma Khan while he was at his compound, surrounded by civilians—his various wives and scores of kids and whatever other bystanders might end up as "collateral damage." The plan was simple, Jimmy explained. The DoD wanted me to make one *last* call on the Samsung, to lure HJK via cell phone to a highway someplace in Nimruz. I begged for some leeway—just a few more months.

"Ninety days," I said to Jimmy. "Give me ninety days."

"Sixty," Jimmy said sharply. "You've got sixty, Ed."

Sixty more days.

For whatever reason, I was still confident I could find another way out, one that'd keep HJK alive, keep him talking, using him to our advantage in these escalating narco-terror wars . . .

Strange as it sounds, beyond his value as a source of useful information, I'd come to care a great deal for HJK—not as a target but as a *man*.

More importantly, I'd always envisioned the inevitable endgame being HJK in my custody—in a federal prison cell—continuing to provide valuable and actionable intel that could save American lives, perhaps lead us to UBL and other high-ranking Al Qaeda and Taliban leaders, not charred to death in a smoldering Toyota on a red-dust highway somewhere in the province of Nimruz . . .

I couldn't share our confidential intel with anyone, of course. Night after night, I imagined what Don Carstensen would have done, what Rogelio and José and all my earliest teachers in Group Four would have done.

Most of all, I thought of HJK, asking me that question in our favorite Persian restaurant.

Why was there no *other* way?

One Thursday, at 3 a.m., eyes wide open, the solution suddenly hit me.

Time had almost run out; I couldn't stall Jimmy or the brass at the Department of Defense any longer. The strike was scheduled in less than a month.

In my dark bedroom, I heard myself mumbling the paradox aloud: "I have to take his life away from him to *save* his life."

■ ■ ■

I picked up the Samsung and reached HJK at his compound in Baluchistan. Without any small talk, I let him know I had a lucrative business opportunity for him, but it was such a sensitive issue, it wasn't safe to talk on the phones.

We had to see each other immediately.

"Meet me here," he said.

"Can't," I said.

"Kabul."

"No, we can't do it in Kabul."

"Where then?"

"Nowhere in Afghanistan."

He was leery. He certainly wouldn't consent to flying to America again, or any country in Western Europe. He finally agreed to meet me in Dubai, but I said that wouldn't do.

For minutes we went back and forth, but he was dug in, insisting that the meeting happen only in the Middle East.

"How about Indonesia?" I finally suggested.

"Indonesia?" He mulled it over.

"Yes, I could meet you in Jakarta."

There was a long silence, and I could sense that his trepidation was softening.

At last the tentativeness left his voice.

Jakarta seemed safe enough to him. Indonesia, after all, is the world's most populous Islamic nation. It was also, from my perspective, a country where, as SES, I'd conducted several friendly and mutually beneficial counter-narcotics operations with local Indonesian authorities.

"Jakarta," he said finally.

"Yes, I'll see you in Jakarta."

I snapped shut the Samsung flip phone and felt a sudden stab of pain.

I knew that had been our last call.

■ ■ ■

It was the blackest of black ops—required our Afghan counterparts to acquire the false passport and visas for Haji Juma Khan. The *twist*: Haji Juma Khan, traveling under a fake identity, would now be thrust into the undercover role as we hustled him on board an Emirates flight to Jakarta.

The operation alone would wind up costing us in excess of $1 million.

He was flying commercial—first class—but we soon found that there was no airline flight that would get me there in time to meet him in Indonesia, on October 22, 2008; DEA had to lease a private Russian-owned G-V jet to scoop me up at Long Beach Airport.

I've never traveled so fast in my life: We flew over the Pacific at 750 knots—so fast that the pilots and navigator had to stand forward most of the time. Stopping to refuel in the Marshall Islands, the G-V overshot the tiny runway, nearly crashing into the drink.

Upon touchdown in Jakarta, I rushed down the tarmac in a sweat.

I saw, coming off the Emirates flight, this lumbering behemoth: all of six-foot-five and 370 pounds, long black beard; wearing his white *shalwar kameez* with a few visible grease stains, brown sandals, his white Haji hat, and a badly fitting black blazer that looked like it had been purchased at a flea market in Kabul back in 1973.

He had no bodyguards or lieutenants around him or any luggage, just a single busted-up carry-on, the wheels of which were so warped that it was *bouncing* toward me . . .

"Mister Ed!" he shouted, smothering me in one of his bear hugs, lifting me off the ground, kissing me twice, in quick succession, on each cheek.

You'd have thought that this fellow was an illiterate peasant who'd stepped out of a village in Nimruz and barely had enough money to pay the visa fee. Not the head of the biggest heroin and opium operation in Southwest Asia, a narcotics kingpin grossing more than $1 billion a year.

The Indonesian cops standing nearby—to a man, devout Muslims—did know the truth: As HJK walked through the airport, wheeling that wobbly carry-on, several policemen fell to their knees in front of "the Great Haji" as if he were some kind of deity.

In the end I managed to fulfill that bizarre paradox.

We were in a diplomatic and jurisdictional gray area: We now had an ironclad indictment against HJK in New York, but the United States has no extradition treaty with Afghanistan, and Haji Juma Khan was traveling with a UAE passport and doctored visas anyway.

I'd prearranged with the Indonesian authorities that they would deny HJK entry to their country so he could not exit the Jakarta airport; we had to get him back on a plane immediately. Would we be accused of snatching HJK in yet another controversial rendition as we'd done with Haji Bagcho Sherzai and Haji Khan Mohammad?

Ultimately, before this could blow up into an international incident, with HJK now in DEA custody, seated aboard the G-V, I made a command decision, yelling at the pilots:

"Take the fuck off!"

I'd absorb the diplomatic and legal flak. Flying back over Asia, our pilot climbed up past 35,000 feet, higher than radar could detect.

The pilot and copilot frantically called me on the sat-phone.

We now faced a more pressing concern: There was not enough jet fuel to get back to New York or any place in Europe where we were authorized to land. The DEA administrator called the State Department directly. Noting that HJK had provided more than $100 million to the Taliban and Al Qaeda, State gave us "top priority" and confirmed our previously authorized clearance to land and refuel in Malta.

Ultimately, we got HJK safely into LaGuardia.

As soon as he landed, he was arrested under the 2006 US narco-terrorism statute, facing a multiple-count indictment of "Conspiracy to Distribute Narcotics with Intent to Provide Material Support to an Organization Engaged in Terrorism" and housed in the Metropolitan Correctional Center in Lower Manhattan.

He was behind bars, but from my point of view, at least he was alive.

EPILOGUE

H aji Juma Khan is currently still incarcerated at the Metropolitan Correctional Center in New York City. Facing a life sentence in federal prison, Haji Juma Khan has officially pleaded "not guilty," but no trial date has yet been set.

HJK's current judicial status is officially categorized as "sealed" for reasons of national security.

The full extent of the information HJK provided us has never been told—may never be told—because the details remain under seal by federal prosecutors in the Southern District of New York.

My conversations with Haji Juma Khan led to actionable movement against the Taliban's third-in-command and to capture-or-kill operations against the very uppermost level of Al Qaeda figures, including Usama Bin Laden, who was hiding in Pakistan.

"Narco-terrorism," a word first coined by Peruvian president Fernando Belaúnde Terry in 1983 and made infamous with Pablo Escobar's violence targeting the government and people of Colombia, has now vastly expanded from being a crisis limited to Latin America.

Indeed, narco-terrorism is now the face of twenty-first-century organized crime. Far-flung groups like the Taliban, Hamas, Hezbollah, and FARC (Fuerzas Armadas Revolucionarias de Colombia) are two-headed monsters: hybrids of highly structured global drug-trafficking cartels and politically motivated terrorists.

Increasingly, the sale of narcotics is the first line of financing for acts of terrorism. For example, the March 11, 2004, coordinated train bombings in Madrid that killed 191 people cost relatively little—an estimated $70,000—and were financed primarily through the sale of hashish and Ecstasy.

On our own shores, the 2014 death of actor Philip Seymour Hoffman from a heroin overdose shed new light on the rapidly growing crisis of opiate abuse and addiction across the United States. The most current estimates are that first-time heroin use has increased in the United States by nearly 60 percent over the past decade. Many of us in the DEA and local law enforcement have seen it firsthand: Young people first get hooked on prescription opiates—often legally prescribed to their parents, pilfered from family medicine chests—and then start looking to buy five- and ten-dollar bags of heroin on the street.

The Centers for Disease Control and Prevention reports that, in recent years, opiate overdoses claimed more lives than any other injury. The CDC also reports that 75 percent of prescription drug overdose deaths involve opioid painkillers, heroin, and morphine. A 2011 study found that prescription opioid abuse costs the United States more than $55.7 billion per year in lost productivity, not to mention the incalculable costs in health care and criminal justice spending. Death by heroin overdose has recently become alarmingly common in the northeast; the DEA reported a 67 percent increase in heroin seizures and a 59 percent increase in heroin charges in New York alone.

Abuse of legal pharmaceutical painkillers may be the first step, but to stem the flow of heroin, we must continue to strike at the warlords of the Golden Crescent. Despite all our best efforts—and billions in counter-narcotics funding—the drug crisis is at an all-time high in Afghanistan. Opium cultivation continues to spike year after year, and heroin production accounts for approximately $3 billion, or 15 percent of the Afghan GDP.

Nobody fought the scourge as tirelessly as my dear friend General Mohammad Daud Daud. Even after I returned to my posting as SES in Los Angeles, we continued to talk regularly and to share advice, strategy, and intelligence. General Daud often told me—with immense frustration—that, in addition to the thousands of Taliban-linked opium producers and smugglers, there were numerous government officials implicated and arrested in the illegal opium trade.

The Taliban heroin warlords behave much like traditional Mafia extortionists: The United Nations said that in 2010 the Taliban had made $100 million the previous year by levying a 10 percent tax on independent opium-growing farmers.

Mohammad knew that he simply did not have the financial resources or manpower to fight the battle alone. In December 2008, General Daud spoke at a United Nations conference in Kabul and said that Afghan law enforcement agencies desperately needed international assistance in training and equipment. He talked bravely about the lack of security and the linkage between drug-trafficking and terrorism, as well as the profound corruption he had witnessed within the Afghan police and the army.

I was fortunate enough to be part of the DEA team providing Mohammad with that needed international assistance.

Mohammad was a fearless man and a warrior—remained a lifelong mujahideen—in the truest sense of that word. He was ready to give up his life to help transition Afghanistan from a rogue state, under the thumb of the murderous opium warlords, into a functional modern democracy governed by the rule of law.

"Ed, I've already accepted that I may be killed while serving my people," he once told me. "I say a prayer every morning when I leave my home because I'm ready to be killed."

Those words struck a deep chord with me, of course. How many days on the job had I said to myself—like so many of my fellow DEA agents:

You want to die today?

Tragically, my dear friend's words proved prophetic.

In May 2011, during the Taliban's so-called Spring Offensive, General Daud was assassinated in a suicide bomb attack, after a meeting held in the headquarters of the provincial governor of Takhar Province. Six others, including two German soldiers serving in Afghanistan, were also killed. The commander of ISAF troops in North Afghanistan, General Markus Kneip, was gravely wounded.

The Taliban immediately claimed responsibility for the terror bombing.

I was driving down the freeway when I heard the report on

all-news radio. I immediately pulled my car off the road and shut off the engine. My hands were trembling on the steering wheel, and I sat in a daze, crying, staring at the traffic speeding past.

The prayer rug that General Daud gave me—the same one I had carried from mosque to mosque while undercover with HJK—remains my most prized possession.

Undercover is an art. But make no mistake: It's a dark and *dying* art. Working with intelligence operatives, flesh-and-blood undercover agents—they even have Orwellian shorthand for it now: "Hum-Int" (for "human intelligence")—requires time, patience, and refined managerial skills. We're relying more and more on cutting-edge technology.

For nearly three decades, undercover was my entire life. Call me old-school. Self-effacement, subterfuge, and vigilance are the keys to outmaneuvering and outplotting those who'd like to do the same to you. Knowing how to be that facade. Knowing how to become that hologram. Knowing how to get inside people's concentric circles without them even knowing you're doing so.

Undercover work requires you to rub skin with another person. When you contribute skin, you are the collateral. You are the person they are trusting with their lives. And that's what DEA does. Very few of us are left. The recipe is almost gone. Jimmy Soiles is the undisputed master of it. I was lucky enough to learn from the best.

All of that, sadly, will soon be a thing of the past. Within a few short years, I believe, undercover will be an entirely lost art.

Why? Primarily, it's due to the astonishing new technology that allows for a virtual presence *absent* of soul. Listen, I've been there as we send up our unmanned aerial vehicles—or UAVs. I had one young DEA agent working for me—a US Army reservist—who's one of the pilots. Our UAVs are remotely flown from various locations, mostly out of Edwards Air Force Base.

Our drones aim to replace the human element. We have surveillance vehicles so small—like the micro RQ-11 Raven—that they weigh less than five pounds and can fit inside a soldier's backpack. If you've watched the drone pilots like I've done, it's eerie: they wear flight suits, strap into virtual "cockpits." But it's all a sophisticated video game, like playing *Halo* or *Call of Duty* on Xbox 360.

The pilot signals from Edwards up to a satellite, and the UAV takes off. The drone hovers at ten thousand feet and, with its state-of-the-art infrared optics package, sees day, dusk, night, and dawn, zeroing in on the targets and deploying missiles—usually to devastating effect. More Al Qaeda command-and-control figures have been killed by Predator strikes than by any other weapon in our arsenal.

I was there personally, on the ground, to set up these actions. Yes, I did manage to save Haji Juma Khan from a lethal drone strike, but others weren't so lucky.

I would be in the field in Afghanistan, undercover, working as the lure for the Department of Defense. When the time was right, I'd be told I needed to engage certain Taliban and Al Qaeda figures on my cell phone. Make that last call.

We'd talk for a few minutes, then *silence*.

The guy at the end of the line—for me, at least—is a ghost.

That's the way things are done today—it's certainly effective but it damn sure isn't *undercover* work. In light of the vastly changed landscape of law enforcement, and the fact that we have an entire generation relying almost solely on advanced technology to "get them in the room," I've come to see myself as having been privileged to be one of the last links in the chain of the dark art.

ACKNOWLEDGMENTS

For their invaluable assistance in completing this book, the authors wish to thank Richard Abate, Mike Bansmer, Charlie Conrad, Mike Holm, Leslie Hansen, Andrea Santoro, William Queen, José Martinez, and Steve Whipple.